THOMAS HOBBES

MODERNITY AND POLITICAL THOUGHT

Series Editor: Morton Schoolman
State University of New York at Albany

This unique collection of orginal studies of the great figures in the history of political and social thought critically examines their contributions to our understanding of modernity, its constitution, and the promise and problems latent within it. These works are written by some of the finest theorists of our time for scholars and students of the social sciences and humanities.

THOMAS HOBBES:

SKEPTICISM, INDIVIDUALITY AND CHASTENED POLITICS

RICHARD E. FLATHMAN

Modernity and Political Thought
VOLUME 2

SAGE Publications
International Educational and Professional Publisher
Newbury Park   London   New Delhi

For information address:

 SAGE Publications, Inc.
2455 Teller Road
Newbury Park, California 91320

SAGE Publications Ltd.
6 Bonhill Street
London EC2A 4PU
United Kingdom

SAGE Publications India Pvt. Ltd.
M-32 Market
Greater Kailash I
New Delhi 110 048 India

Printed in the United States of America

Library of Congress Cataloging-in-Publication Data

Flathman, Richard E.
    Thomas Hobbes : skepticism, individuality and chastened politics
  / Richard E. Flathman.
        p. cm.—(Modernity and political thought ; 2)
    Includes bibliographical references (p.   ) and index.
    ISBN 0-8039-4080-7 (cl).—ISBN 0-8039-4081-5 (pb)
        1. Hobbes, Thomas, 1588-1679—Contributions in political science.
    I. Title. II. Series: Modernity and political thought ;
vol. 2.
    JC153.H66F53 1993
    320'.01—dc20   92-43390

93 94 95 96 97 10 9 8 7 6 5 4 3 2 1

Sage Production Editor: Astrid Virding

in each mans self . . .
It is, to fashion his owne lyfes estate
Spenser

fiction, not falsehood
Clifford Geertz

Contents

Series Editor's Introduction

Richard E. Flathman's *Thomas Hobbes: Skepticism, Individuality and Chastened Politics* is the second volume to appear in the Sage Series **Modernity and Political Thought**. Flathman's work follows the recent publication of the inaugural volume in the series, William Connolly's *The Augustinian Imperative: A Reflection on the Politics of Morality*, and shortly will be joined by Fred Dallmayr's study of G.W.F. Hegel and by Michael Shapiro's inquiry into the thought of Adam Smith. The series will continue with books on selected past political thinkers by leading contemporary political theorists. These will include a study of Hannah Arendt by Seyla Benhabib, of Edmund Burke by Stephen White, Michel Foucault by Thomas Dumm, Sigmund Freud by Jean Elshtain, Friedrich Nietzsche by Benjamin Barber, Jean-Jacques Rousseau by Tracy Strong, Ralph Waldo Emerson by George Kateb, and Henry David Thoreau by Jane Bennett. As those who are familiar with the previous works of these authors will expect, these studies adopt a variety of approaches and pose importantly different questions. As contributors to **Modernity and Political Thought**, however, their efforts also are commonly devoted to effecting critical

examinations of the contributions that major political theorists have
made to our understanding of modernity—its constitution, problems,
promises and dangers that are latent within it.

The intellectual strategy informing *Thomas Hobbes* highlights this
objective of the series. Flathman aims to force a confrontation between
Hobbes's thinking and "ours," a confrontation between Hobbes and the
architects, critics and reformers, and everyday participants of modern
liberal democracies. For Flathman, Hobbes is not removed from us
contextually. Rather, Hobbes shares a language that allows him to share
our world and to enter into dialogue with modernity about that which
Flathman, along with many other theorists who are not all like-minded,
take to be the most seminal achievements of modern politics. Flathman's
approach effectively abolishes Hobbes's distance and otherworldliness.
It is inspired, in part, by the belief that the perspectivism central to
Hobbes's work is too little present in our liberal theory and practice.
By foregrounding Hobbes's perspectivism and related features of his
thinking, Flathman uses his engagement with Hobbes to apply intellectual pressure on our communities, aiming to alter not only our leading
ideas but the very framework within which our ideas are conceived and
translated into action. Through the intensity of this engagement Flathman
presses us to become, self-consciously and despite opposing tendencies
in our public cultures, the Hobbesians he thinks we already are in part
and at our best.

Flathman has long been engaged with the challenges presented by
Hobbes's political theory. Perhaps more than any other single political
thinker, it has been Hobbes who has provided him with the theoretical
tools to reconstruct liberal theory and practice, a project that in one form
or another has occupied Flathman's attentions for much of his intellectual life. Because Flathman's study of Hobbes is deeply rooted in his
preoccupation with liberalism, our appreciation of it can be enhanced
by consideration of his most recent work in liberal theory (which he
himself describes as a "companion" to the present volume), *Willful
Liberalism: Voluntarism and Individuality in Political Theory and
Practice* (Ithaca, NY: Cornell University Press, 1992).

Willful Liberalism develops and defends a theory that moves aggres-
sively against tendencies in and around liberal theory and practice in
late modernity. The sharply controversial character of the voluntarist

liberalism Flathman there endorses prompts him to anticipate that some will regard his argument as illiberal and therefore antiliberal. Although in his estimation (and in mine) such a response would be mistaken, Flathman recognizes that the aversion of most liberals to Hobbes's authoritarianism will dispose them against a view that owes so much to Hobbes.

Though liberal theorists may mistakenly attribute an antiliberal stance to *Willful Liberalism,* they will be correct in discerning a certain skepticism, much indebted to Hobbes, toward democracy. Although inverting Hobbes's view that monarchy is the best and democracy the worst possible form of government, Flathman finds persuasive Hobbes's argument that an active and embracing democratic politics tends to add to the dangerous power and authority of the state. Thus Flathman argues that we should maintain democratic institutions and procedures but adopt what he refers to as Hobbes's "chastened" conception of the state and politics. On this conception, we seek important but few benefits from the state, and we view our political participation more as a means of protection against state excesses than as a means of putting its authority and power to our own uses or as a form of activity that is good in itself. Accordingly, Flathman opposes liberals who argue for a fervently participatory democracy and who promote a deepened and politically intensive conception of justice, social cooperation, and community. Also accordingly, he applauds Hobbes's view that we have a right—albeit not a "natural" one—to dissent, disobedience and rebellion, and goes beyond Hobbes in urging that we maintain a vigilant, defensive stance toward government.

An important part of Flathman's mission is to disrupt those currently influential tendencies in liberal thinking that celebrate reason and encourage and perhaps yearn for social and political unity based on rationally grounded and widely shared beliefs and values. He does so by confronting such views with Hobbes's powerful emphasis on difference, separation and incompatibility, indeterminacy, opacity and incomprehensibility. For Flathman, these features of Hobbes's thinking reorient liberal theory away from stifling homogeneity and conformity, away from those aspects of politics and political involvement that diminish the individual, and move it toward a conception of political association that protects and promotes individuality, plurality, and hence group interactions that are at once mutually productive and as little intrusive as may be.

Although acknowledging that Hobbes's thinking contains objectionably authoritarian tendencies, Flathman exonerates the great English political philosopher of the charge that he was a statist and incipient totalitarian who wanted to impose absolute rule on virtually all of social and political life. In Flathman's reading, Hobbes's *Leviathan* was meant unequivocally to serve individuality and the plethora of "felicities" that are individuality's yield and its exclusive good. Hobbes rejects both the possibility and the desirability of a common good and seeks no more legal and political order than is necessary to facilitate the activities of human beings pursuing a great and constantly changing variety of goods. What is decisive here is the very special meaning of Hobbes's individuality. Flathman shows that he is primarily a theorist of self-making, self-assertion, self-reliance, and self-responsibility, and only secondarily and instrumentally a theorist of ordered and ordering political arrangements.

It is by reason of their relation to God that Hobbes's individuals are fated to this "robust individuality," as it is called by Flathman. A question of fundamental importance with which Hobbes contends is by what means an omnipotent God has permitted individualities. Hobbes reasons, Flathman argues, that God endows humans with the capacities to form the firm belief that She exists, but narrowly limits their ability to know the particulars of Her will. For if God's will were perfectly known, human relations—what individuals can and cannot, should and should not do—would be as unproblematic, and hence as routinized and lacking in enthusiasm and gratification, as relations among the ants and bees. Acting in part on knowledge and belief and not on divinely implanted instincts, but having severely limited knowledge of God, individuals can neither knowingly obey nor disobey, order their affairs by Her will or rebel against it. Whether divines, rulers, or private individuals, each human being must *interpret* and *apply* such commands as God has issued and must make his or her own decisions concerning that broad range of questions on which God has chosen to remain silent. In no uncertain terms these Hobbesian persons are on their own. Belief in the existence of God together with the ineliminable necessity of interpretation establishes God's rule as absolute but not total; and the rule of the state, justified with reference to an imperfect knowledge of God's commands, can be absolute but not total(itarian).

As Flathman shows, the epistemic constraints that characterize the relationship between God and humans and by so doing lay the groundwork for individuality and for jurally absolute but practically limited rule, are reproduced and in important respects deepened in relations among individuals. Owing primarily (but not exclusively) to the ineliminable ambiguity of language and to the quite definite limits on our capacities to understand, assess, and influence one another's thinking, it is rare for us to be able to understand one another or to act with certitude or even confidence on one another's wishes and directives. Unable to know one another as we are unable to know God, we are represented to each other in our thought and action by uncertainty and unpredictability. We are therefore continually faced with the need not only to interpret the beliefs and desires of others but often enough to act in ignorance of the responses others will make to us.

Limited in these and other ways, for Hobbes individuals are primarily creatures of their own making, creatures of "artificings" that flow first and foremost from their passions and their wills, and only secondarily and instrumentally from their reason. Hobbes's political theory, Flathman contends, is thus "deeply voluntarist." The Leviathan, as the supreme example of this will-begotten human artifice, *necessarily* reflects the limits set by human nature and *ought to* limit itself to ameliorating the most debilitating of the human difficulties. Leviathan's task, Flathman argues, is primarily to create and maintain conditions favorable to individuals' self-making and to their never-ending struggle to achieve felicity. In Flathman's estimation the single most important contribution of Hobbes's political thinking resides here. Rather than adding force to the "misconceived and destructive enthusiasms" concerning the state and politics—as prevalent in our time as they were in his—Hobbes's estimations of human and therefore of state limitations does what political theory can do to protect us against them.

Flathman's willful liberalism rests on a voluntarism where passion and will rather than reason are the predominant moving forces of human conduct. On this view, reason is but the "scout" for the passions, as Hobbes famously said. Flathman's liberalism presupposes, as he puts it, individuals whose conduct is for the most part voluntary in the familiar sense of not being determined, coerced, or compelled by other agents or agencies and that occurs because of passions and desires, interests and values, deliberations and decisions that are in some sense the individual's own. By comparison with Hobbes, for Flathman most liberal thinkers have embraced no more than heavily qualified versions of voluntarism, versions too "weak" to account satisfactorily for the kinds of voluntary conduct that *all liberalism* (tacitly) *presupposes.* Moreover, these weak versions of liberal voluntarism are antagonistic to the yet more vigorous forms of individuality for which Flathman finds support in Hobbes. From the interpretive nature, unpredictability, and uncertainty of human affairs issues an inexplicable diversity of thinking and acting, a perpetual newness of human relations and events. In short, there issues what Flathman celebrates and describes aesthetically as life's "wonder-ful," "mysterious" qualities.

It is evident, in light of Flathman's reading of Hobbes, why a Hobbesian inspired willful liberalism would find anathema a single, substantive, and life encompassing ideal, whether defined by the state, the deliberations that occur in a public sphere, or an inspiration to politics and political participation. On his view, for their purposes liberal states, public cultures, and politics must foreground not reason but the passions and the wills that carry us to action; must privilege opacities rather than transparencies and shared beliefs and understandings, unpredictability and uncertainty rather than regularity and predictability, self-making and self-command. Liberal states must seek no more order than is necessary to the activities of diverse human beings pursuing a diversity of goods.

Willful Liberalism attempts a reconstruction of liberal theory only in part through engagement with the thought of Hobbes. It draws equally upon the voluntarist elements of the work of such philosophers as Ockham and Scotus, Schopenhauer, William James, Oakeshott, Arendt, and especially Nietzsche. With *Thomas Hobbes* Flathman escalates the terms of his earlier debates about Hobbes and liberalism. The aspiration here is to show emphatically and comprehensively that Hobbes is a precursor of not just any liberalism, but of one that promotes plurality and above all individuality. These ideas and ideals, Flathman shows, are vibrant throughout Hobbes's thinking, from his metaphysics and epistemology through his philosophy of mind and language right up to his morals and especially his politics. It is Flathman's own ideal that without individuals who are capable of self-making and self-command, self-discipline and self-control, self-reliance and self-responsibility, liberalism is hopelessly utopian. With *Thomas Hobbes,* Flathman looks to the thought of a philosopher often believed to be the enemy of liberalism to save it from the utopianism it seems historically on the verge of becoming.

In the course of developing this interpretation, Flathman leads us through a series of passageways that opens to new perspectives on the cornerstones of Hobbes's thinking. With respect to Hobbes's politics, to cite the most striking example, Flathman shows that although Hobbes takes the right of nature (the fundament of his political theory as Flathman reads it) to an absolutist conception of formal authority, he wants an inactive state, supports a much wider religious toleration than a liberal such as Locke, and readily licenses disobedience and even rebellion.

It is easy to appreciate the combination of thoroughness and innovation with which Flathman crafts his approach to Hobbes. It is reflected in his complex relationship to predecessors whose studies have set the terms of scholarship on Hobbes and his bearing on all of the important facets of liberal and democratic theory. *Thomas Hobbes* is based on a reading closest to that of Michael Oakeshott and partially overlaps the interpretations offered by C. B. Macpherson and Leo Strauss. But Flathman's appropriations and valorizations of Hobbes are radically at variance with those of the latter two thinkers.[1]

As does Flathman's *Thomas Hobbes,* William Connolly's *The Augustinian Imperative: A Reflection on the Politics of Morality* (Sage, 1993) has a strong bearing on liberal theory and practice. And like Flathman's contribution, too, its concerns are also rooted in its author's earlier work on liberalism, *Identity\Difference: Democratic Negotiations of Political Paradox* (1991).[2] Among other concerns, *Identity\ Difference* shows how liberalism forgets the role politics plays in the very construction of personal and collective identity and its conversion of difference into otherness. Connolly pinpoints how liberalism unconsciously devalues the differences created by the identities it nurtures, and how liberal individualism and liberal individuality obscure the politics of identity and difference and deflate efforts to infuse these relations with the spirit of "agonistic respect." A politics of agonistic respect appears when contending identities mutually sacrifice their demands for self-certainty, exercising forbearance on their ambiguous relations of interdependence and strife. Only such a politics of "critical pluralism," as Connolly calls it in this study, can avert the conversion of difference into otherness and the naturalization and normalization of fixed identities that this conversion helps to effect. Politics now becomes the vehicle through which we locate threats to diversity and difference in the state, civil society, and in the interior of the individual. A politics of critical pluralism becomes the medium through which we come to terms with the contingency of our own identities and the violence to others we produce by the effort to conceal this contingency. This is a politics through which difference can begin to flourish, or at least not be converted into otherness and victimized. Through such a politics, liberalism would be reconstituted, drawing inspiration from an unlikely combination of liberal skepticism, Nietzschean agonisms, and Foucauldian care.

A question of fundamental importance becomes, then, why does it seem so difficult for liberalism to make this decisive move to an agonistic politics? Although not explicitly concerned with liberalism, *The Augustinian Imperative* casts light on this question as it challenges the ideal of "intrinsic moral order" still implicit in some versions of liberalism. *The Augustinian Imperative* is an archeological investigation into the intellectual foundation of liberal societies. Connolly excavates and deciphers a complex of discourses that, because of the extent to which they have become insinuated into our linguistic practices, possesses an inertia, not simply toward the determination, but toward the overdetermination of our identities. Augustinian in theory and practice, these discourses contribute to the formation of identity, to the sort of powers by which it is formed and the sort of power it becomes.

If we were to place *The Augustinian Imperative* side by side with *Identity\Difference,* we would learn this: The "Augustinian Imperative" is the moral infrastructure exercising hegemony over our words and thoughts and deeds. It is the structure that pulls identity toward its self-validation and dogmatization. It is the particular structure that constitutes order as intrinsic and identity as integral to the true order of things. The Augustinian Imperative is the holy father of moral order. And this imperative that there be an "intrinsic moral order" is lodged in the subterranean levels of liberalism.

In its theoretical insights and rhetorical power, *The Augustinian Imperative* compares with Michel Foucault's *Discipline and Punish* and his earlier *Madness and Civilization,* although in its genealogical stance Connolly's study has more in common with the later text.[3] As does Foucault with madness and punishment, Connolly locates the points in Augustine's work where knowledge and power intersect, where they are imposed upon the body to constitute an authoritative identity and moral order taken to be intrinsic. Through his examination of Augustine's discourses—on god's will and human will, faith, mystery, divination, confession, condemnation, conversion, healing, self-discipline, heresy—the moral imperative, the tactics for its definition, the cultural forms the imperative assumes and the mechanisms of its cultural reproduction, and the extent to which it can order and organize our lives unfold before us as a densely textured universe of concepts, arguments, proofs. Of words, within which each of us becomes entangled because, as Connolly puts it, "the Augustinian Imperative assumes a larger variety of forms in modern doctrines that relax the demand for eternal life but relocate the spirit of eternity in the cultural identities they endorse and the conceptions of intrinsic moral order they represent."

So compelling is Connolly's image of the imperative that we come to recognize where Augustine's framework has impressed itself on our own cultural practices, where it is at work in contemporary philosophical and theoretical positions. Along the way we recognize, too, that Connolly himself is implicated in the confessional complex and moral imperative he exposes, perhaps all the more as he contests, combats, attempts to lighten its influence, to extricate his own thinking from its identitarian web. That Connolly cannot escape being drawn into the Augustinian maelstrom offers ironic support for his thesis. It also illustrates the departure he represents in contemporary studies of Augustine. Whereas Charles Taylor, for example, argues in his *Sources of the Self: The Making of Modern Identity,* that Augustine's design is to move our attention away from the sensible to the insensible order, Connolly reveals how focusing our attention on the insensible is instrumental to riveting our attention on the order of the sensible world.[4] If Connolly's expose of Augustine's hidden agenda spells its failure, then the paradox is that Augustine succeeds even where he fails.

It will be apparent to the reader of both Flathman's and Connolly's books that there are areas of agreement and disagreement on the problems and prospects of liberalism and its relation to modernity. As future series' volumes appear we will have occasion to revisit liberalism and its critiques in the broader thematic context developed by each new study, and to take an accounting of the view of modernity the contributions to **Modernity and Political Thought** afford.

Members of the Sage Publications editorial staff have been particularly helpful over the nearly four years of labor required to produce this series. I am grateful to Blaise Donnelly for his contribution as in-house series missionary, to C. Terry Hendrix for acting as overseer, and to Carrie Mullen for the professional care she has devoted to nurturing the concept underlying **Modernity and Political Thought**, and for moving series volumes into and through all stages of the production process.

—Morton Schoolman
—*State University of New York at Albany*

Notes

1. For these and other authors whose works Flathman finds instructive, refer to his annotated bibliography, particularly section III, "Works Concerning Hobbes."

2. William E. Connolly, *Identity\Difference: Democratic Negotiations of Political Paradox* (Ithaca, NY: Cornell University Press, 1991). My discussion of Connolly's book focuses on arguments in its third ("Liberalism and Difference") and sixth ("Democracy and Distance") chapters.

3. See Michel Foucault, *Madness and Civilization* (New York: Random House, 1965) and *Discipline and Punish* (New York: Vintage: 1979).

4. Charles Taylor, *Sources of the Self: The Making of Modern Identity* (Cambridge: Harvard University Press, 1989), pp. 127-142.

Preface

Book prefaces being spaces in which authors are permitted a certain overt self-indulgence, I will try to orient readers to this work by commenting briefly on my own objectives in writing it.

In one conspicuous respect this book represents a departure from the studies in political philosophy that I have published over the last couple of decades. Those works are addressed to ideas and issues and are organized in terms of the concepts in which thinking about those topics for the most part takes place. There are no proper names in their titles and only rarely do such items appear in chapter and section headings. Discussions of various thinkers are frequent in my sentences and paragraphs, but this is because I have found their ideas and arguments pertinent to the issues I am discussing. In evident contrast, the present work directly addresses the ideas of Thomas Hobbes and takes much of its organization from categories into which Hobbes's thinking divides.

Because of my preference for the former of these procedures, I much appreciated but was initially hesitant to accept Morton Schoolman's invitation to contribute a book on Hobbes to the series he is editing.

Two connected considerations overcame my reservations and have informed my writing of the book.

Of the proper names that figure in my previous works, few appear more frequently or with more favorable inflections than that of Thomas Hobbes. In writing about and in teaching courses concerning issues in political philosophy, I have repeatedly found both welcome provocation from and a good deal to agree with in Hobbes's trenchant formulations. There was therefore reason to think that a more sustained engagement with his ideas would contribute to rather than deflect me from the purposes I have been pursuing. This consideration was reinforced by the admirable conception that guides the series of which the book is part. It conceives of political philosophy as an attempt to confront, critique and in various ways to alter political practice. It also recognizes and respects the fact the most of those who undertake this activity conduct it in important part through engagements, sometimes more, sometimes less explicit, with its past practitioners. The authors contributing to the series study the thinkers they address with the seriousness owed to those who have demonstrated exceptional prowess in the difficult kinds of thinking the authors are themselves attempting.

In writing about Hobbes my chief purpose is to intensify confrontations with his thinking—on my own part, on the part of seasoned political theorists, and particularly among those in the early and perhaps most entrancing moments (how warmly they are remembered) of their own engagements with political philosophy.

Achieving these objectives requires close and receptive attention to Hobbes's extraordinarily complex and encompassing reflections. I address and construe Hobbes in order to pursue my own agenda, an agenda set by issues that are alive here and now. This objective has led me to discuss a wide range of Hobbes's ideas and arguments. As I read him, Hobbes speaks provocatively to a remarkably large number of the controversies that are current in political philosophy and philosophy more generally. In many instances this is because he speaks in a language and out of assumptions that, while sharply controversial, remain very much with us. In others it is due to the great distance between him and us, to the ways in which he obliges us to contend with possibilities that merit attention they are not presently receiving. I also take seriously a chastened version of his own view that he constructed a philosophy that was systematic in the strongest sense he thought possible. He was wrong to claim that, given a small number of unprovable assumptions and stipulations, the major propositions of his system stand in logically necessary relationships to those assumptions and to one another. But his moral and political ideas, which are my chief concern here, are part of an outlook or sensibility that puts morals and politics in a distinctive and to my mind distinctively valuable perspective.

I have very little to say about topics typically discussed under headings such as "Hobbes's life and times," Hobbes's place in "the history of political philosophy" and the "context" of Hobbes's thought. Sidestepping controversies concerning these evocative but inherently problematic notions, there is much to be learned from, much that can only be understood on the basis of, studies conducted under their inspiration. At the risk of distorting Hobbes's intentions and/or the meaning of Hobbes's texts, my purpose is (to overstate the matter) to do to (or for) Hobbes what he for the most part did to his philosophical predecessors, to wrench him out of his context, to thrust him into ours, to make his texts speak to questions of present philosophical and especially moral and political concern.

For the somewhat less welcome reason of strict limitations on space, I have also had to omit explicit discussion of the large and often excellent literature concerning Hobbes's thought. Because a considerable part of this literature approaches Hobbes in much the same spirit as I have tried to do, this omission is at undoubted cost to my objectives. The Annotated Bibliography lists some of the standard bibliographic sources and enumerates a sampling of the numerous books and articles that speak to questions discussed in the various chapters of this book. I have also recorded in it the debts and disagreements of which I am most aware. I hope that the latter comments will help to elicit some of the further engagements that I had originally intended to carry on in the text itself.

A further and equally regretted omission is of explicit discussion of the large and excellent recent literature that speaks to the issues here discussed. For those familiar with that literature, the terminology I use will signal some of the connections as I see them.

There is one respect in which a Hobbes true to himself would have to be pleased by the treatment he has been accorded by his commentators. An always pungent writer and an often caustic critic of his predecessors and contemporaries, from his own time to ours his ideas have repeatedly provoked vigorous and strongly felt responses. At least for this reason, and despite his reputation as a proponent of a political authoritarianism long since discredited among those likely to read this book, Hobbes has remained very much alive among us, is never absent for long from the pages of political philosophy that have been composed since his death.

There are more than a few recent and not so recent political thinkers who credit him with the far greater success of educating his descendants to the fundaments of his way of thinking, of implanting his most basic ideas deeply and pervasively in the political culture or cultures that have been most aware of his thinking. Convinced that this success on Hobbes's part represents a great failure on the part of the rest of us, these critics are all the more spirited in combating Hobbes's ideas.

In its largest dimensions, the reading of Hobbes developed here agrees with much in the accounts that these last-mentioned critics have given of his thinking. I am also inclined to share their view that, whether or to whatever extent it is due to Hobbes's influence on us, much in our thinking and acting is recognizably Hobbesian in character. My estimations of his ideas and their echoes or counterparts in our own practices and activities are very different from theirs. I welcome rather than deplore his undoctrinaire but pervasive skepticism, his individuality-affirming psychology, prudence and morality, his conception of what can be achieved and should not be so much as attempted through politics and government. I urge that we appropriate more not less from his thinking.

I end the discursive portion of these prefatory remarks on a yet more self-indulgent note. I have tried to point out weaknesses in Hobbes's arguments and to argue against those of his positions that are central to my discussions but that I find unacceptable. On a larger number of issues I have recorded my agreements but left the arguing largely to my Hobbes. To the extent that I have better or different arguments for the same or analogous conclusions, the reader will find them in my book, which I perhaps alone in the world regard as a companion to this volume, *Willful Liberalism: Voluntarism and Individuality in Political Theory and Practice* (Ithaca, NY: Cornell University Press, 1992).

In the absence of standard editions of Hobbes's main texts, and in particular because of the proliferation of widely used editions of *Leviathan,* where possible I refer to chapters as well as to the pages of the particular editions I have used. Page references are to the following editions. *Leviathan,* Michael Oakeshott, ed. (London: Collier Books, 1962) (hereafter *Lev.*). *Elements of Law* (hereafter *Elements*), *De Corpore* and *Of Liberty and Necessity,* in *Body, Man, and Citizen: Selections from Thomas Hobbes,* Richard S. Peters, ed. (New York: Collier Books, 1962). (The work that became *Elements* consists of two sections, "Human Nature" and "De Corpore Politico," that were originally published separately. In the edition used here, this original separation is reintroduced, "Human Nature" running from pages 182 to 244, "De Corpore Politico" from 277 to 390. In addition, "De Corpore Politico" is divided into "Part the First" consisting of Chapters 1-6 running from pages 277 to 311 and "Part the Second" consisting of Chapters 1-10 running from pages 312 to 390. In citing *Elements* I have used "I" for "Human Nature" followed by chapter and page, "II" for "De Corpore Politico" followed by "A" for "Part the First" and "B" for "Part the Second" and then by chapter and page numbers.) *De Homine* and *De Cive or The Citizen,* (hereafter *DC*), in Bernard Gert, ed., *Man and Citizen: Thomas Hobbes* (Atlantic Highlands, NJ: Humanities Press, 1972). *A Dialogue Between a Philosopher and a Student of the Common Laws of England,* Joseph Cropsey, ed. (Chicago: University of Chicago Press, 1971), (hereafter *Dialogue). Hobbes's Thucydides,* Richard Schlatter, ed. (New Brunswick, NJ: Rutgers University Press, 1975) (hereafter *Thucydides*). *Decameron Physiologicum* and *Six Lessons to the Professor of the Mathematics* (hereafter *Six Lessons*), in Sir Thomas Molesworth, ed., *The English Works of Thomas Hobbes of Malmesbury,* Vol. VII. Reprint of the edition of 1845 (Scientia Aalen, 1962) (hereafter *Molesworth). A Physical Dialogue of the Nature of the Air,* Appendix, in Steven Shapin and Simon Schaffer, *Leviathan and the Air-Pump: Hobbes, Boyle, and the Experimental Life* (Princeton, NJ: Princeton University Press, 1985) (hereafter *Physical Dialogue). The Autobiography of Thomas Hobbes,* translated by Benjamin Farrington, *The Rationalist Annual,* 1958 (hereafter *Autobiography). Behemoth or The Long Parliament,* Ferdinand Tonnies, ed. (Chicago: University of Chicago Press, 1990) (hereafter *Behemoth). The Answer of MR Hobbes to SR William D'Avenant's Preface Before Gondibert,* in William

D'Avenant, *Gondibert 1651* (Menston, England: Scolar Press Limited, 1970) (hereafter *Gondibert*). "Third Set of Objections [to Descartes's Meditations] With the Author's [Descartes's] Replies," Vol. II, pp. 121-37, *The Philosophical Writings of Descartes,* John Cottingham, Robert Stoothoff, and Dugald Murdoch, trans. (Cambridge: Cambridge University Press, 1984) (hereafter "Objections.")

These and other texts not cited by page number are listed in alphabetical order in the Annotated Bibliography.

I am much indebted to Bill Connolly, Kirstie McClure, Jerry Schneewind and Morton Schoolman for spirited discussions and many valuable suggestions. Cornell University Press granted permission to use materials from Chapter 1 of *Willful Liberalism.*

1

Of Making and Unmaking

Thomas Hobbes is first and foremost a theorist of individual human beings as the *Makers* of themselves and their worlds. He is also and equally a theorist of failed attempts at makings, of mismakings, and of unmakings or destroyings. Himself the maker of an elaborately constructed system of ideas, Hobbes's writings depict a densely material universe pulsating with energy and movement but largely lacking in humanly intelligible or serviceable order or purpose. Into this universe he thrusts individuals and loose and fluctuating groups who struggle to give shape and impart direction to themselves, their environment, and one another. Often futile or worse, occasionally partly successful, these efforts cease only at death and largely constitute the human experience.

The most famous such making is that with which Hobbes opens his masterwork, the devising of an "artificial animal," "that great LEVIA-THAN called a COMMONWEALTH." Hobbes likens this act to no less than the "**fiat,** or **let us make man,** pronounced by God in the creation" and goes so far as to say that it begets a "mortall God." This astonishing figure is the emblem of his reputation as an uncompromising proponent of absolutist and authoritarian government.

Surrounding, informing and—I argue—finally subordinating the making of the Leviathan are a plethora of images of individual human beings each of whom he invites us to regard as at least God-*like* in their capacities to construct, out of their own passions and desires, beliefs and purposes, themselves and their worlds. The omnipotent God of the various Judeo-Christian mythologies made Adam out of dust and Eve out of a bone. In what we and perhaps Hobbes himself might regard as his transposition and transvaluation of this tale, Hobbesian human beings impose form and purpose upon the matter that is themselves— their own bodies and minds—and their universe.

The thematic of human beings as God-like makers of themselves stands in a never fully relieved, often sharply drawn, tension with other pronounced tendencies in Hobbes's thinking. Hobbes was for the most part scornful of prevailing conceptions of humankind as Knowers of or Believers in something apart from themselves, as active or passive instrumentalities of Reason or Truth. At the same time, he insisted upon respects in which human beings are Sufferers from forces they did not produce and could little alter, respects in which they are captives of a Fate. Whereas Hobbes credits the omnipotent God with having created the universe ex nihilo or out of nothing but Herself, the comparable task confronting human beings is the more difficult one of crafting their selves and things serviceable to those selves out of materials that they know to have certain unalterable characteristics but about which there is otherwise much that they do not and cannot comprehend.

Hobbes thought that the universe consisted of whirling atoms of matter and believed that the motions of these particles formed an unbroken and unbreakable network of strictly causal relationships. Along with his metaphysical materialism and determinism, he thought that there are quite narrow limitations on what human beings can know about and do with and to their world. An opponent of the various doctrinaire or programmatic skepticisms with which he was familiar, he nevertheless contested the soaring religious, philosophical and scientific claims and aspirations of his own and previous ages and he repeatedly drew attention to the defects and liabilities of perception, reason, language and the other sources and resources on which his own most affirmative arguments and conclusions relied.

For these and related reasons, the "givens" bequeathed to humankind by God and Nature, while necessary to the possibility of human "being" and potentially contributive to human well-being, are insufficient for the former, radically so for the latter, and often recalcitrant to human purposes. In order to so much as identify and perpetuate themselves, and more emphatically in order to achieve a degree of "felicity" and "commodious living," women, men and some difficult to classify figures who make brief but intriguing appearances in Hobbes's works, must themselves give form and course to the opaque and often resistant materials that are their experiences and their lives.

It is a daunting task.

The most fundamental artifice of all is inventing names and assigning them to nameless and largely incomprehensible things. This is done quite arbitrarily in that initially it is by their choosing alone that individual human beings invent names and stipulate their meanings. By performing acts of naming they endeavor to impart a degree of stability and intelligibility to themselves and their world. As they cumulate names into languages and form them into conceptions, further thinking and acting become possible, in particular those modes of thought and action that produce the vastly more complex makings that are the sciences and the arts, moral and legal rules, the institutions of government.

If only because of its extraordinary prominence in *Leviathan,* this feature of Hobbes's thinking is familiar to his most casual readers. Partly because Hobbes's influence has extended well beyond his considerable readership, this bracing, invigorating, but apparently also deeply disturbing conception of humankind has become a main though never dominant element in the thinking ("modern," "antimodern," "postmodern," and other) that he did much to inaugurate; a chief albeit never triumphant competitor for the intellectual and spiritual allegiances of the women and men of the ages that he has influenced. In ways that we sometimes find inspiriting and gratifying but that often leave us anxious and fearful, in much of our thinking we conceive of ourselves as Hobbesian creatures.

A self-esteeming and cheerful, certainly a buoyant if only intermittently optimistic man, Hobbes was not one to regret what might be regarded as the insouciance or even malice of God, the fact that the "Author of Nature" had written human beings into largely unfriendly circumstances and left them to cope as best they could by their own inventings and devisings. If God or Nature had done more *for* human beings (as much more, for example, as She or It had done for subhuman animals) they would thereby also have done much more *to* them; certainly they would have diminished the challenge and the zest that Hobbes savored as unique to the human estate. Hobbes did not stint in detailing the difficult, troubled character of human affairs. He nevertheless believed that there are a number of respects in which human beings have done quite well in and with their makings, yet other respects in which by his time they were positioned to do markedly better for themselves than their predecessors had managed.

The clearest case of successful making is what we would call mathematics and its application to the natural sciences and through them to "arts" such as navigation and engineering, agriculture and medicine. Hobbes thought that the set of human inventions that he called geometry had been brought to the status of a genuine science. He describes geometry as an extensive (albeit incomplete and presumably uncompletable), unambiguous, and internally consistent body of propositions (definitions, axioms and deductions therefrom) that are beyond cogent dispute. He was also convinced that the conclusions of geometry and applications of the geometric method in science more generally had imposed substantial intelligibility on the matter of nature. If not deflected or corrupted by the misconceived "experimental science" that was burgeoning around him and that he fiercely combated, science could progressively tame nature's motions and forces, could harness them to human purposes. If as a practical matter there remained far more to lament than to celebrate in politics, morals, and the other modes in which human beings attempt the inveterately difficult task of "keeping company" with one another, Hobbes believed that implementation of his own civil philosophy would set things as straight as there is any reason to want them to be.

In short, Hobbes thought that artificing has sometimes been and in appropriate respects can increasingly be efficacious and durable. Despite their radically subjective character, the stipulations that create language, and the inferences drawn from and actions taken on the basis of those stipulations, could be additive and hence progressive, could diminish the necessity and the desirability of further makings or later re-makings. Along with insisting, often vehemently, that many of the "fabrications"[1] inherited from previous generations had been ill-made and needed remaking and even eradication, he thought that some among them had been skillfully constructed and could and should be received and used rather than forgotten, destroyed, or refashioned by those who come later. Hobbes was nearly Heraclitian in his conception of a natural universe pervaded by a flux that defied human comprehension; as regards the humanly made world he resisted the despairing pessimism commonly associated with such cosmologies and seemingly impelled by his own deeply skeptical temperament.

It is arguable that this refusal on Hobbes's part was no better than the desperate act of a man who had thought himself into an untenable position. Certainly it has often been argued, against Hobbes and recognizably Hobbesian views, that the combination of positions thus far sketched is incoherent and hence self-invalidating. A "world" constructed out of nothing more substantial than the arbitrary wills and artifices of radically particularized individual beings could hardly be orderly, stable or durable. Worse, because by Hobbes's own insistence each of these "beings" is by nature nothing more than a swirling, fluctuating concatenation of particles, the notion that "they" could be God-like makers is altogether incredible. How could such beings produce and use language; how could they form, elaborate, and employ conceptions and theories; construct and operate elaborate machines; devise and maintain effective institutions? By denying the humanly knowable divine, natural or rational order posited by his main theological and philosophical opponents, by claiming to liberate human beings to devise an order of their own making and liking, Hobbes cast humankind into an abyss of self- and mutual unintelligibility. Insofar as the women and men of later centuries have followed Hobbes, that is where their self-conceptions and self-understandings leave them.

Hobbes did sometimes understate and perhaps underestimate the difficulties implied by his most general philosophical positions, did exaggerate the possibility of making good the enormous deficits left in the human condition by God, nature and thus far by human history. Of course this judgment does not itself invalidate his biting critiques of

opposing and apparently more encouraging views, critiques that do
much to expose the illusory or rather delusory character of the strong
assurances of order and intelligibility that others have offered themselves and us. Accordingly, we should show our gratitude for the
lessons Hobbes has taught us by bringing them to bear on the more
affirmative aspects of his thinking. We should subject his own propos-
als and prescriptions to the same skeptical attack that he launched
against the too sanguine and overly zealous religious, philosophical and
political dogmatists of his time.

Unquestionably a part of the present task, Hobbes has done much of
this critical work for us. He sometimes understated or diminished the
skeptical and other circumscribing implications and complications of
his cosmological and theological, metaphysical and epistemological
views; but his works also contain extended discussions that are more
than candid in insisting on the limitations on and obstacles to our
knowing and understanding, our thinking and acting. Hobbes is not a
dogmatic skeptic or passive nihilist who asserts the impossibility of
warranted beliefs or efficacious purposeful action. No attentive reader
can miss the powerfully skeptical tendency of his thinking concerning
the divine and its relation to the human, language and the possibilities
of communication and mutual understanding, reasoning and knowing,
science and the understanding and control of nature.

There is a related point that is yet more important for present purposes.
Hobbes sometimes indulged himself in overstatement as to the possibility
and desirability of achieving political and moral order through contract,
covenant and the rule of the Leviathan. But we have to consider the
possibility that the common or public order he thought possible and
desirable would encompass no more than limited aspects of human life,
was neither meant nor expected to impose any very extensive controls
on the thinking and acting of individual human beings. The view that
he is first and foremost a theorist of individual makings and unmakings
suggests that public order is for the sake of the multiplicity of partial,
personal, and internally conflicted orders that each of us makes and
remakes for ourselves.

Hobbes puts substantial difficulties in the way of entertaining this
possibility. Leaving for later discussion a certain ambivalence that he
betrays concerning the desirable scope and purposes of the form of

association that he called a commonwealth, the most serious among these difficulties reside in his infamous description of the state of nature. Taken at face value, this frightening and often decried account teaches that human relations governed by nothing but individual self-command and self-control ineluctably deteriorate into a destructive "war of all against all." If this is the case, the notion that individual persons should for the most part be left to their own self-making and self-governance is no better than a reckless fantasy. The human beings he describes had better be governed, rigorously and perhaps entirely so, by someone or something else. It seems that if we credit Hobbes's analysis of the state of nature we must also take at face value his argument for a sovereign with the authority and power not only to rule but substantially to remake its subjects. Or rather we could resist this conclusion only by taking the deeply pessimistic view that Hobbesian human beings are ungovernable, fated to misery if not to mutual annihilation. On this familiar and understandable view of his thinking, Hobbes reduces us to a choice between two equally repugnant options: peace, order and a measure of commodious living at the price of docile submission to authoritarian government; assertive self-making and self-direction at the cost of disorder, conflict, and mutual destruction. Because, if these exhaust and are the mutually exclusive alternatives, Hobbes has an unmistakable preference for the first, it is absurd to think of him as a theorist of robust individuality and abundant diversity, of minimal governmental control and discipline.

I contest this reading in the pages that follow. By way of preparation, I here mention a consideration that is partly available in the discussion thus far and that has often been advanced by critics who think that Hobbes's position, whether evaluated as appealing or repulsive, is untenable because internally contradictory or incoherent. The line of criticism to which I refer goes as follows: For all of Hobbes's talk about the absolute authority and fear-inspiring power of the Sovereign, his Leviathan is and on his premises can only be a paper tiger, is and must be incapable of cogently demanding or effectively compelling more than minimal obedience from its subjects. His Leviathan couldn't begin to impose the order and control he wanted.

This critique of the most specifically political aspects of Hobbes's thinking is a particular version of the objection that, quite generally, his views cannot account for regularity or order sufficient to intelligible experience. If human beings as he depicts them cannot so much as make sense of themselves, one another, and their world, they can hardly construct and maintain a politically organized society. As with the more general formulation of this objection, it may be that those who advance it are governed—whether knowingly—by assumptions that Hobbes has good reason to reject. As Hobbes most often deploys them, concepts such as regular-erratic, order-disorder, intelligible-incomprehensible/mysterious (and therefore also peace, security, stability, felicity and their opposite, obverse, and contrasting terms) operate over ranges or along continua. They do not form binaries or dichotomies, are matters of more and less, not all or none. There are real difficulties with his epistemology and his philosophies of language and science, but he should not be castigated for failing to meet criteria of knowledge, meaning and explanation that he repudiated and that, partly for reasons he brought against them, have not fared notably well in subsequent discussions. Most pertinent here, acknowledging the objections against his theory of making and maintaining a politically organized society does not excuse us from asking whether some of those objections proceed from conceptions of the character and proper purposes of governance and politics that deserve the scorn that (remarkably few lapses aside) he heaped on them.

Hobbes was, as we might put it in this preliminary discussion, a pretty smart fellow. If it is obvious to us (from his descriptions of and prescriptions for it!) that the gimcrack contraption that he calls Leviathan could have little effective authority and even less power over its subjects, it might not be unreasonable to assume that he wanted it that way. We will see that he gives us more definite reasons for this inference. (And thereby gives us reasons for preferring a state and a politics something like the one he proposes to the vastly more potent and hence immeasurably more dangerous varieties that had begun to emerge in his time and that now threaten our very existence.)

Hobbes is a spirited participant in debates that are alive and urgent here and now. If we attack or defend his ideas we had better be prepared to support our own.

My claim is that the primary unit of Hobbes's thinking is the individual person and her makings, unmakings and remakings of herself and her worlds, the primary objective of his political and moral thinking is to promote and protect each person's pursuit of her own felicity as she herself sees it. My objective is to defend this reading of Hobbes (including against those aspects of his own thinking that oppose it) and to assess and in considerable part to recommend the continuing merits of the elements of his thinking on which it is based.

Note

1. Because artifacts such as words, conceptions, and theories make rather than present or represent "things," for Hobbes they themselves cannot be fabrications in the sense of lies or deceits (albeit he was intensely aware that language enables lying and that lies are often told and deceptions frequently perpetrated concerning artifacts). For the same reason, that they are "made up" by their creators, for those who oppose this Hobbesian view they will be fabrications in the pejorative sense and will never be without a taint of falsification.

2

Of God, Matter and Mind

I begin by considering a reading of Hobbes sharply at variance with the one I have thus far sketched, one according to which his thinking was founded on and contained within "somethings" that are given to and quite passively but advantageously received by humankind.

Hobbes asserts that "God Almighty hath given reason to . . . man to be a light unto him" (*Elements,* II, A, Ch. 5, p. 305). Whatever else we might do with this divine gift, he claims that anyone who uses their "natural" reason will reach the conclusion that there is a God that created the universe and all that is in it, a God that is the origin of all of the causal chains that together make the universe what it is. It seems that, without any makings or artificings of her own, each person can know that there is a God, that there is a universe, and that the multifarious parts of the universe are held together by causal forces and relationships all of which trace ultimately to God.[1] We may supplement and augment these as it were natural knowings by science and various other artifices, but without them no artificings would be possible.

There is at least one passage in which Hobbes appears to say that there was a moment in human history at which God's providence sufficed for both the being and well-being of mankind (albeit apparently not humankind). In one of the numerous discussions in which he insists upon the artificial character of language and everything that is done in and with it, Hobbes considers the question of how the biblical Adam, prior to the time that he had been given or had invented any words, could understand what God said to him. "But when . . . God is said to have prohibited the eating of the fruit of the tree of knowledge of good and evil . . ., in what manner could Adam have understood that command . . . when he did not as yet know what was meant by **eating, fruit, tree, knowledge, . . . good** or **evil?** It must be, therefore, that Adam understood that divine prohibition not from the meaning of the words, but in some supernatural manner, as is made manifest a little later from this: that God asked him who had told him that he was naked." Injecting a couple of ominous notes as he drives home the point that immediately concerns him, Hobbes goes on to ask "how could Adam, the first mortal, have understood the serpent speaking of death, whereof he could have had no idea? Hence these things could not have been understood in any natural [as distinct from supernatural] way; and as a consequence, speech could not have had a natural origin except by the will of man himself" (*De Homine,* Ch. 10, pp. 38-39. Eve makes no appearance in this discussion).

The arresting idea in this beguiling passage is that God had provided Adam with "supernatural understandings" that are sufficiently like unto God's to allow Adam to comprehend and respond to God's thoughts and commands. Of at least some of the things of his world (fruits, trees), of actions (eating), of no less than the vexed philosophical questions of what knowledge is and what good and evil are, Adam was furnished with what we have to presume to have been unblemished understandings. (In traditional philosophical vocabularies these understandings would extend to the Essences or Real natures of the things understood.) Given Hobbes's view that understanding and knowledge are preeminent sources of power over their subjects, it appears that God gave Adam not only his self and his world but substantial powers over them. The story— and its sequel—suggests that these powers were sufficient not merely for felicity and commodious living (the best for which post-Adamic

humankind can hope) but some (putatively) more exalted condition. (I
say putatively because it may be a mistake to assume that Hobbes
envied Adam's edenic condition or regretted its loss. Perhaps he regarded it as a kind of *oblomovka*. If the estate of the pre-lapsarian
woman lacked some of Adam's advantages, it is possible that Hobbes
thought—or that we should think—that Eve's was the more estimable
of the two lives.)

Angered by uses Adam made of these powers,[2] God took these great
gifts away from Adam, deprived him of the flooding lights of supernatural understandings.

As Hobbes retells this gripping tale, God not only held yet more
severe punishments in reserve but gave something in partial compensa-
tion for Adam's loss. That something, this time given to all of the
members of humankind, was the ability to invent, remember, and
communicate with one another in a single language. Human beings
could no longer hope for understandings supernatural of the divinely
ordained Order of Things; they could construct various partial and less
secure but nevertheless serviceable orders for themselves. Because they
all spoke the same language, they could act in concert and thereby
engender powers at least weakly analogous to those Adam had originally enjoyed.

Once again displeased with the uses to which these powers were
being put, God intervened anew and more drastically. Although leaving
individual women and men with the capacity to invent words for their
own uses, at Babel She effected a "confusion of languages" that from
that time forward would disable the grandiose and aggrandizing projects that Her creatures had hybristically conceived and undertaken.

As with his discussion of Adam, Hobbes invokes the Babel story to
drive home to his scripturally obsessed readers his argument that all
language is fabricated not natural.[3] But his uses of these still potent
mythologies have a far wider and deeper significance. They tell us how
matters now stand with and among us, disabuse us of illusions concerning our resources and possibilities, dramatize the difficulties with
which we are confronted and the challenges we have to face. They deny
us the security and comfort of a divinely ordained or naturally given
world, of a consonance or harmony between us and our world and
among ourselves, a consonance that enables knowledge and under-

standing, cooperation and effective action. The "confusion of tongues" that God has effected among us is at once a main source and the very emblem of our "fallen" condition.

The passages I have been considering have to be regarded as adjacent to not a part of Hobbes's philosophical thinking. He presents himself as a man of Christian faith, as a man who *believes* in the Christian revelation.[4] Insofar as he is addressing other Christians he can draw on scriptural resources to win their acceptance of his views. If his philosophy has no place for the essences and supernatural understandings of the Adam story, if it casts deep doubt on the possibility of so much as widely shared to say nothing of the universally intelligible pre-Babel language, the teachings of that philosophy largely coincide with the Christian doctrine concerning our post-Adamic and post-Babelian condition.[5]

I

In elaborating and defending this claim, I begin with some of the main affirmative and negative claims of Hobbes's metaphysics and physics and then consider the epistemology and philosophy of science in and through which he attempts to explain and justify those claims. Aspects of his philosophy of language and his philosophical and empirical psychology cannot be entirely avoided in this discussion but exposition and critique of those topics will for the most part be postponed until Chapters 3 and 4 respectively. These discussions will prepare the ground for treatment of his moral, political, and jurisprudential theories in Chapters 5, 6 and 7.[6]

Hobbes was a "plenist," he held that the universe is "full" of matter, that there are no empty spaces in it. In protracted and often acrimonious controversies with Robert Boyle and the experimental scientists of the newly established Royal Society, he argued against the reality of vacuums in nature and the possibility of creating a vacuum by artificial means such as pumping the "air" (i.e., the plethora of what we might call submicroscopic particles) out of a globe or other vessel. The pumping devices crafted by Boyle and his co-workers altered the motions of the particles in the vessel and thereby caused various effects, for example, the killing—though by "the force of tenacious air," not by asphyxiation as

Boyle claimed (*Physical Dialogue,* p. 347)—of animals placed in the globe, but neither these nor any other forces could empty it.

He was also a metaphysician of motion and a causalist to the point of being a thoroughgoing philosophical determinist. Against Aristotle's view that the matter of nature is "naturally" and therefore properly at rest and that motion is what has to be explained and justified, he argued that the particles of which the universe consists are in incessant motion and that particular movements of any aggregation of particles can be altered or halted only by collision with the movements of some other.[7] The motions of these particles of matter were "placed in the things themselves by the Author of Nature" (ibid., Ch. 25, p. 145). Arguing in part from the "supposition" that this "Author" is an omnipotent God whose power extends throughout the universe that She created, in part from the notion that moving bodies in a "full" universe could not but have incessant and consequential causal impacts on one another, Hobbes hypothesizes that these bodies form an immensely complex but unbroken network of causal relationships.

On his own philosophical theology, Hobbes is in no position to affirm more than "beliefs" about God's uses of Her powers. His metaphysics may warrant the claim that there will be constant contact among the moving particles of which the universe consists but it provides no support for the claim that those contacts will form an integrated system of relationships. Despite these shaky foundations, the positions thus far discussed, strongly analogous to those of his theological, philosophical and scientific opponents, would appear to offer grounds for optimism concerning the possibilities of human knowledge of and control over nature. Having banished indeterminism (chance or mere coincidence) and hence contingency from the universe,[8] having hypothesized that the universe is orderly, and believing that God has gifted humankind with natural reason, Hobbes would seem to have given himself and us reason to expect considerable success in understanding and perhaps in achieving mastery over our world and ourselves as among the objects in that world.

In considerable if unwarranted part, Hobbes permitted himself these conclusions from his reasonings. But the more sanguine parts of his thinking about science and its practical applications must be read in the light of the cautions, or rather the many further cautions, that he enters.

In Hobbes's view, the proposition that God "placed" or impelled the motions in the things of the world contains the corollary that these motions are merely "by us observed in them," that is, that the "principles" of "PHYSICS," or the study of "the Phenomena of Nature" "are not such as we ourselves make" (ibid., Ch. 25, pp. 145-46). No doubt heartening to those who think that a given, an objectively existing, universe is a necessary condition of genuinely scientific knowledge, this proposition and the implication Hobbes finds in it are for him reason for a robust skepticism. The hypothesis that the universe is orderly is generated exclusively by the abstract considerations mentioned above, it *cannot* be warranted by our "observations." Rather, we observe and "make use of" bodies and their motions "in single and particular, not universal propositions" (ibid.). Nothing in these radically particularized observations dictates the names we do or should assign to them. Because generalizing is always on the basis of the meanings of names and other words previously assigned, "Nor do they [the observations] impose upon us any necessity of constituting theorems; their use being only . . . to show us the possibility of some production or generation" (ibid.). However it may be to the eye of God, to human "observers" the universe presents itself as a plethora of particulars that are connected only in that they regularly bash against one another. The "theorems," generalizations, and explanations that we construct out of our stipulations are and can only be "conditional" and "hypothetical," never "categorical."[9]

Signaling yet deeper doubts and narrower limitations, when discussing our capacity for "observing" Hobbes routinely denominates the results we obtain by terms such as *appearances, seemings* and *fancies, affections, apparitions,* and *phantasms.* Consistent with his unremitting metaphysics of matter in motion, for Hobbes all perception— that is, seeing and hearing as well as feeling, tasting and smelling—consists in interactions, which take place in "organs" of sense, between and among motions coming from without and others from within the body that perceives. "The cause of sense is the external body, or object, which presseth the organ proper to each sense, either immediately, as in the taste and touch; or mediately, as in seeing, hearing and smelling; which pressure, by the mediation of nerves and other strings and membranes of the body, continued inward to the brain and heart, causeth there a resistance, or counter-pressure, or endeavour of the heart to deliver itself, which endeavour, because **outward**, seemeth to be some matter without. And this **seeming**, or **fancy**, is that which men call sense."[10]

Notwithstanding his use of apparently pejorative or dismissive words like "seeming" and "fancy," Hobbes does not intend to discredit the senses and the data they yield, does not mean to supplant them by some allegedly superior source of information about or means of access to the world. Claims of the latter sort, whether philosophical as in Plato and Descartes, religious and demonological as in claims of direct or personal divine inspiration and powers of witches and witchcraft, or yet more crassly hypocritical and self-serving as with money-grubbing astrologers and soothsayers, are main sources of confusion, mystification and indeed destructive civil war. In attacking these deeply deluded and deluding doctrines, Hobbes sometimes writes as if he were a psychological empiricist à la John Locke and John Stuart Mill.[11] He regards his account of perception as accurate, as giving the only tenable account of an undeniable and indispensable feature of the experience of all sensate beings.

He is at least as keen to discredit the unrealistic estimations of the reliability and efficacy of perception offered by other philosophers and to insist upon the limitations on what we can know and do on the basis of what our senses tell us. In their treatment of sense and the senses, Aristotle and the numerous philosophers who have followed him compounded an error that we have already seen Hobbes combating, namely thinking that the things of the world are naturally intelligible to us, that they speak to us in a language that we are naturally fitted to understand. Having either rejected or severely qualified Plato's doctrine of Forms or Ideas knowable by Reason or Rational Intuition, these thinkers thought themselves obliged to defend, against Plato's assault, the reliability of the senses as transmitters or conduits of the objects or things of the world. They did so, as Hobbes somewhat tendentiously reports them, by putting "for the cause of **vision**, that the thing seen, sendeth forth on every side a **visible species** . . . the receiving whereof into the eye is **seeing**. And for the cause of **hearing**, that the thing heard, sendeth forth an **audible species** . . . which entering at the ear, maketh **hearing**. Nay, for the cause of **understanding** also, they say the thing understood sendeth forth an **intelligible species**, that is, an **intelligible being seen**; which, coming into the understanding, makes us understand."

All of this is so much "insignificant speech." The "species" and "beings" that this doctrine posits are no better than fantasies dreamed up for our (false) comfort (ibid., p. 22). The vibrations produced by the clash of inward and outward motions become "somethings" as opposed to "anythings,"[12] become distinct perceptions or experiences only when individual human beings differentiate among them.[13] Because the senses themselves and the motions that impinge upon them are multiple and unruly, making differentiations is a difficult and uncertain business. In its natural condition the world of the senses is very much as William James was later to characterize the "stream of consciousness," a "blooming, buzzing confusion."[14]

The activity of distinguishing and imposing order upon sense impressions is propelled and partly directed by another and quite special set of forces, the "Voluntary Motions, commonly called the Passions" (*Lev.,* Ch. 6, p. 47). If human beings lacked the powers that their passions provide, their experience and hence they themselves would be little better than a chaos. To understand the difficult work that the passions (and its agent or "scout," reason) have to do, we have first to consider the ways in which sense experience is augmented but also immensely complicated by what Hobbes calls the imagination.

Despite passages already discussed, Hobbes does consider and attempt to refute versions of the yet more skeptical doctrine that our senses themselves do not exist, that our belief in so much as their reality is a delusion. His first rejoinder is that we must "acknowledge" the reality of the senses and sense data because their existence is the only possible explanation for something else that we cannot deny, namely that we do in fact form "apparitions" of ourselves and our world. What if these apparitions are no more than his term for them seems to imply, what if they come and go in an instant, leaving no trace to give us continuing assurance of their reality? As Hobbes puts the difficulty, "But you will say, by what sense shall we take notice of sense?" His answer, a kind of *petitio* in that it presupposes the reality of a species of the very thing that is in question, invokes the "sixth sense" that is memory and leads him to imagination.

"I answer, by sense itself, namely by the memory which for some time remains in us of things sensible, though they themselves pass away. For he that perceives that he hath perceived, remembers."[15] Bearing in mind that we do not yet have an account of how memories can be of "somethings" rather than "anythings," Hobbes affirms (or, again, "acknowledges") that memories collect or are stored in the mind. But they remain discrete, connected with one another only in that they arrive in a particular succession. Because as a matter of inexplicable fact these successions sometimes repeat themselves, memory not only assures us of the reality of sense but allows us to form "conjectures" concerning the future. For this reason, memory and its failings are essential ingredients in what Hobbes calls prudence and imprudence.[16]

These conjectures, and the prudence they enable and the imprudence for which they are partly responsible, are far more limited than either the best or the worst of what even the least potent among us sometimes manage.[17] To understand the excesses—in both directions—we must consider the imagination.

A philosophical psychologist (because a metaphysician) of motions and processes, for Hobbes the "faculties" or "states" of memory and imagination as well as the "organs" of sense are simply names for confluences of motions held together by their own centripetal forces. Memory is the continuation of the motions that were the initial sense datum. Its clarity or dimness, reliability or unreliability, depends on the extent to which those motions are "obscured" or diminished due to conflict with other moving things. Generically, "imagination" is merely another name for obscured or decayed memory, that is, it does not identify a new process or a different phenomenon.

Hobbes distinguishes, however, between "simple" and "compounded" imaginings. The former, which "is the imagining the whole object as it was presented to the sense," adds nothing to sense-cum-memory and is of no more advantage or danger to us than they. The latter is much more fecund, but of confusion and disorder as or more often than of under-standing. Imaginations compounded are "as when, from the sight of a man at one time, and of a horse at another, we conceive in our mind a Centaur. So when a man compoundeth the image of his own person with the images of the action of another man, as when a man imagines himself a Hercules or an Alexander, which happeneth often to them that are much taken with reading of romances, it is a compound imagination, and properly but a fiction of the mind" (*Lev.,* Ch. 2., p. 24).

Without so much as a word concerning more fruitful compoundings, Hobbes then launches into a discussion of dreams, of the religions of the "Gentiles" and their satyrs, nymphs and other monstrosities, of the ghosts, goblins and witches so frequent in the beliefs and practices of Christians, and of the doctrines of the philosophical schools that are no better than these others but that lend the latter an undeserved tincture of credibility. With the exception of disorders of the senses produced by very bright lights, illness, drunkenness, and the like, all of these confounding fantasies are the products of compound imagining (ibid., pp. 24-27). The trope of his discussion of our natural powers of compound imagination is catachresis. Understanding, order, and power develop primarily to the extent that these natural capacities are brought under control by the passions and more particularly by the master artificings that he calls stipulation and ratiocination.[18]

The "voluntary" motions that Hobbes calls the passions are further and also in part natural psychological forces that sometimes operate to improve thinking and acting, often disturb and confound them. They are of course not voluntary in the sense of being uncaused. By contrast with "vital" motions such as "the **course** of the **blood**, the **pulse**," and so forth, however, "animal" motions such "as to **go**, to **speak**, to **move**" take place only "in such manner as is first fancied in our minds . . .[,] depend always upon a precedent thought of **whither, which way**, and **what**" (*Lev.,* Ch. 6, p. 47).

Some of these "thoughts," and the "appetites" and "aversions," doings and forgoings, to which the passions give rise are natural to humankind and differ very little from one person to the next (*Lev.,* Author's Introduction, p. 20). Indeed there are appetites and aversions (in some instances difficult to distinguish from "vital motions"!) that are "born with men; as appetite of food, appetite of excretion, and exoneration" (ibid., Ch. 6, p. 48). Even with these, *what* food to eat, *which way* to excrete (?!), and *whither* to seek exoneration, that is the "**objects** of the passions" "do so vary" by "constitution individual, and particular education" that generalizing about them is always perilous (ibid., Author's Introduction, p. 20). Yet more pertinent at this juncture, because the passions are the most robust motions of the mind, and because each individual's complement of passions is diverse, fluctuating, and internally conflicted, the "perturbations" the passions produce in the mind "are innumerable" (*De Corpore*, Ch. 25, p. 161).

In dreaming, during feverish illness, and in the circumstances of contagious fear that Hobbes calls "panic-terror," passions well up and discharge themselves in an uncontrolled manner, compounding the fluctuations of the senses and inflaming the imagination. Under their influence the mind "runs from anything to anything" and human behavior becomes random and destructive. There are many people, for example the religious enthusiasts with whom Hobbes was all too familiar and those numerous others who suffer "MADNESS" ("whereof there be almost as many kinds, as of the passions themselves"), who are in such a "distracted" condition much or all of the time. They either "have passions indifferently for every thing" ("GIDDINESS") or "stronger and more vehement passions for any thing, than is ordinarily seen in others." Driven by such passions as "**vain-glory**" or "**pride**," "RAGE and FURY," and "**dejection of mind**" or "MELANCHOLY" such persons diminish or destroy themselves and all too often wreak havoc on those around them (*Lev.*, Ch. 6, pp. 62-63).

If these last passages could have been written by any number of predecessor and successor thinkers who reviled the passions and were terrified of the madness they fomented (Plato, Chrysippus, Saul/Paul, Augustine; Locke, Kant, Rawls, etc.), Hobbes rejected the inference that the passions could or should be extirpated or rigorously subordinated and thought of madness not as a condition different in kind but as multifarious and fluctuating differences of degree from normality or sanity. He regarded the passions as well as the imagination as essential to all effective thought and action and indeed as the dominant party in the perpetually unstable array of forces responsible for both peace and disorder, both great achievements and horrific failures.

A man "who has no great passion . . . but is, as men term it, indifferent; though he may be so far a good man, as to be free from giving offence; yet he cannot possibly have either a great fancy or much judgment. . . . for as to have no desire, is to be dead: so to have weak passions, is dullness." The passions alone cannot yield philosophy, science, or any of their estimable productions. These require "acquired wit" or reason, which is gotten only by "method and instruction," that is, by forms of self-discipline strongly reminiscent of those promoted by philosophical and religious enemies of the passions. But reason and the disciplined thinking that it involves "are to the desires, as scouts, and spies, to range abroad, and find the way to the things desired: all steadiness of the mind's motions, and all quickness of the same, proceeding from thence." And the "causes of the difference of wits, are in the passions; . . . which are different, not only from the differences of men's complexions [e.g., "temper of the brain, and the organs of sense"]; but from their difference of customs, and education" (ibid.).

At the age of 84, Hobbes wrote (in Latin verse) a brief autobiography in which he recounts his intellectual and other adventures. Written in the epic language of heroic struggle against great odds, it captures the two sharply opposed but resolutely affirmed tendencies of his thinking. "One thing only is real, but it forms the basis of the things we falsely claim to be something, though they are only like the fugitive shapes of dreams or like the images I can multiply at will by mirrors; fantasies, creatures of our brains and nothing more, the only reality of which is motion." Yet his *De Corpore* forges "the shackles of reason in which I could bind Proteus to force him to confess the art by which he cloaks his tricks."[19]

We are *assured* of no more than that there is a reality, one that is largely mysterious to us. Our efforts to abate that mystery often serve rather to deepen it. Yet we can force it to reveal its secrets to us, compel it to submit to our wills.

Deep skepticism, pugnacious self-assertion.

Notes

1. Curiosity and the reasoning by which it is satisfied "draws a man from the consideration of the effect, to seek the cause; and again, the cause of that cause; till of necessity he must come to this thought at last, there is some cause, whereof there is no former cause, but is eternal; which is it men call God" (*Lev.*, Ch. 11, p. 85). Cf. "Objections," p. 127, where he calls the "thought" that there is God a "supposition."

2. If Eve was the culprit, did she do her nefarious deeds out of justified resentment of the massive original inequality just described?

3. "For from that time the origins of language are diverse and have been brought by single men to single peoples. What others [e.g., Aristotle] say . . .—that names have been

imposed on . . . things according to the nature of those things—is childish. For who could have it so when the nature of things is everywhere the same while languages are diverse." Radicalizing the argument in ways I consider below, he adds: "And what relationship hath a **call** (that is, a sound) with an **animal** (that is, a body)?" (*De Homine.*, p. 39).

4. From his own time to the present, many readers of Hobbes have thought that his professions of faith are disingenuous, that he was in fact an atheist. If this judgment is based on his philosophical views, if for example it is the claim that his metaphysical materialism and atomism logically exclude the possibility of a God, Hobbes would regard it as a confusion.

Hobbes distinguished sharply between religion and theology on the one hand and philosophy, science and ordinary experience on the other; between our religious *faith* and what we can *know* on the basis of ratiocination or are justified in *thinking* because of what we see and hear, smell, taste and feel. "The **subject** of Philosophy, or the matter it treats of, is every body of which we can conceive any generation, and which we may, by any consideration thereof, compare with other bodies, or which is capable of composition and resolution; that is to say, every body of whose generation or properties we can have any knowledge. . . . Therefore it excludes **Theology**, I mean the doctrine of God, eternal, ingenerable, incomprehensible, and in whom there is nothing neither to divide nor compound, nor any generation to be conceived. It excludes the doctrine of **angels** . . . [and] all such knowledge as is acquired by Divine inspiration, or revelation, as not derived to us by reason, but by Divine grace in an instant, and, as it were, by some sense supernatural" (*De Corpore,* Ch. 1, pp. 29-30). He may have been inconsistent in claiming that reason could tell us so much as *that* there is a God (albeit in the passages that say this he may be doing no more than presenting a series of deductions from previous stipulations followed by a naming of the last inference in the series—an interpretation strongly suggested by the statement in "Objections," p. 126), but he insisted that we could *know* nothing of or about God. Those who conclude that there is a God properly go on to "confess he is incomprehensible, and above their understanding." If they speak about God, they do so "not **dogmatically**, with intention to make the divine nature understood; but **piously**, to honor him with attributes . . . as remote as they can from the grossness of bodies visible" (*Lev.,* Ch. 12, p. 89).

Thus, strictly, his claim that God gave us natural reason is either illicit or has to be viewed as no more than the assertion of one of his religious beliefs. For this reason, in examining Hobbes's philosophy I bracket the question whether in his personal beliefs Hobbes was a Christian or an atheist. If we think the latter, we can treat his numerous discussions of theological and religious questions as Theophrastian or simply as taking advantage of powerful metaphors to articulate and dramatize his reflections. It might be added that if we think the former we have to say that his discussions of Adam and of Babel show him willing to face up to aspects of the Christian story that many Christians have found too strong for their stomachs.

5. This and other parallels between his philosophical doctrine and his religious beliefs, most of us will be tempted to think, are no mere coincidence. Whether Hobbes was a believing Christian, he lived in places and a time suffused with the languages, images, and doctrines of Christianity and he was deeply engaged in the controversies that surrounded and divided it. His was one of the most vigorous and sustained attempts of his time to keep religious faith and dogma apart from philosophical, scientific and practical political thinking, but it would be quite astonishing if he had been entirely successful in this effort. For what little it is worth, my own suspicion is that his belief in

a divinely ordered universe, however inaccessible that order might be to humankind, helped him to maintain at least some distance from the radical and despairing skepticism threatened by much else in his thinking.

6. Because the latter topics are the primary concern of this work, readers may wonder why they are left for so much later, may be tempted to forgo what they—perhaps under the influence of currently fashionable disdain for philosophical "systems" and "foundation-alisms"—regard as preliminaries if not irrelevancies. Hobbes himself sometimes licenses a partial version of this view by arguing that the knowledge and understanding of humankind necessary to "civil philosophy" can be got by introspection and hence without the study of metaphysics or physics. He also seems to suggest that the student of politics, law and morals could get along with only those parts of epistemology that comprise his theory of ratiocination and limited aspects of his philosophical psychology (cf. *De Corpore,* Ch. 6, p. 78; *Lev.,* Author's Introduction, p. 20). His occasional statements to these effects are reinforced by the fact that his most widely read pages, those comprising Parts One and Two of *Leviathan,* pass very quickly over his metaphysics and physics and give highly compressed accounts of his theories of perception and imagination, reasoning and knowing.

The view that Hobbes's political philosophy is independent of the rest of his thinking is at odds with his own frequently reiterated understandings and intentions. Most important, by deflecting attention from his skepticism and in general his sense of the limitations on human capacities and powers, that view has been a chief source of misunderstandings and misappreciations of his most specifically political doctrines. If we mean by Leviathan anything approaching the powerful and intrusive state commonly thought to be Hobbes's aspiration, the human beings Hobbes describes neither could nor should attempt to construct or maintain any such thing. Regrettably, events have proven Hobbes wrong as to the "can"; attention to the full range of his thinking may help us to the conclusion that he was and still is correct as to the "should."

(By his middle or late forties, Hobbes believed that he had thought through all of the main issues of philosophy and had developed a comprehensive and fully integrated system of thought the several elements of which were interdependent and mutually confirming. Political and other developments diverted him from articulating this system in what he regarded as the philosophically proper order [for one of the most delightful of several such statements see *DC,* The Author's Preface to the Reader, pp. 102-3; see also *De Homine,* Epistle Dedicatory, pp. 35-36], but the main components of the system are in his mind and discernible in his writings at least from the *Elements of Law* forward and he did not rest until [with *De Corpore* and *De Homine* together with *De Cive* and *Leviathan*] he had expounded it in its entirety.)

7. "It is therefore manifest, that rest does nothing at all, nor is of any efficacy; and that nothing but motion gives motion to such things as be at rest, and takes it away from things moved" (*De Corpore,* Ch. 15, p. 137).

8. "[E]very act, that shall be produced, shall necessarily be produced; . . . But here . . . some man may ask whether those future things, which are commonly called contingents, are necessary. I say . . . that . . . all contingents have their necessary causes. . . ; but are called contingents in respect of other events, upon which they do not depend; . . . for men commonly call that casual or contingent, whereof they do not perceive the necessary cause. . . . " (ibid., Ch. 10, pp. 122-23. And see *Of Liberty and Necessity,* esp. p. 250).

These assertions are at the level of metaphysics and are hypothetical. As regards physics, Hobbes insisted that for the most part we are and will remain ignorant of the actual movements of and relationships among the matter of the universe. "[S]ince the causes of natural things are not in our power, but in the divine will, and since the greatest part of them, namely the ether, is invisible; we, that do not see them cannot deduce their qualities from their causes" (*De Homine*, Ch. 10, p. 42. See also *Seven Philosophical Problems*, pp. 3-4; *Decameron Physiologicum*, Ch. 2).

9. The "primary propositions" of science, those from which all further conclusions are deduced, "are nothing but definitions, or parts of definitions, and these only are the principles of demonstrations, being truths constituted arbitrarily by the inventors of speech, and therefore not to be demonstrated" (*De Corpore*, Ch. 3, p. 50).

10. Lev., Ch. 1, p. 21. Cf. Ch. 4, p. 40, where he speaks of "affections," and *De Corpore*, Ch. 25, pp. 145ff, where he speaks of "apparitions" and "phantasms." For a more detailed statement, both anatomically and otherwise, see *Elements*, I, Ch. 2, pp. 184-88.

I have not investigated the ordinary or other philosophical uses of these terms in the seventeenth century and it may be that they then had less subjectivistic and illusional or delusional connotations than they now carry. Hobbes uses these same terms when he is discussing deceptions of the senses such as the stick seeming to bend in the water, the confused and misguided thinking of other philosophers (including his contemporary Descartes—see "Objections," esp. pp. 128-30), the allegedly inspired visions of religious enthusiasts, and even the ravings of the mad. I conclude from this and much else that he fully intended the skeptical resonances of these words.

11. The "original" of all of "the thoughts of man . . . is that which we call SENSE, for there is no conception in a man's mind, which hath not at first, totally, or by parts, been begotten upon the organs of sense. The rest are derived from that original" (*Lev.*, Ch. 1, p. 21).

12. Cf. Ludwig Wittgenstein, *Philosophical Investigations*, I, 6. Trans. G.E.M. Anscombe (New York: Macmillan, 1958). Hobbes is not prepared to entertain, however, the more radical Wittgensteinian possibility that they are "nothings."

13. Hobbes was especially proud of his doctrine, for which he claimed originality (thereby arousing the ire and perhaps the enmity of Descartes), of "secondary qualities." (See "To The Right Honourable The Marquis of Newcastle" in Molesworth, Vol. VII, pp. 467-68.) Colors, heat, smells, and so forth, are not in the external objects whose motions impact on the organs of sense, they are in *us;* they simply *are* the new or redirected motions that occur within our bodies as a result of the interactions between the incoming and outgoing motions. This doctrine depends on a distinction between the motions that make up the objects (bodies) themselves—the primary qualities—and the new motions that result from the interaction—the secondary qualities. Hobbes is clearly devoted to this distinction and hence to the notion that the primary qualities, including those that are qualities of our own bodies, have an undeniable reality, one that is independent of our perception of them but that can be experienced by us through our senses. ("The highest causes, and most universal in every kind, are known by themselves. But the causes of universal things (of those, at least, that have any cause [e.g., excluding God]) are manifest of themselves, or (as they say commonly) known to nature" *De Corpore*, Ch. 6, p. 75). The distinction has an insecure place in his theory. If perception and hence the knowings of which it is invariably a condition is always an interaction between incoming and outgoing motions, so far as we are concerned (as distinct, for example, from God) all qualities are secondary and the distinction collapses. (Recurring to Wittgenstein's formulation, objects and their motions that do not interact with outward-going motions are

"nothings." Hobbes's refusal of this disturbing idea may be an instance of his philosophically ungroundable faith.)

14. Looking ahead, we should note that, as with James, Hobbes did not altogether regret the diverse and disorderly character of sense experience. If sense experience were single or uniform, the distinguishing and comparing that Hobbes regards as an essential part of human understanding and knowing would be impossible. He describes those who narrow their attentions to one or a very few of the things they experience as being in a kind of stupor: "it being almost all one for a man to be always sensible of one and the same thing, and not to be sensible at all of any thing" (*De Corpore,* Ch. 25, pp. 149-50). "As for those objects, if there be any such, which do not at all stir the mind, we are said to contemn them" (ibid., p. 162).

15. *De Corpore,* Ch. 25, pp. 145-46. Hobbes appeals to a variant of this argument in rejoining to the argument of Descartes and others that we cannot demonstrate the reality of sense because we cannot distinguish clearly or certainly between the waking and the dreaming state. "For my part, when I consider that in dreams I do not often nor constantly think of the same persons, places, objects, and actions, that I do waking; nor remember *so long* a train of coherent thoughts, dreaming, as at other times; and because waking I often observe the absurdity of dreams, but never dream of the absurdities of my waking thoughts; I am well satisfied, that being awake, I know I dream not, though when I dream I think myself awake" (*Lev.,* Ch. 2, p. 25, italics added). Appropriately given that his argument concedes to dreaming the very characteristic that he says assures us of the reality of waking sense, he concedes that "it is a hard matter . . . to distinguish between sense and dreaming" (ibid.).

16. Hobbes's skepticism is underlined by the fact that he relies entirely on memory for assurance of the reality of our senses and the data they provide but gives an account of memory as essentially the *loss* of information originally possessed. "Seeing then the **conception**, which when it was **first** produced by sense, was **clear**, and represented the **parts** of the object **distinctly**; and when it cometh **again** is **obscure**, we find **missing** somewhat that we expected; by which we judge it **past** and **decayed**. For example, a man that is present in a foreign city, seeth not only **whole** streets, but can also distinguish particular **houses** and **parts** of houses; but departed thence, he cannot distinguish them so particularly in his mind as he did, . . . yet is this to **remember**: when **afterwards** there escape him **more** particulars, this is also to **remember**, but **not so** well. . . . Seeing then remembrance is **more** or **less**, as we find more or less **obscurity**, why may not we well think **remembrance** to be nothing else but the **missing of parts** which every man expecteth should succeed after they have a conception of the whole" (*Elements,* I, Ch. 3, pp. 191-92).

Looking ahead, this doctrine concerning memory is clearly important to his argument that the "natural" capacities of the mind, that is sense, memory, imagination, and some of the passions, need to be augmented by stipulation and reason. Stipulations *fix* the conceptions originally formed by sense and imagination, attach them to a name the remembering of which brings with it the components of the conception better (albeit imperfectly in most cases) than memory of unnamed sense data can do. It seems that we are better at remembering names that we ourselves have made than we are at remembering conceptions themselves. Looking even further ahead, it is plausible to think that this understanding of memory influences his antagonism toward custom as a source of law, his insistence that law is always the present or occurrent will of the Sovereign.

17. At their very best, the faculties and processes thus far considered give us assurances that are "more or less; but never full and evident: for though a man may have always seen the day and night to follow one another hitherto; yet can he not thence conclude they shall do so, or that they have done so eternally: experience concludeth nothing universally" (*Elements,* I, Ch. 4, p. 195). "Universal" conclusions, which are always "hypothetical," depend on that mode of artificing that is the stipulating of names and ratiocination from those names.

18. With the qualification just noted, unlike Nietzsche, Hobbes rarely considers the possibility that imaginative inventings are means by which human beings create inspiring ideals for themselves, project and propel themselves toward ways of thinking and acting more engaging and gratifying than those they have theretofore managed. The perhaps more important similarity between the two thinkers is that improvements in human affairs are achievements of human artifice, not gifts of God or Nature.

19. Around him "the temple of Janus flew open," civil war "raged," "Treacherous Fortune remained in the criminal camp," and the "rebel mob seized power and governed the people without law." Yet his *Leviathan,* which affords no less than "a standard of justice, a check on ambition, a stronghold of kingship, and a guarantee of peace for the people," was "firmly established in favour, and will, I hope, remain so throughout time, defended by its own internal strength" (*Autobiography,* pp. 25-28).

3

Of Language, Reason and Science

The single most widely quoted passage in Hobbes's works is his description of the "state of nature" as a war of all against all in which life is "solitary, poor, nasty, brutish, and short" (*Lev.,* Ch. 13, p. 100). As Rousseau and numerous others have commented, this account is in fact of a highly "unnatural" condition, one in which a great deal of artificing has already occurred. Language has been invented and become widely shared; there are mutual understandings and misunderstandings; desires and purposes have formed that are unknown in other creatures whose natures are little different than that of human beings. The story of this state of nature, in short, is primarily one of artificing gone wrong, of makings that are the unmaking or rather the undoing of their makers.

Hobbes has another account of the "natural" condition of humankind, one that is primarily in epistemological rather than political terms. As with his more famous version, if historical at all it is at best casually so, Hobbes's concern being to call attention to characteristics that have always been and will forever continue to be part of the human condition.

A kind of analogue to the Eden to Babel story already considered, it sets what we might call the anthropological scene for his discussion of stipulation, ratiocination and science, establishes the benchmark that allows him to assess both the improvements effected and the troubles produced by these most consequential among the modes of human making.

"Philosophy seems to me to be amongst men now, in the same manner as corn and wine are said to have been in the world in ancient time. For from the beginning there were vines and ears of corn growing here and there in the fields; but no care was taken for the planting and sowing of them. Men lived therefore upon acorns; or if any were so bold as to venture upon the eating of those unknown and doubtful fruits, they did it with danger of their health. In like manner, every man brought Philosophy, that is, Natural Reason, into the world with him; for all men can reason to some degree, and concerning some things: but where there is need of a long series of reasons, there most men wander out of the way, and fall into error for want of method, as it were for want of sowing and planting, that is, of improving their reason" (*De Corpore*, Ch. 1, p. 23).

These "unimproved" reasoners and their thinking and acting are no more to be despised than the acorns on which some among them live; their "prudence," while "not to be esteemed philosophy," is as much to be preferred to false or fraudulent philosophers and philosophizing as healthful acorns to the poisonous concoctions and effluents of the latter. "And from hence it comes to pass, that they who content themselves with daily experience, which may be likened to feeding upon acorns, and either reject, or not much regard philosophy, are commonly esteemed, and are, indeed men of sounder judgment than those who from opinions, though not vulgar, yet full of uncertainty, and carelessly received, do nothing but dispute and wrangle, like men that are not well in their wits" (ibid., pp. 24, 23). As Hobbes frequently puts it, the judgment of those of "Natural Reason" or "daily experience" is "between" the absurdities of those who abuse language on the one hand and the science or sapience of those who use it properly on the other.[1] Despite his skepticism concerning prudence, Hobbes's philosophy, in particular his civil philosophy, depends deeply on it.

The achievements and improvements that now separate the "people of Europe" and some other places from the hunting and gathering "Americans" are nevertheless due almost entirely to "natural philosophy and geometry." "[T]he greatest commodities of mankind are the arts; namely; of measuring matter and motion; of moving ponderous bodies; of architecture; of navigation; of making instruments for all uses; of calculating the celestial motions, the aspects of the stars, and the parts of time; of geography, &c." (*De Corpore*, Ch. 1, pp. 27-28).

The want of comparable achievements in civil philosophy leaves the Europeans in a little improved, perhaps a worsened condition than the Americans, in their politics and morals (ibid). "If the moral philosophers had as happily discharged their duty, I know not what could have been added by human industry to the completion of that happiness, which is consistent with human life. For were the nature of human actions as distinctly known as the nature of **quantity** in geometrical figures, the strength of **avarice** and **ambition**, which is sustained by the erroneous opinions of the vulgar as touching the nature of **right** and **wrong**, would presently faint and languish; and mankind should enjoy such an immortal peace, that unless it were for habitation, on supposition that the earth should grow too narrow for her inhabitants, there would hardly be left any pretence for war."[2]

In addition to making his own contributions to natural science, then, Hobbes's self-assigned task was to extend the methods of natural philosophy to its "civil" branch. Partly due to his powerful urge to systematic thinking, partly because the question of what those methods properly are had become a matter of sharp controversy, he felt obliged to give an orderly account of science and its procedures. Predicated as it is on his views concerning matter and motion, sense and imagination, memory and the passions, this account cannot and does not feature observation and hypothesizing, experimentation and inductive generalization. Rather, it is in what he takes to be the geometric terms of stipulation, axiomatization and the deductions therefrom that he calls ratiocination. In important respects anticipating views now prominent in the philosophy of science, it is not an account that is likely to warm the hearts of the apostles of science—whether natural or the so-called science of politics.

I

The bodies and motions of the universe do not present themselves to us in intelligible form. For this reason, and because memory is of dissonant and decaying sense experiences that are further disturbed by imagination and passion, something must be done to fix or stabilize our experiences. "How unconstant and fading men's thoughts are, and how much the recovery of them depends upon chance, there is none but knows by infallible experience of himself. . . . From which it follows, that, for the acquiring of philosophy, some sensible moniments are necessary, by which our passing thoughts may be not only reduced, but also registered every one in its own order." This need is initially met by individuals who invent for their own use what Hobbes calls "marks" to stand for the apparitions that have formed in their minds.[3] Because the objects of sense are "senseless," that is as yet without meaning, this inventing is "at pleasure" or "arbitrary." Post-Babelian experience itself shows "the original of names to be arbitrary," but there is the deeper point that it is "impossible . . . either to observe similitude, or make any comparison betwixt a name and a thing" (*De Corpore,* Ch. 2, p. 34). Marks are not of the natural world of particulars that they single out, they are added to or imposed on that world by human beings. Those who make them do not receive warrants or directives to do—or how to do—so from any quality or characteristic of the things named, they are themselves possessed of the requisite *author*ity and they invest it in the names they invent. Marks are like the "Author" of Nature's own creations, ex nihilo, from nothing except the fiat of those who create them.

The primary agencies of initiation and movement of thought being the passions, the work of originating marks must be done mainly by those potent but unruly forces. For this and the other reasons discussed, it is therefore no surprise that the naming process yields great diversity and fluctuation, that "new names are daily made, and old ones laid aside; that diverse nations use different names" (*De Corpore,* Ch. 2, p. 34). Later we see Hobbes trying to contain the resulting confusion by a combination of habit and convention, reason and political authority, but we should immediately note two respects in which he wavers little if at all from the account as I have thus far followed it. The first is that each individual's passions play a decisive role in the making of that especially important subclass of names that identify things as good and evil, desirable and undesirable, virtuous and vicious. If commonality or regularity develop in respect to these parts of language, and it would be easy to exaggerate the extent to which Hobbes either expects or wants it to do so, it is because of the providential fact that in certain respects the passions of human beings are the same and because the workings of the individual's passions can be influenced to some extent by other aspects of her experience. The second is that in doing philosophy, that is in the very activity in which language plays the most crucial role, each person must always be prepared to reject names previously adopted by herself or others, must be ready and willing to stipulate anew and differently as she herself judges appropriate.[4]

In shifting from the terminology of "marks" to "words" and "language" I have gotten somewhat ahead of the story of science as Hobbes tells it. Before returning to the development of his account let us note that in furnishing scientists with instruments that enable access to and reflection concerning nature he has already placed quite dense filters between them and the natural world they investigate. The senses, the imagination, and the passions work their own powerful effects on the data that impinges on them; memory loses much of that data; marks are invented to stabilize and preserve the resulting apparitions and to allow the performance of various further operations on it; being arbitrary devisings, marks reconstitute rather than faithfully re-present the apparitions they single out; and being products of the passions of individuals they are diverse and fluctuating. It would be something of an understatement to say that ratiocination, the task of which is to impose order on these materials, has its work cut out for it.

Perhaps partly in order to deflect or at least to postpone further difficulties that he knows await him, Hobbes nevertheless claims that the resources thus far discussed, if augmented by the "good wit" and "good judgment" that develop when the natural capacity for ratiocination is disciplined by methodical practice, are sufficient to allow individual persons to arrive at scientific truths. It is important to insist that Hobbes's emphasis here falls on "individual," on this or that person working largely independent of other scientists. In passages that strongly parallel his attacks on religious sects and the destructive political factions they so often become, Hobbes expressed both his disdain and his fear of the "group" or "team" research of experimental scientists such as Robert Boyle and his co-workers in the Royal Society (*Physical Dialogue,* esp. pp. 350ff). He treasured his many exchanges with other scientists such as Harvey, Bacon, Mersenne and Gassendi, and he never doubted that the "utility" of science consists in the power it gives to humankind to ameliorate its condition. For this reason science must be taught to others who will put it to use. The *doing* of science is the self-contained, much of the time the solitary, activity of putting one's own thoughts in order. "[C]onceptions of the things without us" are such that "if a man could be alive, and all the rest of the world annihilated, he should nevertheless retain the **image** thereof" (*Elements,* I, Ch. 1, p. 183). Each person's capacity to reason is her own and the stipulations that allow her to use it are originally and in an important sense continuously of her own making. The "child of the world and your mind is within yourself."[5] For these reasons "a man may be a philosopher alone by himself" (*De Corpore,* Ch. 6, p. 82). Much of the language and thinking inherited from previous generations or current among one's contemporaries is corrupted by equivocality and confusion. For these reasons it is better that the philosopher or scientist be alone.

In the perspective of the largest tendencies of his thinking, Hobbes's stress on the personal character of philosophy and science can be viewed as expressing both his deep commitment to individuality and his severe doubts about the possibility and desirability of keeping close or continuous company with any very large number of his fellow human beings. The all but solipsistic character of his account of the human activity that he most enjoyed and admired bespeaks his strongest affirmative preferences as well as his abiding sense that the need to cooperate with others introduces confounding and disagreeable complications and contentions.

Cooperate and contend we must. The most skeptical aspects of Hobbes's epistemology and philosophy of science prepare us for the actual and desirable limitations on political and moral knowing and acting; equally, the more affirmative and interpersonal parts of his thinking concerning natural science anticipate the constructive features of his civil philosophy.

II

Marks are personal mnemonic devices that stand for particular apparitions. They become a personal *language* when the individual who has invented them takes the further step of devising additional *words* or *concepts* that classify and otherwise order relationships among marks: words such as noun and verb; singular and universal; all, many and none; and, if, and then; either and or. These "second-order" words (words about words as Hobbes the philosophical nominalist repeatedly and insistently says) constitute the grammar that regulates uses of the language. This grammar makes it possible to put words together into meaningful sentences and propositions, to distinguish between correct and incorrect speech, true and false propositions. The rules of grammar also enable generalization and abstraction, inference and deduction, negation and contradiction, that is, *ratiocination* in general and specialized forms thereof such as logic and mathematics.

On first invention these words about words are yet more "arbitrary" than the first-order marks. This is because their relationship to the world of matter and motion is yet more heavily mediated by the motions of the mind itself than that of marks and first-order words;[6] and it is this fact about them that is the chief source of both their power or utility, their limitations and the troubles they cause. Being all but wholly made, there is little about them that is not in the power of the person who invented and uses them. In principle, persons stand to their personal languages almost as God stands to the universe She created.

In actuality most persons frequently forget their earlier stipulations, are negligent of and even perversely disobedient to their own rules. To this extent, their language disables their thinking and acting and they become "like men not well in their wits." At the same time, because second-order language is self-made and self-contained, thinking that is entirely in its terms and carefully done (but only such thinking) yields truths that are certain, truths that are rationally indisputable. The highest form of science, geometry, is thinking that is exclusively of this kind.

This account of scientific thinking leaves Hobbes with the difficult question of how such a science can connect with the world that it purports to be about, how such a self-made and self-contained set of truths can yield power and utility. He has to show both that marks bring the world into scientific thinking and that they do so without destroying the integrity of the reasoning that is done with second-order words. Because the marks are not "made" in his strongest sense, are disturbed by the several sources of variability and fluctuation discussed above, it would appear that incorporating them must weaken the scientist's control over her reasoning and hence deprive her conclusions of the certitude that Hobbes claims for them.

The concessions we have seen Hobbes making to this objection are importantly enlarged by the aspects of his thinking now before us. Science as it is now emerging must be very "pure" indeed, must be all but self-standing and self-subsistent. It appears that it can yield truths in Hobbes's strongest sense only if it leaves the world behind. It is no accident that Hobbes thought he could best explain or teach scientific thinking by imagining the annihilation of all of the world save the scientist. (Nor is it any accident, to glance ahead once more, that Hobbes thought his Leviathan should be a monarchy, should be ruled by a single mind that takes data from its experience and may take advice from other persons but that, like the scientific mind on which it is partly modeled, imposes and maintains its own order, invents for itself the coordinated system of propositions that Hobbes calls law. But the Sovereign cannot leave the world behind, must give "rule" not only to her own thoughts and words but to a fractious multitude over which she has yet less control than the scientist has over the motions of mind and nature. A Sovereign could rule "scientifically" only if she were in the politically or jurally self-annihilating condition of having no subjects to rule.)

There is yet another and more nettled dimension to the issue of the power and utility of science. The scientist who aspires to contribute to human well-being must forgo the treasure that is her splendid isolation, must "go public" to the extent necessary to teach her scientific conclusions to others. In order to do so the language in which she does her thinking must cease to be the deeply personal construction/possession that we have been discussing and become a means of communication with others. Marks must become *signs* and words must become *speech;* thoughts and reasonings that had been so exclusively mine as to be mere noises or doodles to others must be put at the disposal of others, must be made available to the use and hence vulnerable to the abuses and profanations of others. Power, command or control in any sense save self-command or self-control can be gotten only at the cost of a kind of exhibitionism, of exposing oneself to others. (It will turn out that self-command also requires such exposure.)

Hobbes's estimation of this treacherous exchange will bring us back to the other aspects of the issue about the utility of science. It will also help us to see the ways in which science must be supplemented by, or rather is dependent on, the (yet!) much less certain business that Hobbes calls prudence.

As with the marks and words of personal languages, signs divide into the classes of first- and second-order, the former being assigned to apparitions, the latter providing classifications of and otherwise imposing order on the former. Whereas marks and words are for my own thinking and would be useful "though a man were alone in the world" (*De Corpore,* Ch. 2, p. 33), signs are for communicating with others. "The difference, therefore, betwixt marks and signs is this, that we make those for our own use, but these for the use of others" (ibid.).

The chief use of the signs that make up the language of science is the teaching of the truths that individual scientists have established. "[T]hough some one man, of how excellent a wit soever, should spend all his time partly in reasoning, and partly in inventing marks for the help of his memory, and advancing himself in learning; who sees not that the benefit he reaps to himself will not be much, and to others not at all? For unless he communicate his notes with others, his science will perish with him. But if the same notes be made common to many, and so one man's inventions be taught to others, science will thereby be increased to the general good of mankind."[7]

Perhaps deliberately and not altogether innocently playing on his own word, Hobbes dramatizes the communicative component of science by going so far as to say that the infallible "sign" of the genuine scientist is the capacity to teach her scientific truths to others. "The signs of science are some, certain and infallible; some, uncertain. Certain, when he that pretendeth the science of any thing, can teach the same; that is to say, demonstrate the truth thereof perspicuously to another; uncertain, when only some particular events answer to his pretence, and upon many occasions prove so as he says they must" (*Lev.*, Ch. 5, p. 46). Just as the Sovereign's rule depends on her capacity to make her laws "perspicuous" to her subjects (failing which she ceases to be Sovereign), so the standing of the scientist and her science depends on her capacity to communicate clearly to others. Failing such communication, she is no more than a pretender and her science no better than a pretence.[8]

Can language and we its makers and users meet these stringent tests, shoulder these heavy burdens? Hobbes thought that it sometimes does and that a few among us sometimes do. Although shaken by his own bitter disputes with geometers of his own day and contemptuous of much that passed for science in his own time, he thought that geometry was a true science and that genuine scientists such as Harvey had brought themselves and aspects of their subject matters as close to this standing as work with an "empirical" dimension can come. Hobbes was nevertheless vividly aware that his teaching requirement greatly compounded the difficulties we have already seen, imposed substantial further limitations on the possibilities of science and of everything else that he makes to depend on shared language.

III

In the *De Homine* discussion of Adam and Babel, Hobbes begins by arguing that humankind's unique capacity for speech explains its superiority over all other animals. He nevertheless acknowledges that his own account of language seems to put speech and its advantages in jeopardy. "Because, however, I would say that names have arisen from human invention, someone might possibly ask how a human invention could avail so much as to confer on mankind the benefit speech appears to us to have. For it is incredible that men once came together to take counsel to constitute by decree what all words and all connexions of words would signify." His immediate response (not irrelevant to his account of the emergence of politically organized societies) is that human beings did little by little what they could not do all at once. "It is more credible, that at first there were few names and only of those things that were the most familiar. Thus the first man by his own will imposed names on just a few animals . . . then on other things, as one or another species of things offered itself to his sense; these names, having been accepted, were handed down from fathers to their sons, who also devised others" (Ch. 1, p. 38).

It is difficult to resist saying that Hobbes either evades altogether or gives a manifestly unsatisfactory answer to the hard part of the question as he himself first posed it. The important issue is not whether all or some substantial number of "men once came together" to establish a language common among themselves; rather, it is how human beings as he describes them could successfully invent and use language at all. The bland, matter of fact character of his description of the gradual accumulation of common language will hardly be convincing to anyone who has taken seriously his powerful insistence on the commotion that is without, within, and among human beings. It is indeed "incredible" that mere human inventions could capture such disorder and flux, could "impose" a more or less stable and for the most part mutually understandable language on it.

Hobbes's primary concern in the *De Homine* discussion is to discredit the notion of a language that is supernaturally or naturally intelligible. Perhaps for this reason, in that place his affirmative response to the objection I am considering consists entirely of the few sentences I quoted. It is important to underline that it is Hobbes himself who poses the objection and that his immediately following Adam to Babel story strengthens the objection by rejecting what might be thought to be a more convincing rejoinder to it. If the capacities necessary to invent and sustain a common language were known to have been provided by God, human beings could hardly question their efficacy.[9]

These considerations raise the question whether Hobbes was: (a) aware that the response he there made to the objection left it with considerable force; (b) convinced that it is the only tenable kind of response available; and (c) content or even pleased with the limitations on language and communication that would remain even after the response had been presented in a more developed and satisfactory form.

(Of course there is also the more profound "Wittgensteinian" objection that a language as deeply private as that of Hobbes's "first man,"

indeed of the "originals" of the languages of each and every human
being, is a logical impossibility. Absurd as it would be to suggest that
Hobbes considered this objection in the refined forms now available,
we will see that the best articulated of his responses to the objection
that he did address have some bearing on it.)

IV

If we could hardly dignify Hobbes's casual remarks in *De Homine* as
historical, his use of terms such as *accepted* and *handed down* supplement his theory of stipulation with notions of custom or convention.
Augmented by a quite strong doctrine of habit, by the more active ideas
of consent and agreement, and finally by the notion of definitions
invested with the authority of the Sovereign and taught by her command, custom and convention are yet much more prominent in his more
extensive discussions of speech in other works.

Hobbes distinguishes "error" from "falsity," "absurdity," and "insig-
nificance." The first is due to misperception and poorly conducted
"silent" and apparently extra-linguistic "cogitation." The far more
consequential other three arise from "pronouncing rashly; for names
have their constitution . . . from the will and consent of men. And
hence . . . men pronounce falsely, by their own negligence, in departing
from such appellations as they have agreed upon" (*De Corpore*, Ch. 5,
p. 65). Good reasoning concerning "all questions of right and philosophy"
is "drawn from the covenants of men, and definitions, that is to say,
significations received by use and common consent of words." Or
rather, there is *no other way* to reason about such questions, nothing
else on which such reasoning can be based. "[W]hen in matter of right
it is questioned, whether there be **a promise** and **covenant**, or not, that
is nothing else but to demand whether such words, spoken in such a
manner, be by common use and consent of the subjects **a promise** or
covenant; which if they be so called, then it is true that a contract is
made; if not, then it is false: that truth therefore depends on the
compacts and consents of men." Driving home the categorical character
of his position (in case, for example, someone thinks that it is limited
to "performative utterances" or to settings in which there are "consti-

tutive rules") Hobbes continues, "In like manner, when it is demanded in philosophy, whether the same thing may entirely be in diverse places at once; the determination of the question depends on the knowledge of the common consent of men, about the signification of the word **entire**. For if men, when they say a thing is entirely somewhere, do signify by common consent that they understand nothing of the same to be elsewhere; it is false that the same thing is in divers places at once. . . . And they who do judge that anything can be determined, contrary to the common consent of men concerning the appellations of things . . . do also judge that the use of speech, and at once all human society, is to be taken away. . . . Nay, they take away reason itself; which is nothing else but a searching out of the truth made by such consent" *(DC,* Ch. XVII, pp. 367-68. As the last sentences make clear, this passage is much more than a restatement of Hobbes's nominalism. First-order words start out as marks for apparitions produced by sense and imagination; when they become speech their meanings and hence the truth or falsity of the propositions they compose depend on common consent, not the things that they mark.)

Both the affirmative and philosophical and the negative and polemical force of this powerful passage (it is a part of one of Hobbes numerous assaults on "inspired" or otherwise deeply personal interpretations of Scripture) are underlined in Hobbes's—highly idiosyncratic!—rendering of the notion of conscience. When two or more persons attentively consult common language and reason their way to the truths implicit in it, they become "CONSCIOUS of it one to another; which is as much as to know it together. And because such are fittest witnesses of the facts of one another, or of a third, it was and ever will be reputed a very evil act, for any man to speak against his **conscience**; or to corrupt or force another so to do: inasmuch that the plea of conscience, has been always hearkened unto very diligently in all times." Much to Hobbes's disgust and dismay, in the conflicts of his own time this esteemed notion was appropriated to linguistically deviant, epistemologically absurd, and politically destructive purposes. "Afterwards, men made use of the same word metaphorically, for the knowledge of their own secret facts . . . and . . . thoughts; and therefore it is rhetorically said, that the conscience is a thousand witnesses. And last of all, men, vehemently in love with their own new opinions . . . gave those their opinions also that reverenced name of conscience, as if they would have it seem unlawful, to change or speak against them; and so to pretend to know they are true, when they know at most, but that they think so" (*Lev.,* Ch. 7, p. 57).

Disagreements and conflicts such as those that prompted these violations of "ordinary language" should be resolved not by descent into the maelstrom of private experience and opinion but by "**trac**[ing] and **find**[ing] out, by many experiences, what men do mean by calling things [for example] just and unjust" (*De Corpore,* Ch. 4, p. 196); by seeking "equipollence" among their propositions through close attention to the established but often distorted meanings of the words of which they consist (ibid., Ch. 3, pp. 51-52).[10] The equivocality and confusion that so often afflict thought and the actions it informs stem not from "names, for some use them properly and accurately for the finding out of truth," but from the regrettable fact that "others draw them from their proper sense, for ornament or deceit" (ibid., p. 39).

In these and related passages, Hobbes exudes confidence concerning the interpersonal standing of the languages that he has in mind, manifests assurance that those who speak the same languages can communicate effectively in them. These languages are governed by rules or norms that distinguish between correct and incorrect speech, between meaningful and meaningless uses of words and true and false propositions made up of words. Because the criteria by which these distinctions are drawn arise out of custom and convention, by the consent and agreement of those who speak the languages, there is every reason to think that they are known to and accepted by those speakers. Language is a serviceable instrument not only for individual thinking but for the interactions necessary to keeping company. Because ratiocination is nothing more than the working out of what is implied in names already known to those who engage in it, there is every reason to think that human beings can reason effectively, can arrive at truths and teach them to one another.

Hobbes knows that human beings often misuse and deliberately abuse their languages. Falsity and absurdity are widespread and are chief sources of the confusion and conflict that disturb and disrupt human affairs. But these misuses and abuses are identifiable as such and are subject to correction. Much of Hobbes's own philosophizing is aimed at effecting these corrections, at subjecting to "tractation" that which is distracted and distracting. The very fact that language starts with stipulation, that it is made and can be remade by human fiat, means that it can be enlarged and extended to deal with new questions and problems as they present themselves. Human beings can augment their capacity to make language by devising institutions vested with the authority to extend and enhance their uses of it. Government, in the hands of that great stipulator the Sovereign, is the chief such devising.

Hobbes neither has, nor given his premises can have, any very plausible account of how consent and agreement develop, how others can come to know and hence agree to the uses I make of words that I have invented. If this is a defect in his theory, he doesn't let it deter him from insisting that speech and everything that depends on it presupposes substantial agreement in and fidelity to the established uses of language.[11] In the passages just surveyed he writes as if this condition is, or at any rate could easily enough be, largely satisfied.

In the wider setting of Hobbes's thought these passages take on a quite different coloration. The possibilities I have been canvassing are never denied but the probability of steady success in communication is assessed very differently than I have just suggested. Hobbes repeatedly insists on views that make his own sometimes optimism concerning language, reason and science difficult to credit. Yet more arresting, he often treats the very considerations that support his most favorable estimations as sources of difficulty and disturbance, as reasons for thinking that language makes human affairs more difficult rather than easier (which may not be to say worse rather than better).

Marks, words, and speech are to fix and stabilize both intra- and interpersonal experience, to quiet the turbulence of the mind and diminish the disorders of social life. Language can do these things only if there is fidelity to customs, conventions, and agreements. We are therefore pulled up short (or thrown back to his view of science as personal, as done in solitude) when we find Hobbes saying that those who "make custom and example the rule of . . . [their] actions . . . [are] like little children, that have no other rule of good and evil manners, but the correction they receive from the parents and masters." Likening such people to "the lawyers which only use this false measure of justice" and "barbarously" call it "precedent," Hobbes seems to extend to custom and customary behavior generally the same scathing disdain that he had for the common law and those who celebrate it (*Lev.,* Ch. 11, p. 84; *Dialogue,* passim).

In another and yet harsher passage, Hobbes writes as if all speech, indeed all thinking that occurs in language, becomes so "habitual," so mechanical, that it reduces those who engage in it to something close to the merely corporeal entities of inanimate nature. Whereas much of what we considered above would lead us to expect Hobbes to approve of habit and habitual behavior, certainly of training, education and their results, Hobbes here treats them as involving or producing particularly objectionable forms of mindless behavior. The remarks in question are in a section of *Elements of Law* revealingly subtitled "Translation of the discourse of the mind into the discourse of the tongue, and of the errors *thence* proceeding." "It is the **nature** almost of every **corporal** thing, being **often moved** in one and the same manner, to receive continually a **greater and greater easiness** and aptitude to the same motion, insomuch as in time the same becometh so **habitual**, that, to **beget** it, there needs no more than to **begin** it. The **passions** of man, as they are the beginning of **voluntary** motions; so are they the beginning of **speech**, which is the motion of the tongue. And men desiring to show others the knowledge, opinions, conceptions, and passions which are in themselves, and to that end having invented **language**, have by that means transferred all that **discursion** of their **mind** . . . by the **motion** of their **tongues**, into **discourse of words**: and **ratio** now is but **oratio**, for the most part, wherein custom hath so great a power, that the mind suggesteth only the first word; the rest follow **habitually**, and are not followed by the mind; as it is with beggars, when they say their **paternoster**, putting together such words, and in such manner, as in their education they have learned from their nurses, from their companies, or from their teachers, having **no images** or **conceptions** in their mind, answering to the words they speak; and as they have learned themselves, so they teach posterity" (I, Ch. 5, pp. 201-2, italics added). Recalling his remark that cursing is the "movement of a tongue accustomed," we are tempted to say that Hobbes stands with Caliban; all speaking is cursing and speech itself is a curse on humankind.

Nor does the predictability of these automata render them sufficiently tractable to be fit for keeping company; certainly it does not make them reliably contributive to any worthy end or purpose. The noises they severally make, while repetitive, do not cohere in their own speech or mesh intelligibly with the speech of others. Because their minds do not keep pace with their tongues, they cannot adjust to or coordinate their speech and action with those of others, cannot adapt appropriately to changes in their circumstances. Whereas the children they resemble are at least "constant" to the routines to which they have been programmed, those who "have grown old, and stubborn, . . . appeal from custom to reason, and reason to custom, as it serves their turn; receding from custom when their interest requires it, and setting themselves against reason, as oft as reason is against them: which is the cause, that the doctrine of right and wrong, is perpetually disputed, both by the pen and the sword" (*Lev.*, Ch. 11, p. 84).

As prevalent and destructive as Hobbes evidently thinks they are, the misuses and abuses of speech that these passages describe are just that and hence are in principle corrigible. They are difficulties not with language as such, language as it can and should be, but with those who use it badly. Hobbes seems to be making exactly this point when he continues the passage just quoted by contrasting the abominable condition of the "doctrine of right and wrong" with the admirable order and utility of the "doctrine of lines, and figures." Because he sometimes claims that his own doctrine of right and wrong is as clear and as beyond dispute as geometry, he appears to be saying that political and moral thinking and speaking could in principle be purged of disorder.[12]

The possibility of a fully deductive, indisputably true doctrine of right and wrong would seem to turn on whether such a doctrine necessarily includes words that mark apparitions partly derived from the senses and the imagination. If so, and assuming that Hobbes can show how first- and second-order words can be successfully integrated in coherent speech, it would be "mixed" as is physics, not pure as in the case with geometry. Hence some at least of its propositions could never be more than probable. Hobbes's civil philosophy, despite his frequent claims to the contrary, is in fact mixed in this way.

This characterization of the issue ignores (as Hobbes himself often does) much deeper doubts that he himself raises about speech and language, doubts that reach to speech and language that are the best they can be.

The distinctive certainty of geometry results from the fact that it is (all but) entirely *made,* that its only debt to the raucous world of matter in motion is to motions in the minds of its human makers. As Hobbes puts it, this means that the language of geometry is "abstract" rather than "concrete." The manner in which he draws this distinction signals an important part of his further and deeper doubts.

Manifesting aspects of his skepticism already considered, he says that "**concrete** is the name of anything which we *suppose* to have a being, as **body, moveable, moved,** . . . **hot, cold,** . . . and the like" (*De Corpore,* Ch. 3, pp. 45-46, italics added). Even if they are names of no more than supposititious things, concrete names must be in place before abstract names can be used or even invented. "There is also this difference betwixt **concrete** and **abstract** names, that those [i.e., concrete] were invented before propositions, but these [abstract] after; for these could have no being till there were propositions, from whose **copula** they proceed" (ibid., p. 46). In this respect, abstract names and the ratiocinative operations we perform with them are dependent on apparitions.

Perhaps because of his materialism and his concern to establish the utility of science, but in any case manifesting his unorthodox notion of causation, Hobbes then gives a definition of "abstract" that deepens this dependency. "[A]bstract is that which in any subject [i.e., in any concrete name] denotes the *cause* of the concrete name, as **to be a body, to be moveable, to be moved** . . . **to be hot, to be cold** . . . **&c.**" He explains this somewhat elusive idea as follows: "But **abstract names** denote only the causes of **concrete names**, and not the things themselves. For example, when we see any thing, or conceive in our mind any visible thing, that thing appears to us, or is conceived by us, not in one point, but as having parts distant from one another, that is, as being extended and filling some space. Seeing therefore we call the thing so conceived **body**, the cause of that name is, that that thing is **extended**, or the **extension** or **corporeity** of it" (ibid., italics added).

V

Looking for other things, we have stumbled onto Hobbes's explanation of how abstract and artificing science brings material reality along with it, of the ways in which stipulation and ratiocination connect with and yield power over the world of sensuous experience. The notions of body, extension, corporeity and hence causation are *not* given by experience itself. They are inventions or devisings by or through which we human beings *give* meaning to otherwise confused and even unintelligible concatenations of particular or "concrete" events and happenings. If we were without these "abstract" conceptions we could not "compute the properties of bodies; for when we would multiply, divide, add or subtract heat, light or motion, if we should double or add them together by concrete names, saying (for example) hot is double to hot, light double to light, or moved bodies double to moved, we should not double the properties, but the bodies themselves that are hot, light, moved &c. which we would not do" (ibid., p. 47). These further invented or second-order conceptions not only presuppose (generically as it were) but in every instance are used with reference to some number of particular sensuous/imaginative experiences.[13] By a process of subsumption, ratiocination that employs them brings those particulars with them. Thus Hobbes claims that science as he understands it connects with and can in principle yield power over material nature.

For the self-same reason, this science is vulnerable to the vagaries of material nature and of the senses, imagination and passions. As it is sometimes said that every revealing is a concealing, every illuminating a darkening, for Hobbes every empowering is necessarily also a disabling, every controlling or commanding a submission. (It will be well to bear these points in mind when thinking about that form of controlling that is political rule.)

The abuse of philosophy and the sciences it properly informs "proceeds from this, that some men seeing they can consider . . . the increasings and decreasings of quantity, heat and other accidents, without considering their bodies or subjects (which they call **abstracting**, or making to exist apart by themselves) they speak of accidents as if they might be separated from all bodies. And from hence proceed the gross errors of metaphysics; for because they can consider thought without the consideration of body, they infer there is no need of a thinking-body; and because quantity may be considered without body, they think also that quantity may be without body, and body without quantity; and that a body has quantity by the addition of quantity to it. From the same fountain spring those insignificant words, **abstract substance, separated essence** . . . and other the like barbarous terms" (ibid. p. 47).

These abuses, which not only weaken but positively disable science, are corrigible. What seems to be ineliminable from ratiocination and science is the equally disabling defect that Hobbes usually calls equivocality, that he sometimes characterizes as the lack of perspicuity, occasionally labels unintelligibility. Although hardly one to think that bodies and their motions inscribe themselves, item by item and without loss or addition of meaning, on our marks and first-order words, it is clear from his animadversions against illicit abstractions that the stipulating by which we form second- as well as first-order words needs constraining or circumscribing by sense. The vice that is the inescapable concomitant of the virtue of second-order or abstract words is that they are *less* disciplined by these constraints.

In a remark that deepens immeasurably the skepticism implicit in his query as to "how a human invention could avail so much as to confer on mankind the benefit speech appears to us to have," Hobbes considers (with second-order words explicitly in mind) whether "from the liberty which a man may take of so defining as seems best to himself, he may conclude any thing from any thing," thereby almost certainly *increasing* the disagreement and disorder among human beings. His response, faithful to everything in his thinking *except* what we might call his collective or even collectivistically "Promethean" tendencies, is as follows: "I think it no hard matter to demonstrate that this definition [of philosophy and its proper procedures] agrees with the sense of all men." Hobbes knows full well that his "definition" agrees little if at all with the "sense" of most of the "men" he has in mind. More important, the most prominent and insistent elements in his own thinking tell him that agreement on such matters, if it can develop at all, does so against all odds.

What are the chances that his (or anyone else's) definition of philosophy and science will agree with those "of all men"? It would seem that they are poor at best. "The appellations that be universal, and common to many things, are not always given to all the particulars (as they ought to be) for like conceptions, and like considerations in them all; which is the cause that many of them are not of constant signification, but bring into our mind other thoughts than those for which they were ordained." "[T]here is scarce any word that is not made equivocal by divers contextures of speech, or by diversity of pronunciation and gesture" (*De Corpore,* Ch. 5, p. 199). The words that others use, "besides the signification of what we imagine of their nature, have a signification also of the nature, dispositions, and interest of the speaker" (*Lev.,* Ch. 4, p. 40). "[W]ords have no effect, but on those that understand them: and then they have no other, but to signify the intentions or passions of them that speak" (ibid., Ch. 37, p. 322). Even those whose own stipulations are carefully made and well remembered can in "words and speech" so "easily counterfeit" their intentions and meanings (*Elements,* I, Ch. 13, p. 240).[14]

Does Hobbes regret and want to ameliorate this state of affairs? No doubt this is one of his objectives. But consider whether the following remarks should be regarded as Hobbesian *norms* of communicative behavior: in using words "we limit them not ourselves, but leave them to be applied by the hearer" (*De Corpore,* Ch. 5, p. 199). "It is . . . always to be supposed, that he which intendeth not to deceive, alloweth the private interpretation of his speech to him to whom it is addressed" (*Elements,* I, Ch. 13, p. 244).

Unlike some of those "contemporary theorists" toward whom I gestured above, the chastening doctrines just reviewed brought Hobbes neither to solemn despair (passive nihilism) nor to an apparently frisky but often quite febrile gamesmanship. He did what he thought possible and desirable to clarify and otherwise improve language and thought. Out of his deep commitment to individuality he also extended to all of humankind his view that "philosophers . . . had always the liberty, and sometimes they both had and will have the necessity, of taking to themselves such names as they please for the signifying of their meaning." Anticipating the objection that his own use of this "liberty" is likely to be a "cause of dispute betwixt me and them" he "undertake[s] no more than to deliver the elements" of his own conceptions and urges "they who search after other philosophy . . . to seek it from other principles" (*De Corpore,* Ch. 1, p. 31).[15]

Notes

1. "Nature itself cannot err; and as men abound in copiousness of language, so they become more wise, or more mad than ordinary" (*Lev.,* Ch. 4, p. 37).

2. *DC,* Epistle Dedicatory, p. 91. Hobbes claims to make good on this failing with his own civil philosophy, and these and comparable statements in *Elements* (see I, Ch. 14, p. 241), *Lev.* (see Ch. 5, p. 45) and perhaps especially *Gondibert* (p. 79) are the high water marks of his view of humankind as Promethean, as able to generate knowledge and power sufficient to *make* their world and their affairs to their liking and their advantage. Note, however, that the *De Cive* passage (from what is easily his most pessimistic albeit not his most skeptical work on politics and morals) enters cautionary or chastening notes ("as is consistent with human life," "hardly")—including one that is more resonant now than when he wrote it. There is no doubt that Hobbes participated in the confidence concerning science and its technological applications that was burgeoning in his time, but those who read him as an evangelist of knowledge and power underestimate both his philosophical skepticism and his more general sense of human limitations. Hobbes himself retells the tale of Prometheus, emphasizing the suffering that Prometheus' pride, or rather his vain-glory, brought upon him (see *Lev.,* Ch. 12, pp. 87-88).

3. In the first chapter of *De Corpore* and again in Chapter 3 of *Leviathan* Hobbes writes of thinking that occurs "without words," that is, prelinguistically, and he credits all human beings and some other animals with this capacity (the capacity for "deliberation"). For the reasons I have indicated, in respect to human beings it is highly implausible to construe these passages to mean thinking without the use of "marks," better to treat them as referring to thinking that uses marks that have not yet been formed into what he calls speech and language. (Note that the "moniments" are "sensible," i.e., objects of sense perception.) But if we do interpret the passages in the former way, we must emphasize yet more strongly the limits on what can be accomplished by this kind of thinking. For Hobbes, thinking can become orderly and productive only after it has become linguistic at least to the extent of employing marks.

4. "Moreover, whatsoever the common use of words be, yet philosophers . . . had always the liberty, and sometimes they had and will have the necessity, of taking to themselves such names as they please for the signifying of their meaning. . . . Nor had mathematicians need to ask leave of any but themselves to name the figures they invented, **parabolas, hyperboles, cissoeides, quadratices, &c.** or to call one magnitude A, another B" (ibid., p. 34).

As he became increasingly aware of the impact of science on politics and vice versa, Hobbes did enter a disturbing qualification to this doctrine. If a philosopher's Sovereign forbade or commanded her to speak or write in a certain way the philosopher has an obligation to obey. See Chapter 7 below for further discussion of this point.

5. *Physical Dialogue,* p. 348. For a more extended statement of this point see *De Corpore,* Ch. 7, pp. 93-94 where Hobbes actually conducts the Cartesian-like thought experiment anticipated in the passage from the *Elements of Law,* that is, "feigning the world to be annihilated" of a sudden, leaving but one person. He argues that the remaining person would have the resources necessary to do philosophy and science and says that he presents the experiment because there is no better way of teaching the correct philosophy and methodology of science.

6. When he is attacking metaphysical realism and its doctrines of real essences Hobbes writes as if second-order words have *no* relationship to matter and motion (or rather they relate only to a subset of the motions that are internal to the minds of those who invent them). He qualifies this position in ways highly consequential for his view of reason and science.

7. Ibid., pp. 32-33. In *Leviathan* and in other writings not primarily concerned with natural science, Hobbes adds that signs are also "to make known to others our wills and purposes, that we may have the mutual help of one another" and "to please and delight ourselves and others, by playing with our words, for pleasure or ornament, innocently" (*Lev.*, Ch. 4, p. 34). (As to the pleasing and delighting, see especially *Gondibert,* passim.) He then identifies the misuses and abuses that correspond to each of these functions.

Being arbitrary, there is no such thing as the mismaking of marks, but their misuse is "inconstancy" and the confusions in thinking that it produces. Second-order words and signs can be mismade, as when misguided philosophers such as Aristotle treat them not as words about first-order words but as marks of presumed but nonexistent entities such as essences and substances. Signs can also be abused in ways corresponding to their uses, to deceive rather than to teach, to mislead so as to hurt rather than help one another, and to "grieve" rather than please or delight (*Lev.*, Ch. 4, p. 34). There are also profanations of speech, for example "cursing, swearing, reviling, and the like, [that] do not signify as speech; but as the actions of a tongue accustomed" (ibid., Ch. 6, p. 55).

8. One of Hobbes's main complaints against Boyle and the inductivists was that the experiments on which they based their scientific conclusions were conducted "in private," that is, in workshops and laboratories inaccessible to the general public. Because their conclusions rested on sense data unavailable to "others," it was impossible for them "to demonstrate the truth thereof perspicuously to another" (see *Physical Dialogue,* p. 350).

9. This may be an appropriate juncture to underline a general point that I hope is emerging with some force. For Hobbes, language is no neutral or unproblematic medium in which we deal with other problematic things; it is no mere and transparent epiphenomenon that we can readily see through to the non- or extra-linguistic realities that are our true concerns. He agreed with Plato that language is fundamentally problematic, shared much of the latter's sense that it distorts and obfuscates. But he rejected what he took to be Plato's belief that we can and should think without language. For this reason he labored to show that and how language could be made *less* distorting, *more* serviceable than for the most part it in fact is. Much of the skepticism that pervades his thinking is due to his conviction that this effort can never be more than partly successful. In these respects Hobbes anticipates the most powerfully skeptical theorists of our own time whose thinking has taken "the linguistic turn," who have made language itself a if not the chief focus of attention.

10. Hobbes counsels that this kind of "ordinary language analysis" be carried out "silently by themselves, or betwixt them and their masters only; for it will be thought both ridiculous and absurd, for a man to use such language publicly"! (ibid.). Presumably this is because others will *think* the analysis redundant on the ground that "everyone already knows" the meanings of words or irrelevant because something so superficial as ordinary language can hardly settle philosophical or other serious and disputed questions. In Hobbes's view they are often, in an important sense always, mistaken in thinking these things.

11. Are there any theories of language that entirely escape or overcome this difficulty, this *ur*-mystery? No doubt Hobbes darkens counsel by insisting so strongly on the turbulence of experience, the entirely arbitrary character of the stipulations out of which shared language develops, the many ways in which human beings are inaccessible to one another, and so forth through the doctrines we have been considering. No doubt brighter light is cast upon it by theorists who are more patient with and steadily respectful of

custom and convention, more careful and detailed in their explorations of grammar and its rules and norms, of training and technique, of agreements in judgment, shared practices and institutions. The best among such theorists, for example Wittgenstein (whose critiques of more optimistic and mutually or at least self-congratulatory positions often echo those of Hobbes), are far from claiming to have banished the mystery altogether (and share some of Hobbes's considerable savor for it).

12. Ibid. Albeit Hobbes's optimism concerning geometry is itself at least qualified. He "doubt[s] not, but if it had been a thing contrary to any man's right of dominion, or to the interest of men that have dominion, **that the three angles of a triangle, should be equal to two angles of a square**; that doctrine should have been, if not disputed, yet by the burning of all books of geometry, suppressed, as far he whom it concerned was able." He was soon to learn that works of geometry, particularly his own, are also heatedly disputed.

13. That is, every instance of speech that is not metatheoretical or *third order*. Hobbes's entire account of the reasoning distinctive to science is discourse about second-order discourse and hence is third order in character. It connects to first-order discourse only through the mediations of second-order words.

14. Cf. *Dialogue:* "It is a hard matter, or rather impossible, to know what other men mean, especially if they be crafty" (p. 37). "Hypocrisy hath indeed this great prerogative above other sins, that it cannot be accused" (p. 48).

15. Although Hobbes himself would never countenance doing so, we might well regard his account of language, reason and science as the construction and projection of an ideal. If we do so, the passage just quoted may remind us of Friedrich Nietzsche's characterizations of his own comparable efforts: "This is what **I** am; this is what **I** want: **you** can go to hell!" (*Will to Power,* Para. 349, p. 191. Trans. Walter Kaufmann and R. J. Hollingdale, Vintage, 1967). "May your virtue be too exalted for the familiarity of names: and if you must speak of her, then do not be ashamed to stammer of her. Then speak and stammer, 'This is my good; this I love; it pleases me wholly; thus alone do **I** want the good. I do not want it as a divine law; I do not want it as human statute and need: it shall not be a signpost for me to overearths and paradises.' " (*Thus Spoke Zarathustra,* First Part, Section 5, p. 36. Trans. Walter Kaufmann, Penguin, 1966).

Is this "going too far"? Hobbes ends *De Cive* with the following verse from Paul's *Epistle to the Romans:* "**Let not him that eateth, despise him that eateth not, and let not him that eateth not, judge him that eateth; for God hath received him. One man esteemeth one day above another, another esteemeth every day alike. Let every man be fully persuaded in his own mind**" (Ch. XVIII, p. 386).

4

Of Prudence and Morality:
The Right and the Laws of Nature

Hobbes gathers many of his thoughts about mind and matter, language, reason and science in a passage in *Elements of Law* that I have already quoted in part. "Now, if we consider the power of those **deceptions** of the sense . . . and also how **unconstantly** names have been settled, and how subject they are to **equivocation**, and how **diversified** by **passion** (scarce two men agreeing what is to be called good, and what evil; what liberality, what prodigality; what valor, what temerity) and how subject men are to paralogism or fallacy in reasoning, I may in a manner conclude, that it is impossible to **rectify** so many errors of any one man, as must needs proceed from those causes." But this is only one possible manner of concluding. At once embracing and distancing himself (a "pathos of distance") from this despairing conclusion, he goes intrepidly on: "without beginning **anew** from the very first grounds of all our knowledge and sense; and instead of books, reading over orderly one's own conceptions: in which meaning I take **nosce teipsum** for a precept worthy the reputation it hath gotten" (I, Ch. 5, p. 202).

Deep skepticism, pugnacious *self*-assertion.

It is striking that we encounter this disturbing combination in the highest of the noetic realms, in the domains apparently most favorable to science and hence to the possibility of universality, certitude and indisputability. Must we not expect yet narrower limitations, yet more disabling difficulties in the realm of daily experience and prudence; in respect to those matters that Hobbes, from first to last, insists are affairs of belief and opinion, of the mutable, the capricious and the disputatious? Or can these be made to submit to the imperium that is the "science of morality," the power generating "philosophy" that Hobbes calls "civil"?

I

We have seen that Hobbes qualifies his distinction between demonstrative, truth-producing science and nondemonstrative, belief-engendering prudence. It follows from his account of language and science that all philosophy, hence the "civil" variety, has to be "mixed" rather than entirely "pure" (or that "purity" is a matter of degree, with geometry being the most pure, natural philosophy such as physics and civil philosophy less so, and non- or prephilosophical thinking having only that degree of purity or "madeness" provided by the fact that the names in which it occurs are arbitrary human inventions). On this rendering of the relationship between prudence and morality, the question is not whether prudence and scientific morality are combined in his thinking but rather the particular ways in which he brings them together, tries to make them support or qualify one another.

These considerations provide perspective on Hobbes's repeated insistence that his is a civil *philosophy,* a system of moral and political thinking that is truly demonstrative in character.[1] As we would expect from these claims, much of his writing on morals and politics is in the deontic and jural languages of binding law, of obligation and duty, of justice and injustice, and of rights as qualifications of the former. As we would also expect, it is often in the idioms of stipulation and axiom, deduction and theorem.

These characteristics of Hobbes's writing have encouraged a number of his commentators to view him as a natural law thinker, even as a precursor of the powerfully deontic thinking of Kant. His skepticism obliged him to reject the "classic" and medieval Christian versions of natural law or natural right doctrine. According to some versions of the latter, Nature itself delivers to our reason or other of our powers of apprehension a sufficient grasp of the principles that ought to govern our moral and political lives; enables us to discern the good and the right and the virtues necessary to achieving them. According to others, God and God's Nature delineate, in a manner accessible to our reason, the obligations and duties, the rules of justice and injustice, such rights as we may have against one another. Rejecting these views, Hobbes held that we must make or devise for ourselves our principles and laws, our rules of justice and injustice, our obligations and rights. As with other "modern" natural law thinkers such as Hugo Grotius and Samuel Pufendorf, he believed that we can accomplish this devising with sufficient certitude to warrant the strongly deontic or imperatival languages of law and justice, obligation and duty, right and rights.

In part for this reason, he assigns little importance to benevolence and altruism, compassion and sympathy; virtue and vice appear to play a subsidiary role in his thinking; there are extended stretches of discussion in which notions such as "practical reasoning," "judgment," "casuistry" and the like make little or no appearance. We adopt principles and laws and reason directly from them to conclusions concerning our proper conduct here and now, to our duties and our rights, to what we must, must not, and may do in these or those circumstances. Insofar as our human weaknesses prevent us from discharging our duties or exercising our rights, we are to turn to the equally law and obligation privileging devices of sovereign authority and its binding commands, devices that are themselves derived from and justified in terms of the laws of nature that we have previously devised.[2]

Happily, this construal of Hobbes leaves open the question of how comprehensive or encompassing he intends the system of laws, duties and rights to be, what range of human actions and interactions are to be subsumed under and controlled by it. Such a deontic system might be quite strict or rigorous within the range of its operation and yet leave much of human life to be conducted in other terms, according to other principles or none. We can say that Hobbes is a "modern natural law" theorist and accommodate both his preoccupation with desires and interests, ends and purposes, good and evil and the fact that he renders all of these notions in agent-relative and otherwise deeply individuating ways. We can also make room for his evident concern to assure liberty to pursue personal ends.

This reading has the further merit of providing by now reassuringly familiar places for these several aspects of Hobbes's thinking. The demonstrative science of civil philosophy institutes a disciplining structure of indisputable and binding principles and laws, obligations, duties and rights. Within the constraints and requirements of the basic moral and jural structure that it installs, individuals and groups are at liberty to conceive and pursue a great diversity of particular ends and purposes, qualities of character and experiments in living, projects and ideals. It might be a primary purpose of a deontic and hence enframing or constitutive civil philosophy to accommodate, enable, and otherwise *safely* to encourage the human proclivity to individuation and diversity. Civil *philosophy* delineates the parameters of the categorical, reasonable or just, the agent-neutral or critical and hence mutually (or side-) constraining aspects of moral and political life. By doing so it defines spaces that protect but also and more importantly protect others against the merely rational, the agent-relative, ordinary, end-, interest-, preference-, and utility-seeking tendencies in human conduct.

This picture encompasses much of what Hobbes says about morals and politics. Because Hobbes is a "boyishly candid" writer, it no doubt conveys important aspects of his thinking about these topics.

As I have thus far presented it, the picture distorts more than it clarifies Hobbes's thought, misdirects more than it instructs or improves our own responses to his views. The elements it foregrounds are indeed present in Hobbes's thinking, but their order and directionality, the weightings Hobbes gave and we should give the several among them, are other than this account asserts.

Against it, I argue that Hobbes was first and foremost a strong individualist. He was neither a philosophical nor a psychological egoist in the strict sense according to which benevolence, altruism or even other-regarding conduct are conceptual or psychological impossibilities. But he was convinced that in fact individual human beings are moved to act primarily by their self-regarding desires and aversions and by the ends and purposes that their desires and opinions lead them to form and adopt. Also convinced that these desires and opinions will continue to vary widely from person to person, he transposed if he did not confute understandings of the distinction (in a register other than the epistemic one discussed above) between prudence and morality that were, then as now, widely received. From a normative as well as an historical and logical standpoint, individual desires and objectives and the liberty-cum-right to pursue them are the first things. Moral and legal obligations and duties are devised and enforced not for their own sake but in order to facilitate success in seeking felicity. Various virtue- or *virtu*-like qualities of character and disposition, with which Hobbes was more concerned than most of his commentators and critics have recognized, are to be cultivated primarily for the same reason.

II

In arguing for this view our attention must first focus on Hobbes's various and complexly related discussions of "nature." Whether aligning civil philosophy with geometry and physics or using the "introspective" method that makes it partly independent of them, Hobbes insists that moral and political thinking require knowledge of human and extra-human nature, of aspects of our affairs that are devised by us only in that we identify and otherwise think about them in languages of our own making. If human beings were importantly different than Hobbes claims they are, either there would be no need for morals and politics or the arrangements appropriate to them would be quite different than those Hobbes proposes. For one example, the ants and the bees live in "natural concord" without laws and justice, obligations and rights; for another, for those few human beings who genuinely disdain pain and death and relish the strife and hazards of war, the heroic virtues of courage and magnanimity might suffice as guides to and constraints upon conduct. On the other hand, there are respects in which, human nature and its circumstances being what they are, certain quite definite and quite clearly moral judgments or conclusions must be drawn, cannot be cogently disputed.[3]

Despite the last-mentioned claim, in these respects Hobbes's own criteria require him to regard his moral and political thinking as primarily or at least substantially prudential in the epistemic sense that contrasts with philosophical, as first and foremost a gathering of "daily" experience rather than the drawing of deductions from stipulations or axioms. The propositions it advances and that provide the basis for the ratiocinations of civil philosophy are subject to qualification, do not themselves state truths that are certain or indisputable. Despite his sometimes contrary statements, this understanding is manifest in the most salient aspects of his moral doctrine and in important aspects of his political argument.

The most momentous of these manifestations is his famous distinction between the state of nature and the condition of politically organized and ruled life that he calls *common*wealth. Of course he claims that basic aspects of human nature remain constant between these two sets of circumstances. In both settings all human beings are sharply individuated, desire-forming and passion-driven creatures whose primary objective is their own good (felicity) as they severally and variously see it. Also, for most human beings most of the time the single most powerful of their affirmative desires is self-preservation, their most potent aversion is to the "contra-natural dissolution" that is a premature and especially a violent death.[4]

It is nevertheless essential to Hobbes's argument that the actualities of human conduct can and should change dramatically when or to the extent that the transition is made from the state of nature to commonwealth. In his most flamboyant discussions of the state of nature Hobbes says that life in it excludes moral considerations altogether, indeed that human beings in this condition do not form so much as a concept of morality.[5] His more usual view concerning the moral laws of nature (other than those that forbid cruelty and revenge and require us to regard one another as equals) is that these laws, being constructions of human reason, are (or can be) known to those in the state of nature but are binding only *in foro interno* or (roughly) as to motive or intention. From the advent of commonwealth and the elimination of the pervasive insecurity that characterizes the state of nature, the obligations imposed by the laws of nature bind *in foro externo* or as to conduct. Hobbes's belief that there are important continuities between the two conditions leads him to place various qualifying or excusing conditions on these obligations; there is no doubt that he regards human "nature" as adaptable or even malleable enough to make their discharge *de possibilus,* as much of the time within the capacities of most of humankind. In this respect there is one pattern of thinking and acting in the state of nature, quite another one in commonwealths. The worst form of imprudence (in both his epistemic and the now more familiar normative senses, which Hobbes distinguishes but repeatedly melds together) is to fail to recognize and to act on this difference.

III

The importance of this complication in Hobbes's account of human nature is underscored when we recognize that the state of nature/commonwealth distinction is between conditions and their associated human characteristics both of which *always* obtain—and in Hobbes's view always *should* obtain—in the affairs of all human beings. His clearest statements of this point concern international relations. Without exception Hobbes describes the international arena as a condition in which the likelihood of actual warfare is so great that every sovereign must view all others with suspicion (with the same suspicion appropriate to relations among individuals who are not members of the same commonwealth) and must constantly be prepared for battle. Prudence and not scientific or any other form of morality is the appropriate "norm" in this domain. Because wars and the constant prospect thereof among commonwealths affect, more or less, all individual citizens or subjects, in this respect all those who live in such societies are constantly in a state of war with a very large number of other persons.

International relations are no more than the most obvious of the respects in which the state of war and the condition of civil society coexist. Perhaps the next most salient such respect concerns the relationship between sovereigns and their own subjects. Hobbesian sovereigns enter into no contract or covenant with those over whom they rule.

The latter covenant with one another to create and obey a political order and they then (in the *Leviathan* formulation of his argument) "authorize" some person to rule over them. The person who becomes ruler does no more than accept or acknowledge this authorization.[6] Having entered into no agreements with her subjects, she remains in the state of nature vis-à-vis them. Accordingly, in the epistemic sense of the prudence-morality distinction the basis of her conduct toward them must be prudence *not* morality (albeit Hobbes regards it as special and in some respects higher prudence. Hobbes does also say that by virtue of her office the Sovereign has various duties the conscientious discharge of which will benefit her subjects. He insists that those duties are *to* God not to her subjects.). Subjects have *in foro externo* obligations to the Sovereign and to one another, but by now we will not be surprised to find Hobbes counseling them to a certain caution in deciding how and indeed whether to discharge these civic duties. He repeatedly claims that life in commonwealths is less dangerous than in the state of nature, arguing that it is better to be subject to the unconstrained authority and power of a single sovereign than to be at risk to a whole multitude of hostile others. Given that sovereigns qua natural persons have the same human nature as everyone else in the state of nature, human beings who have taken Hobbes's teachings to heart will be circumspect in relating to them.

The foregoing remarks still do not reach the most important respects in which the state of nature and commonwealth coexist. The transition to the latter leaves the basic characteristics of human nature unchanged. It is the task of sovereigns to educate their subjects against acting in the mutually destructive ways characteristic of the state of nature, to prohibit such actions by law, to deter them by threats of punishment, even to deceive and manipulate them if there is no other way to maintain peace and order. But (a few florid passages aside) Hobbes knows full well that no ruler has ever been or will ever be more than partly successful in these efforts.[7] If properly constructed and conducted, the institution of a commonwealth can effect significant improvements in human affairs. It cannot eliminate all of the "inconveniences" attendant upon human nature itself, certainly cannot bring about that perfection of the human estate imagined or at least wished for by "pleasant men."[8] Even when the laws of nature have been demonstrated and political rule properly instituted, there is plenty of room, or rather an abundant need, for the prudence of daily experience as distinct from philosophically derived obligations.[9]

IV

As with prudence/science, pure/mixed and passion/reason, "the state of nature" and "commonwealth" are ideal types or ideal characters that Hobbes uses to organize and present his thinking. From an empirical or existential standpoint they stand for intermingled and fluctuating combinations of elements, mark variable contrasts not strict dichotomies. To substantiate these claims and the claims of the foregoing pages I have to look more closely at Hobbes's derivation of the laws of nature.

Hobbes's arguments for these laws begin from a number of empirical generalizations concerning the sources and character of the difficulties experienced by human beings who live without the effective constraint and direction of those laws. These generalizations vary somewhat among his several presentations but the following list includes those that recur and are otherwise given emphasis. (1) All normal human beings are desiring, purposive, end-seeking creatures; insofar as they avoid giddiness, melancholy, panic-terror and like degenerations they act to satisfy their desires, achieve their ends. Due to differences in their natures and experiences, the individuals that make up the human species develop a considerable diversity of desires and interests, pursue a multiplicity of ends and purposes. (2) These interests and objectives sometimes harmonize sufficiently to permit cooperation, are sometimes sufficiently compatible to permit independent and successful action, but they often conflict, leading to competition and contention, disagreement and strife. (3) The resources and weaknesses that individuals bring to these conflicts, their physical strength, intelligence, cunning, and wealth, their frailty, fearfulness, gullibility, and indigence are roughly equal in one dramatic respect, namely that it is relatively easy for any one person to kill and hence to be killed by any other.[10] This rough equality of powers and vulnerabilities guarantees the failure, usually sooner than later, of all attempts to achieve security by self-help or alliances with some number of others who appear to be like-minded. (4) Natural equality also encourages a tendency to vain-conceit and breeds what Hobbes (oddly to our ears) calls "diffidence." Although seemingly mutually exclusive, these behavioral tendencies coexist and intensify competition and conflict. Because I see my "own wit at hand, and other men's at a distance," I "will hardly believe there be many so wise" as myself, and this conceit leads me both recklessly to overestimate my own prowess and to frighten and antagonize others by my pretensions.[11] On the other hand, insofar as you and I recognize the "equality of ability" between us, there "ariseth" in each of us "equality of hope in the attaining of our ends," a misplaced optimism that leads us to "become enemies" to one another.[12]

On the basis of these generalizations (all of which are subject to qualification and are significantly qualified), as supplemented by discussions of careless speech and wayward reasoning, Hobbes draws his famous conclusion that lives lived in the state of nature are (this time in the language of *De Cive*) "few, fierce, short-lived, poor, nasty, and deprived of that pleasure and beauty . . . which peace and society are wont to bring with them" (Ch. I, p. 118).

This conclusion is the grounding for what deserves to be regarded as the "primary" element in his civil *philosophy,* the axiom that he calls "a precept, or general rule of reason" and from which he claims to derive the right and all of the laws of nature and much of his justification for politically organized society. As formulated in *Leviathan,* this "rule" reads as follows: **"that every man, ought to endeavour peace, as far as he has hope of obtaining it; and when he cannot obtain it, that he may seek, and use, all helps and advantages of war**."[13]

The first or 'ought' "branch" of this the most general rule of reason relevant to social life "containeth [that is, is an inference from the rule] the first, and fundamental law of nature; which is, **to seek peace, and follow it**."[14] The other such laws are derived from the rule and the first law when "derived from" means that it is only by obeying the further laws that peace can be obtained. In this perspective, if the other laws of nature are imperatives they are of the form that would later be called "hypothetical" or "if-then" as opposed to "categorical." On this understanding they would bind unqualifiedly only if it could be shown that abiding by them is always the only or at least always the best means to the end of peace, that any and all violations of them engender war (propositions that have very little to be said for them!). Because by Hobbes's own criteria this is partly a question of daily experience or fact, on his epistemological views we could never have certain knowledge that this condition is satisfied. Thus, anachronistic as doing so may be, we can better understand and assess Hobbes's argument if we call all but the first of the laws of nature "rules of thumb"; "maxims" of conduct that intelligent seekers of peace will be disposed to follow and will in fact follow except when circumstances give them strong reasons for not doing so. This feature of his argument, together with his readiness to allow the obligation to obey the laws to be overridden by the second branch of the general rule, provides considerable reason for saying that these "laws" are part of prudence not of philosophy; they are also reasons for thinking that those who are prudent in the sense of intelligent in the conduct of their affairs will often have good reason to depart from the laws.[15]

This conclusion is both supported and extended when we look more closely at the axiom, seek peace, from which the laws of nature are "derived." It is for each person to judge for herself whether she has any "hope" of actually obtaining peace and hence whether she should follow the laws of nature or instead exercise her right of nature. Because the resolution of this question is left to each individual, there is an important sense in which the enabling, empowering, or warranting "may" of the second clause is the one unqualified or "categorical" element in the general rule of reason. If we follow Hobbes in treating the second clause as the promulgation of a right, the view according to which his civil philosophy is deontic or imperatival yields the conclusion that he is first and foremost a theorist of individual rights, secondarily and qualifiedly a theorist of duties or obligations. As a matter of logic and of right, individuals can always trump the laws of nature and the duties they establish by asserting their right of nature.[16]

Hobbes insists that the right of nature cannot be alienated or transferred, and he never wavers from his view that it both will and should be exercised whenever push comes to shove in the struggle for self-preservation. His works are nevertheless substantially taken up with arguments against reliance on this right and the modes of conduct it licenses, arguments for obedience both to the laws of nature and the

Sovereign's laws and commands. Actions contrary to these laws usually defeat the immediate purposes for which they are taken and, to the extent that such violations become widespread, are both self- and mutually destructive.

V

Is there a way of reconciling these apparently incompatible features of his thinking? The most straightforward means of doing so, which Hobbes does much to encourage, is to say that arguments for the right of nature and its exercise are meant to apply in the state of nature, the arguments for natural and positive laws and obedience thereto are meant to apply to life in commonwealths. With limited exceptions, to obey the laws of nature when in the state of nature is gratuitously and irrationally to sacrifice or at least to jeopardize one's own interests and quite possibly one's life. Also with limited exceptions, those in commonwealths who violate either the laws of nature and/or the Sovereign's laws and commands either destroy the conditions that give them their best hope of felicity or make themselves enemies to a power that has the right and may have the power to destroy them.

This interpretation is encouraged by Hobbes's famous discussion of the "fool," the person who makes her own direct calculations of how to serve her interests, accords no independent conduct-guiding significance to the laws of nature (*Lev.,* Ch. 15, pp. 114-16). Condensing and in some respects augmenting Hobbes's main arguments against reliance on self-help and the right of nature, this passage appears to argue that this strategy *always* fails, is never rational for human beings as Hobbes describes them.

It is striking, however, that as Hobbes sees it "the question" between him and the fool "is not of promises mutual, where there is no security of performance on either side; as when there is no civil power erected over the parties promising; for such promises are not covenants: but either where one of the parties has performed already; or where there is a power to make him perform." It would appear that, excepting the special and indeed rationally anomalous case of the person who performs her part of an agreement without assurance of reciprocity, Hobbes agrees with the fool as regards conduct in the state of nature.[17] If I am correct about the numerous and extensive respects in which the state of nature and the state of civil society commingle, it follows that in fact Hobbes's position *coincides with* the fool's over a very wide range of human activity.[18]

It will help us to assess this interpretation to note that it informs a widely received criticism of Hobbes, namely that his theory makes rationally inexplicable and indeed indefensible the transition from the state of nature to commonwealth. If in actuality the "fool" is "wise" (is an "idiot savant") as regards conduct in the state of nature, what Hobbes calls "commonwealth by institution" or voluntary agreement (*Lev.*, Ch. 17, p. 133) could emerge and stabilize, if at all, only if some considerable number of human beings make and keep agreements and otherwise obey the laws of nature despite its being deeply imprudent for them to do so.[19]

As this objection indicates, Hobbes's argument with the fool is a dispute with himself, is a clashing point for some of the most highly charged elements in his (and our!) thinking. Staying for the moment with the most specifically political dimension of the difficulty posed by the fool, in dealing with it Hobbes is conducting a war on at least two fronts. Realizing that the construction and stabilization of legitimate government requires a widespread willingness to obey the laws of nature in the state of nature, he tries to make it appear that it is prudent as well as "morally required" to do so. He argues that the fool is a fool. On the other hand, he sees that if fully successful his argument against the fool would make government unnecessary. Human beings who accepted and acted on that argument could achieve a stable peace without submitting to the rule of Leviathan (and would very likely regard Leviathan's power and authority over them as obnoxious). Hence he argues that in fact human beings will reliably obey the laws of nature only if "there is a power to make [them] perform" and that as a matter of prudence and hence natural right they ought to do so only under that condition. It appears that his every victory on the one argumentative front constitutes a defeat on the other.

For reasons already seen in part (above all that the state of nature/civil society distinction is not categorical), as regards the establishment and legitimation-cum-stabilization of government Hobbes rejects the view that he is playing a zero-sum argumentative game. Human beings and their circumstances being what they are, there are "inconveniences" that cannot be eliminated but that with skill and a bit of luck can be ameliorated sufficiently to make life tolerably secure and moderately pleasant. Hobbes is most famous for his horrific descriptions of the state of nature, descriptions intended to frighten us into subscription and obedience to political authority. These self-same accounts are the basis of his insistence that every person has license to act as she individually judges appropriate to preserve and enhance her life. Nor will anyone persuaded by his analysis of human beings need encouragement to view those in power and authority with suspicion.

A closely analogous dynamic is at work even when the issue of government is well in the background of Hobbes's discussions. Hobbes argues vigorously for both the right and the laws of nature (and, yet more generally, for individuality and communality, self-assertion and reason, my language and our language). He clearly believes human relationships devoid of the second member of these pairs to be untenable, and there are extended passages that read as conventional and quite strict law of nature moralizing (and even—when he redescribes those laws as divine commands—familiar Christian homiletics). But these passages invariably come after and are at most partial qualifications of yet lengthier stretches of discussion of a sharply contrasting tendency. Hobbes reviles the excessive ambitions and claims of other philosophers, moralists and sermonizers, describes human beings in ways that make it clear that they neither can nor will submit to any very closely restrictive moral regimen and that prudence in the sense both of daily experience and self-interest is an absolutely essential feature of conduct in the moral and political domains. These discussions establish that prudence, if it can be distinguished from morality, has a value at least equal to the value of the latter.

Notes

1. See the table or classification of the sciences in *Lev.*, Ch. 8, pp. 70-71; *De Homine*, Ch. 10, pp. 42-43: "politics and ethics (that is, the sciences of **just and unjust** of **equity and inequity**) can be demonstrated **a priori**; because we ourselves make the principles—

that is, the causes of justice (namely laws and covenants)—whereby it is known what **justice and equity** . . . are" (*Six Lessons,* p. 102).

2. Hobbes claims that his laws of nature are also divine laws, laws that God has enunciated and made known to us. If we take this claim at face value we will say that Hobbes was *both* a "modern" and a (admittedly unorthodox) "Christian" natural law thinker, that he thought that his versions of these positions, even though independently grounded, complementary one to the other.

3. For example Hobbes repeatedly argues that cruelty, that is, inflicting suffering on others or even taking "pleasure in other men's great harms" "without other end of his own," is wrong everywhere and always, and he extends this to an unqualified condemnation of backward-looking revenge as distinct from forward-looking punishment. (*Lev.,* Ch. 6, p. 52-53 and Ch. 17, p. 129; *DC,* Ch. I, p. 117; Ch. III, pp. 142, 149.)

4. "For every man is desirous of what is good for him, and shuns what is evil, but chiefly the chiefest of natural evils, which is death; and this he doth by a certain impulsion of nature, no less than that whereby a stone moves downward" (*DC,* Ch. I, p. 115).

5. "For moral philosophy is nothing else but the science of what is **good**, and **evil**, in the conversation, and society of mankind. . . . And . . . so long as a man is in the condition of mere nature, which is a condition of war, . . . private appetite is the measure of good, and evil" (*Lev.,* Ch. 15, pp. 123-24).

6. The individual who has thus become the "artificial person," that is a sovereign, is also a natural or private person and continues to have obligations under the laws of nature. But these obligations bind only *in foro interno.*

7. "It may seem strange to some man . . . that nature should thus dissociate, and render men apt to invade, and destroy one another: and he may therefore, not trusting to this inference, made from the passions, desire perhaps to have the same confirmed by experience. Let him therefore consider with himself, when taking a journey, he arms himself, and seeks to go well accompanied; when going to sleep, he locks his doors; when even in his house he locks his chests; and this when he knows there be laws, and public officers, armed, to revenge all injuries shall be done him" (*Lev.,* Ch. 13, p. 100).

"[T]o make men altogether safe from mutual harms, so as they cannot be hurt or injuriously killed, is impossible; and, therefore, comes not within deliberation" (*DC,* Ch. 6, p. 176). For further discussion of these points, see Chapters 6 and 7 below.

8. "Men are troubled at the Crossing of their Wishes; but it is our own fault. First, we wish Impossibilities; we would have our Security against all the World . . . without Paying for it: . . . We may as well Expect that Fish, and Fowl should Boil, Rost, and Dish themselves in our Mouths, and have all other the Contentments and ease which some pleasant Men have Related of the Land of **Coquany**" (*Dialogue,* p. 66).

9. There is the further question of the basis on which to conduct interactions that occur in domains of life within commonwealths that are in legal fact unregulated. If we think Hobbes intended an encompassing and intrusive governance, one that reaches widely and deeply into the thoughts and actions of its subjects, the answer to this question will add little to the discussion above. Prudence will be required or even appropriate in relations among the members of a commonwealth primarily to the extent that sovereigns fail in their attempts to control their subjects. On the other hand, if (a) Hobbes intended an absolute but not very active government, a governance that leaves its subjects legally at liberty in numerous aspects of their lives, then it would seem to follow that (b) the realm of prudence would enlarge substantially. I argue for (a) in Chapters 6 and 7. The success of this argument would not itself establish (b) because there is the possibility that

interactions that are legally unregulated will be closely controlled by the rationally and now (commonwealth being in place) fully binding moral laws of nature. Later in this chapter and in the following one I argue against this view, and for not only (b) but a more radical interpretation according to which the mode of thinking and acting appropriate to much of the activity that occurs within commonwealths is the prudence of the state of nature. Reverting to the point with which I began this chapter, I argue that over large domains of social life the individuals who make up a Hobbesian commonwealth do and should relate to one another in the manner of the sovereigns who contend with one another in the international arena. If the possibility of peace among nations depends on the prudence of sovereigns, so the possibility of felicity and commodious living within nations depends primarily on the prudence of the individual members of society. The extent to which this prudence is also a morality in some less than fully Hobbesian philosophical sense will concern us as we proceed.

10. This is the single most important respect in which, for Hobbes, a rough but highly consequential equality in fact obtains among human beings. In the light of both earlier and later treatments of equality it is of some moment to note that he sees this fact as a source of severe difficulties in human affairs. If, as in the views of Plato, Aristotle and much of medieval moral and political thought, there were clearly defined natural inequalities among human beings, the rule of superiors over inferiors could readily be justified. Rejecting these views, Hobbes must have recourse to notions and devices such as agreement and contract, devices that, by acknowledging and thereby possibly enhancing natural equality, might well exacerbate the very difficulties government is intended to resolve.

But Hobbes does much more than acknowledge and adapt to the rough natural equality thus far discussed. He *promotes* a norm or ideal of human equality in at least two respects: first, all human beings have and ought to acknowledge in one another what he calls the Right of Nature; second and yet more radically, he rejects the idea that some conceptions of the good are intrinsically superior to others. Substantively, this is a very different ideal of equality than those made familiar by thinkers from Rousseau to twentieth century Marxists and socialists, but Hobbes does seem to accord it a standing that we are tempted to call moral as distinct from a maxim of intelligently selfinterested conduct.

11. *Lev.*, Ch. 13, p. 98. Sophistically, Hobbes argues that this phenomenon supports his claim that wisdom is distributed in a roughly equal manner among all human beings: "For there is not ordinarily a greater sign of the equal distribution of any thing, than that every man is contented with his share" (ibid). In fact, it is an important part of Hobbes's argument that vain-conceit, inflated expectations, and the self- and mutually destructive behaviors that go with them are unevenly distributed in the human population. In every society there are a number of people whose false pride and inordinate ambition impel them to disrupt every arrangement that is not distinctively advantageous to themselves. Even though small in number, the activities of such people, compounded by the difficulty more "moderate" types have in knowing whether this or the next person they encounter will prove to be of this tendency, greatly complicate life in the best governed commonwealths. In the state of nature they make peaceful and cooperative conduct virtually impossible.

12. Ibid. The reasons for conflict in human affairs are discussed again and again in Hobbes's works, the three most sustained and extended treatments being *Elements,* II, A, Ch. l; *DC,* Chs. I and VI; *Lev.,* Ch. 13.

13. *Lev.*, Ch. 14, p. 104. In *Elements of Law* and *De Cive* he conflates the distinction between a rule of reason and laws of nature derived from it. The statement in *Elements,* which is worth quoting because it makes explicit the connection between the "rule" and

empirical generalizations such as discussed above, reads as follows: "But since it is supposed by the equality of strength, and other natural faculties of men, that no man is of might sufficient, to assure himself for any long time, of preserving himself thereby, whilst he remaineth in the state of hostility and war; reason therefore dictateth to every man for his own good, to seek after peace, as far forth as there is hope to attain the same; and strengthen himself with all the help he can procure, for his own defense against those, from whom such peace cannot be obtained; and to do all those things which necessarily conduce thereunto." He goes on to say that "there can . . . be no other law of nature than reason" and to treat the more particular laws of nature as "precepts" of reason (II, A, Ch. 1, pp. 280, 281). The basically similar statement in *De Cive* is at Ch. II, p. 119. The change he effects in *Leviathan,* while verbally slight, is important because it clarifies the difference between the laws of nature and the right of nature while sustaining the claim that both are products of ratiocination.

14. The second or 'may' "branch" of the rule is "the sum of the right of nature; which is, **by all means we can, to defend ourselves.**"

Hobbes sometimes writes as if the first and all the other laws of nature are derived from the full formulation of the general rule. Because that rule is bifurcated or rather Janus-faced, nothing can be derived or deduced from "it." Hobbes in effect underlines this point in another passage that will be important to our later discussions: "For though they that speak of this subject, use to confound **jus** and **lex**, **right** and **law**: yet they ought to be distinguished; because RIGHT, consisteth in liberty to do, or to forbear: whereas LAW, determinith, and bindeth to one of them: so that law, and right, differ as much, as obligation, and liberty; which in one and the same matter are inconsistent" (ibid, p. 103).

15. Hobbes may be trying to discourage this reading when he adds "and follow it" to the command "seek peace." If we emphasize this phrase, we could construe "following peace" as *consisting in* obeying the further laws of nature and hence violating them as *constituting* a violation of the first law as well. This would yield a stronger sense in which the further laws of nature are "derived" from the first one and would license his tendency to say that those who accept the first law but violate the further laws thereby contradict themselves and fall into "absurdity." It remains the case that the further laws are hypothetical not categorical imperatives, that not following them is often justified (in which cases there is no contradiction or absurdity), and that the question whether to follow them, while arising in a philosophically constrained context, is prudential in its material character and will often and properly be decided in the negative. Indeed at one point in *De Cive* Hobbes goes so far as to say that violations of the laws of nature conduce to peace and that obeying them increases the probability, if not of war itself at least of its being deeply harmful to those who imprudently obeyed the laws. Having stated his usual doctrine that "It is not . . . to be imagined, that by nature . . . men are obliged to the exercise of all these laws," he later added the following footnote: "Nay, among these laws some things there are, the omission whereof, provided it be done for peace or self-preservation, seems rather to be the fulfilling, than breach of the natural law. For he that doth all things against those that do all things, and plunders plunderers, doth equity. But on the other side, to do that which in peace is a handsome action, and becoming an honest man, is dejectedness and poorness of spirit, and a betraying of one's self, in time of war" (Ch. III, pp. 148-49). If doing equity is a moral requirement as distinct from a maxim of self-interested conduct, violating particular laws of nature is sometimes a moral requirement.

I discuss some of the further laws below but will not follow Hobbes's articulation of the entire list. In *Leviathan* the second law is formulated and defended in Ch. 14, numbers

3 through 19 in Ch. 15, and a 20th is added in "A Review, and Conclusion," p. 504. Gregory Kavka has provided a concise list of the first 19 laws that calls attention to the extent to which they are familiar maxims of moral conduct. He restates them as follows: "1. For peace 2. For mutual and reciprocal surrender of natural rights 3. Against injustice, i.e., against violating obligations . . . . 4. For gratitude 5. For accommodating others (including giving up one's luxuries for their necessities . . .) 6. For pardoning offenses of those who repent and guarantee future good conduct 7. Against punishing for revenge 8. Against declaring contempt or hatred for others 9. For acknowledging others as one's natural equals 10. Against claiming for oneself rights that one denies to others 11. For equity by judges 12. For common use of resources that cannot be divided 13. For alternating use, or assignment by lot, of what cannot be used in common 14. For primogeniture or first seizure as a form of natural lottery in distributing goods 15. For safe conduct for mediators 16. For submitting controversies to an arbitrator 17. Against being a judge in one's own case 18. Against using arbitrators who are partial 19. For using witnesses to settle controversies of fact[.]" Gregory S. Kavka, *Hobbesian Moral and Political Theory* (Princeton, NJ: Princeton University Press, 1986), p. 343.

16. It may be objected that Hobbes's right of nature is not truly a right because it entails no obligations for others. My right to seek and use all of the advantages of war, to do almost anything that I judge to be necessary to my preservation, does not restrict your right to do the same. Hobbes himself repeatedly emphasizes that, for this reason, the right of nature worsens our estate by licensing and hence emboldening aggressive and war-engendering conduct. But the claim that Hobbes's right of nature entails no restrictions on others is importantly incorrect. Because all of us have this right, none of us (not even the Sovereign) can say that any action of any other person is morally wrong, is reason for them to be morally ashamed of themselves. General respect for Hobbes's right of nature would protect all of us against one of the most pervasive, insidious, and mutually debilitating means by which we attempt to control one another's thinking and acting. Hobbes's insistence on the right of nature, maintained in the teeth of the shame culture promoted by the Puritans and numerous other Christians of his much regretted acquaintance, is a major manifestation of his deep commitment to individuality.

17. Despite recent efforts of rational choice theorists to argue the contrary (see the Annotated Bibliography), the person who performs first in the state of nature is grievously deficient by Hobbes's standards of prudence and rationality. "For it suits not with reason, that any man should perform first, if it be not likely that the other will make good his promise after; which, whether it be probable or not, he that doubts it must be judge of" (*DC*, Ch. II, p. 127).

18. In his "rejoinder" to the fool and elsewhere Hobbes seems to bolster what appear to be his arguments for respecting the laws of nature in the state of nature with considerations concerning the afterlife, going so far as to say that there is "but one way imaginable" of "gaining the secure and perpetual felicity of heaven . . . and that is not breaking, but keeping of covenant" (*Lev.*, Ch. 15, p. 115). Together with his slightly earlier remark that "the same fool hath said in his heart there is no God" (p. 114), this invocation of religious considerations could be taken to mean that in a truly long-term and hence fully rational perspective the fool's position is irrational in respect to both the state of nature and the civil condition. It could hardly be rational to assure one's own eternal suffering.

Hobbes signals his own considered position in this respect when he says that the fool's expectation of gaining eternal felicity by injustice, rather than being mistaken by comparison with some other strategy such as living a just life, is "frivolous." There is evidence that Hobbes was a predestinarian, that it was part of his religious belief that the question of the salvation or damnation of every human being who would ever live had been decided by God at the time of the Creation (see, e.g., *Lev.,* Ch. 29, p., 239). In any case he clearly rejects the view that human beings can "earn" either salvation or damnation and he is of course unrelenting in his opposition to political disobedience justified in such terms. (See Chapter 7 below for further discussion of this question.) It is undeniable that he sometimes augments his "secular" arguments for obedience by issuing threats and promises concerning post- or extra-mundane life; on his own epistemological and theological views these passages must be viewed as rhetorical in the most diminishing sense of the term.

19. Equally, he could justify or legitimate the continuing *in foro externo* obligation to obey "commonwealths by acquisition," that is, those established by mere but overwhelming power (ibid.), only if he could satisfy a strongly analogous condition. Commonwealths by acquisition arise either by conquest or as gradual enlargements of maternal and later parental domination over children. Taking the latter case first, because the child's preservation depends initially on the mother and later the parents (and hence in most anthropologically known cases primarily the father), there is a certain raw plausibility to his view that children have a "natural" obligation to obey parents for as long as the latter remain physically dominant. Why should children continue to obey, as he says they are obligated to do, after they achieve that rough equality that enables them to resist and if necessary to kill their parents? (see *Elements,* II, B, Ch. 4; *DC,* Ch. IX; *Lev.,* Ch. 20). Why should adults who submit to conquerors in order to preserve their lives continue to obey them, as with qualifications Hobbes says they should, if they later come to be able effectively to resist or escape? It seems that these commonwealths by acquisition can be legitimated only by appeal to laws of nature that bind *despite* being against the fool's wisdom. Looking ahead, it may be Hobbes's realization of this fact that led him to admit that "there is scarce a commonwealth in the world whose beginnings can in conscience be justified" and to advise both sovereigns and subjects to look to the future not the past in their thinking and acting concerning government and politics (ibid., "A Review and A Conclusion," p. 506. On this view, we stumble or are bludgeoned into commonwealths but then find to our surprise that it is to our advantage to remain there).

5

Of Prudence and Morality:
Desires, Ends and Character

Because they are irreducibly dissonant, Hobbes never fully harmonizes the two substantially deontic dimensions of his thinking, never gives general or final priority to the right of nature or the laws of nature and the obligations they impose. As suggested at the outset of the previous chapter, however, he diminishes the tensions between them by placing both the right and the laws of nature in the larger setting of a teleological and axiological theory concerned with desires and their satisfaction, purposes and their achievement, and with the qualities of character conducive to success in end-oriented activities.

As steps toward examining this larger conception, we have first to consider two further aspects of Hobbes's theory of obligation. The first is his contractarian doctrine that (a) all obligations must be voluntarily undertaken; hence (b) can and should be undertaken only if judged, by those whose obligations they will be, to serve their desires and interests.

The second concerns additional complications and qualifications in his account of the role that obligations, once duly undertaken, can and cannot, should and should not play in day-to-day human conduct. Here the remaining task is to bring the more skeptical aspects of Hobbes's thinking about language to bear on the formulation and following of rules.

I

The core claim of Hobbes's contractarianism is the proposition that there is "no obligation on any man, which ariseth not from some act of his own; for all men equally, are by nature free" (*Lev.,* Ch. 21, p. 164. Cf. *DC,* Ch. VIII, p. 207). He also holds that all human actions, while caused, are voluntary in the sense that the agent's own passions and deliberations are (conceptually as well as empirically) necessary links in the causal chains that produce them. Finally, he holds that "of the voluntary acts of every man, the object is some **good to himself**" or the avoidance of some evil and that "these words of good, evil, and contemptible, are ever used with relation to the person that useth them: there being nothing simply and absolutely so; nor any common rule of good and evil, to be taken from the objects themselves" (*Lev.,* Ch. 14, p. 105; Ch. 6, pp. 48-49).

Taken together and at face value, these propositions place several thick layers of subjectivity or agent-relativity between actually acquiring an obligation and the objective, agent-neutral philosophical ratiocination that yields the laws of nature (or any other obligation-generating) rule or imperative. However rigorous that reasoning may be, its conclusions become—properly as well as in conduct-influencing belief or psychological fact—imperatives for assignable persons only if those persons endorse or subscribe to them. If civil philosophy "takes" agents to action-producing conclusions, it takes them to that destination by the elbow not by the throat. In a deep sense, all agents do and must make their own obligations for themselves.

Hobbes surrounds this radically voluntarist doctrine with a considerable variety of qualifying, complicating and hence taming considerations. In addition to the argumentation already considered, he regularly construes concepts such as "voluntary" and "assent," "consent" and "agreement" in ways that permit him to say that, despite what most of us would regard as substantial evidence to the contrary, these voluntarist conditions have been satisfied by an agent's actions and hence that an obligation has become binding upon her. Most important, his latitudinarian criteria for the "consenting" or "covenanting" necessary to commonwealth (whether by institution or acquisition) makes it all but impossible for anyone in the claimed jurisdiction of such a political association to show that she *hasn't* given her consent to its authority. Because he insists that this consent is to virtually any law or command that the Sovereign chooses to promulgate, it seems that the consent condition is so easily and so generally satisfied as to be nugatory.

Even if this last judgment were fully correct (we see in the next chapters that as just stated it is about as exaggerated as is the view that the consent requirement nullifies all the other arguments for the laws of nature),[1] we would have to ask why Hobbes introduces this complication into his political theory. If consent, covenant, and the like do no real work in establishing *in foro externo* obligations, if the obligations he thinks most important can be shown to be fully binding by his general arguments for the laws of nature and for political authority, why does he provide the human beings he describes with grounds on which they can reject or escape from them? After all, these folks don't seem to be in need of encouragement in this regard.

On the reading/cum/appropriation of Hobbes that I am developing throughout this book, the answer to this question is that he adopts a voluntarist or self-assumed theory of obligation because of his commitment to individuality and individual self-making. Obligations or any other binding requirements that owed nothing to, that depended not at all upon, the individual's own desires and beliefs, ends and purposes, would unacceptably diminish those on whom they are imposed. Believing as he does that there are certain minimal but basic respects in which almost all human beings have the same desires and purposes, are well served by certain shared arrangements and more or less standardized patterns of conduct, he thinks that they can and should be persuaded to accept rules that establish those arrangements and make those patterns of conduct obligatory. But it is not enough that *he* believes this or that objective or impersonal reason demonstrates it to be the case. They, *each of them,* must be satisfied that the rules will enhance their own safety and felicity as they conceive them. They must testify to this conviction by their own speech and action (albeit with respect to subscription to political authority and occasionally the laws of nature Hobbes compromises his position with his version of the obnoxious notion of tacit consent).

If they remain unconvinced, if they refuse to subscribe to arrangements and rules that a substantial number of others accept, they must accept the consequence that those others will regard them as enemies and, by the same right of nature that the nonsubscribers have exercised in their refusing, may succeed in controlling or even destroying them. None of this shows that they have an obligation to submit or that they do wrong and should be ashamed of themselves for not submitting. Nor does Hobbes ever so much as consider the notion that the way of individuality is an easy way to go.[2]

As we have thus far followed Hobbes's discussion of moral obligation, he has opened up substantial reason for doubt whether this or that person will or should undertake, and if so whether they will or should actually discharge, the obligations articulated by the laws of nature. In the passages thus far considered, however, he for the most part writes as if there is little or no doubt as to what actions these obligations forbid or require. There remains room for decision *whether* to undertake and discharge this or that obligation, but taking that decision obviates the necessity and even the possibility of further decisions as to *how* to do so.

In writing this way, Hobbes is in effect claiming to have accomplished one of the most difficult tasks of his civil philosophy. He thinks that his proposition "LAW, determineth, and bindeth to one . . . [act]: so that law, and right, differ as much, as obligation, and liberty; which in one and the same matter are inconsistent," has always been true as an account of the ordinary and proper uses of the concepts it explicates. Regrettably, it has often been denied or misconstrued by previous philosophers. For this reason, and because of the further and morally substantive absurdities and confusions introduced by philosophy, theology, and religious and political sectarianisms, the question of the content of the moral obligations has become a matter of uncertainty and disagreement. Hobbes sometimes claims to have rectified this situation. He has placed morality on its proper foundation in human nature and has provided an indisputable derivation of the obligations relevant to

life in company with other human beings. Henceforth it will be possible
to act in a fashion fully consonant with the logic of our moral concepts.

This claim (and indeed his claim concerning the unequivocal meanings of "law" and "obligation," "right" and "liberty") coheres badly
with his own views concerning conditions necessary to all thinking and
communicating. Questions concerning these matters cannot be so much
as formulated without use of the ultimately arbitrary, ineliminably
agent-relative device that is language. When Hobbes or anyone else has
formulated his own thoughts concerning them, has "promulgated" to
himself laws or rules to govern his own future thinking and acting
concerning them, he can abide by his own prescriptions to himself only
to the extent that he remembers and otherwise remains constant to his
initial stipulations (he should or ought to do so, moreover, only to the
extent that he *now* finds those thoughts acceptable). He can so much as
communicate those prescriptions to others, certainly can win the acceptance of his prescriptions by others, only if these uncertain processes
are faithfully replicated in the language and thinking of those others.

In Hobbes's most general discussions of language and speech his
estimation is that steady success in such activities is, at best, highly
problematic. "[T]here is scarce any word that is not made equivocal by
divers contextures of speech, or by diversity of pronunciation and
gesture" (*De Corpore,* Ch. 5, p. 199); understanding others requires
attention not only to the *words* that others use which, "besides the
signification of what we imagine of their nature, have a signification
also of the nature, dispositions, and interest of the speaker" (*Lev.,* Ch.
4, p. 40); "words have no effect, but on those that understand them: and
then they have no other, but to signify the intentions or passions of them
that speak" (ibid., Ch. 37, p. 322); even those whose own stipulations
are carefully made and well remembered can in "words and speech"
"easily counterfeit" their intentions and meanings (*Elements,* I, Ch. 13,
p. 240). The names that make up a language are "indefinite" in the never
to be eliminated respect that "we limit them not ourselves, but leave
them to be applied by the hearer" (*De Corpore,* Ch. 5, p. 199).

Hobbes's own account of language and speech concerning the "doctrine of right and wrong" and hence obligation, right and liberty, does
much more than merely acknowledge that these general difficulties are
at their most severe in this highly charged domain. That account puts

further and much heavier strain on the boast that we are considering. Much of his moral and political philosophy is in the language of rules and rule-following, but he himself casts deep doubt on the possibility of conducting human affairs in this regularian mode.[3]

These doubts extend to the form of rules and rule-following on which Hobbes apparently places his greatest reliance, the laws and commands issued by the Sovereign and the strict obedience thereto by all of the Sovereign's subjects. Can the Sovereign make her laws sufficiently "perspicuous" to her subjects such that it is possible for them to know how to go about obeying them? Can the Sovereign herself be certain of what counts as obedience and disobedience such that she can know whether to punish her subjects and thereby make future disobedience less likely?

These further questions will concern us in the next chapter. Having noticed them, we can see that Hobbes's claim to have rendered the laws of nature "intelligible even to the meanest capacity"[4] involves him in a variant of the argument with himself that we encountered earlier. If the laws of nature and the obligations they entail are vague, equivocal or otherwise indeterminate, assent to them will not do much to end the state of war. Quarrels that had been taking place under the rubric of the right of nature will continue unabated, the only change being that they will now be conducted in the name of what is forbidden or required by the laws of nature. Recognizing this, Hobbes attempts to provide those laws with content that is sufficiently definite to diminish the uncertainty and disorder of the state of nature. Insofar as he succeeds in this effort, however, he weakens one of his own main arguments for commonwealth with the absolute authority to promulgate laws and commands (and more especially for that form of commonwealth called a monarchy). As with good geometry, on this among his views peace cannot be achieved through general convention or agreement; it is possible only if the ambiguity and disagreement that pervade general thinking and acting are eliminated by the stipulations of a sovereign. From this point of view, if taken too seriously Hobbes's own claim to have banished ambiguity from the laws of nature could itself become an impediment to peace. Those convinced by it might draw the conclusion that sovereign authority is unnecessary or of secondary importance. Thus Hobbes makes the claim but surrounds it with a variety of complicating and weakening considerations that (in

addition to expressing his most considered views about language) are
intended to ward off this false and dangerous inference.[5]

II

It seems that Hobbes wants matters both of two mutually incompatible ways as regards the determinateness of the laws of nature. As with
his closely analogous position concerning the rationally undeniable
standing of these laws, this conclusion is correct but incomplete. The
fact is that he wants all of these things and more. The "more" that he
wants might be described as follows: a civil philosophy that (A) identifies individual felicity as the highest if not the only (or only earthly)
noninstrumental value; and that (B) effects the mix of prudence, morality and political governance that, account taken of available powers and
resources, best enables individuals to pursue their felicity as they
severally and variously see it. To get this something more, Hobbes
thinks that his civil philosophy—and hence the beliefs and understandings, practices and arrangements in or through which that philosophy
is implemented—must include and promote (C) qualities of individual
character that have thus far made few and fleeting appearances in our
discussion. It must include and promote virtues and/or *virtus* such as
justice and fidelity, moderation and self-control, magnanimity, and
even a certain rare but distinctively admirable nobility.

III

(A) The most obvious objection to (A) is that life or self-preservation
not felicity is Hobbes's highest value, an objection that takes plausibility from Hobbes's repeated statements that most human beings regard
premature and violent death as the *summum malum,* as that which they
seek to avoid at all costs. The objection takes further force from the fact
that in at least one place Hobbes says that anyone who attempts suicide
shows that she is "non compos mentis," a view that seems to *equate*
putting the preservation of life first with the capacity to make rational
evaluations in any register.

These statements are importantly qualified. The relevant passage in *De Homine* contains the emphasis on physical preservation (avoiding a "contra-natural dissolution" of the body) but allows that "though death is the greatest of all evils (especially when accompanied by torture), the pains of life can be so great that, unless their quick end is foreseen, they may lead men to number death among the goods."[6] Other discussions go much further, according great importance to considerations that have little or no connection with self-preservation or even bodily well-being. He is emphatic that many people think, evidently with his approval, that various kinds of shame and dishonor are worse than death. The laws of nature that are the means to peace forbid expressing contempt of others because "life itself, with the condition of enduring scorn, is not esteemed worth the enjoying, much less peace" (*Elements,* II, A, Ch. 3, p. 293). "[I]nsomuch as most men would rather lose their lives (that I say not, their peace) than suffer slander; it . . . is prescribed by the law of nature, **that no man, either by deeds or words, countenance or laughter, do declare himself to hate or scorn another**" (*DC*, Ch. III, pp. 142-43).

For present purposes much the most important of these qualifications are those by which Hobbes circumscribes the obligation to obey the laws and commands of commonwealths. Political authority being absolute, the Sovereign can adopt any law and issue any command that she judges appropriate. As we might expect given his emphasis on self-preservation, Hobbes nevertheless argues that the right of nature warrants subjects to refuse obedience to any command that directly or certainly threatens their lives (the command to submit to capital punishment being the most obvious but by no means the only example). What is much more striking, he extends this license to cases in which obeying a command would bring dishonor or other nonphysical "pains" to the subject. "For it is one thing if I say, **I give you right to command what you will**; another, if I say, **I will do whatsoever you command**. And the command may be such, as I would rather die than do it. Forasmuch, therefore, as no man can be bound to will being killed, *much less* is he tied to that which to him is worse than death." A son, for example, "will rather die than live infamous and hated of all the world" because he obeyed the command to execute one of his parents (even if the parent be "guilty and condemned by the law"). This is no more than one among many such examples. Strongly suggesting that the subject's own judgment is both necessary and sufficient to trigger the exemption, he adds: "There are many other cases in which, since the commands are shameful to be done by some and not by others, obedience may by right be performed by these, and refused by those; and this without breach of that absolute right which was given to the chief ruler" (*DC*, Ch. VI, pp. 182-83, italics added. Cf. *Lev.,* Ch. 14, p. 105).

Noticing one further and far more radical passage will allow us to move to the next stage of this discussion. In Chapter 15 of *Leviathan* Hobbes gives the following list of rights that subjects must retain when they enter commonwealths: "right to govern their own bodies; enjoy air, water, motion, ways to go from place to place; and all things else, without which a man cannot live, *or not live well*" (p. 120, italics added). The last phrase in particular goes well beyond his remarks concerning shame, infamy, scorn and physical pain. The latter give examples of afflictions and torments so strongly adverse to felicity as to give cogency to the thought that death would be preferable to suffering them. Of course, the potential significance of the remarks is enlarged by the fact that they are presented as examples of which there are apparently a large number of others. But it is one thing for Hobbes to identify evils worse than death, quite another for him to use the notion of "living well" as he here does. If the first of these moves alters an impression that he himself often creates, he could not have created that impression without embracing the idea of a *summum malum,* of a ranking of evils that has or deserves to have interpersonal standing. He is, however, indefatigable in his opposition to the converse notion of a *summum bonum,* stubborn in his insistence on the diverse, fluctuating, irremediably agent-relative character of all noninstrumental conceptions of the "desirable" and the "good," of "felicity" and "living well."[7] In making the notion of "living well" the basis of no less than an inalienable right, he identifies this deeply individuating conception of value as the fundament of his moral and political thinking.

IV

(B) Hobbes means to be taken seriously when he says the right of nature is inalienable. "[I]f a man by words, or other signs, seem to despoil himself of the end, for which those signs were intended; he is not to be understood as if he meant it, or that it was his will; but that he was ignorant of how such words and actions were to be interpreted."[8] He has the same intention when he says that the inalienable rights are categorical in the sense discussed earlier. Any human being prepared to pay the price *may,* has license, to reject or refuse to discharge the obligations of natural and positive law.[9]

In this perspective, those parts of Hobbes's thinking anticipated under (B) and (C) present Hobbes's views as to how to make lives go well, how to improve the chances of achieving felicity. Having fitted us up with the right of nature grounded in our desiring, end-seeking but vulnerable nature, he urges us voluntarily to qualify that right by undertaking various obligations; he does the latter because his experience and reason have taught him that for most people most of the time this is the best way to satisfy our desires and achieve our ends. Because we are inconstant and wayward in our thinking and acting, he counsels all of us to take steps that I will henceforth call prudential/moral: (1) cultivate in ourselves dispositions or qualities of character, traditionally called virtues, that help us to resist temptations to self-defeating actions; (2) construct for ourselves a government that has authority and power to protect us against the worst incursions of others and to provide us with further motivations to prudential/moral conduct. Finally, he tries to inspire any among us who may be receptive to an additional and yet more deeply individuating kind of self-making. Advancing what might be called an ideal of life, this conception of self-enactment transcends the category of prudence/morality and can be partly rendered by the notion of *virtu.*[10]

Hobbes's argument for government is the concern of the next two chapters. The main elements of his argument for undertaking obligations have been discussed above and need only be placed in the perspective provided by the previous sections. Effecting this reconstrual will both introduce the notion of virtue and help to warrant my claim that Hobbes conflates the prudence-morality distinction in both his philosophical use of it and in the sense in which, in his time and ours, it involves a contrast between self-interest and moral obligation or duty. The "virtu" elements in Hobbes's thinking will be considered at the end of this chapter.

Whether reflections of his general skepticism and the powerfully agent-relative theory of value that goes with it, or simply manifestations of his lively and generous character, many of Hobbes's substantive moral and other normative opinions are remarkably tolerant, permissive, or liberal in character. Against the dominant tendencies of his place and time, he rejected the notion that human beings are by nature sinful or guilty, himself indulged and encouraged others to a cheerful enjoyment of the body and its pleasures, and cultivated a "proper self-esteem" complemented by respect for others that led his numerous friends and associates to esteem him for his lively wit and pleasant company.

That human beings are wicked by nature "cannot be granted without impiety" and in any case is false. "For the affections of the mind, [even those] which arise only from the lower parts of the soul, are not wicked themselves" (*DC*, The Author's Preface to the Reader, p. 109. Cf. *Behemoth*, p. 26). "The desires, and other passions of men, are in themselves no sin. No more are the actions, that proceed from those passions, till they know a law that forbids them" (*Lev.*, Ch. 13, p. 101). "The secret thoughts of a man run over all things, holy, profane, clean, obscene, grave, and light, without shame, or blame" (ibid., Ch. 8, p. 61); "To be delighted in the imagination only, of being possessed of another man's goods, servants, or wife . . . is no breach of the law . . . . For to be pleased in the fiction of that, which would please a man if it were real, is a passion so adherent to the nature of . . . man . . . as to make it a sin, were to make a sin of being a man" (ibid., Ch. 27, p. 216). "Proper self-esteem . . . is not a perturbation, but a state of mind that ought to be" (*De Homine*, Ch. XII, p. 60-61). "The question who is the better man, has no place in the condition of mere nature; . . . where all men are equal. . . . I know that Aristotle . . . maketh men by nature . . . some more worthy to command, meaning the wiser sort, such as he thought himself to be for his philosophy; others to serve, meaning those that had strong bodies, . . . as if master and servant were not introduced by consent of men, but by difference of wit: which is not only against reason; but also against experience. For there are very few so foolish, that had not rather govern themselves, than be governed by others: . . . And therefore for the ninth law of nature, I put this, **that every man acknowledge another for his equal by nature**. The breach of this precept is [false] **pride**" (*Lev.*, Ch. 15, p. 120).[11]

"He was marvellous happy and ready in his replies, and that without rancor (except provoked). . . . " "[H]e was well beloved: they lov'd his company for his pleasant facetiousness and good nature." "[B]eing naturally of a cheerfull and pleasant humour, he affected not at all austerity and gravity to looke severe." "'Tis not consistent with [such] an harmonicall soule to be a woman-hater, neither had he an Abhorrescence to good wine but he was, even in his youth (generally) temperate, both as to wine and women" (John Aubrey, "Thomas Hobbes," pp. 153, 154, 155. In Oliver Lawson Dick, ed., *Aubrey's Brief Lives* [Ann Arbor: University of Michigan Press, 1957]).

If we had nothing more from Hobbes than the passages quoted here and in Note 12, they would be sufficient reason to cherish him as Aubrey did.

Perhaps in part because he held these views and had these personal characteristics, Hobbes distinguished sharply between the justice or injustice of actions on the one hand and the justness or "guiltiness" of persons and their intentions or character on the other (see Elements, II, A, Ch. 3, pp. 290ff; DC, Ch. III, pp. 138-39; Lev., Ch. 15, pp. 116-17). He occasionally writes as if the latter matters are largely inaccessible to observers, he reviles the intrusive inquisitorial practices that afflicted his age, and he makes it clear that his primary concern (particularly in the most specifically political aspects of his thinking) is to influence the former.[12]

These aspects of Hobbes's thinking may appear to reinforce his reputation as a primarily deontic thinker who embraced a rule-dominated and hence highly legalistic conception of morals. He "codifies" morality into 20 laws of nature, says that in its most generic sense virtue consists in actions that conform to those laws, and gives pride of place to the most legal-like of the specific virtues, that is, justice (which is at once obedience to law and fidelity to the agreement to do so and to all other agreements that are consistent with law). When combined with the fact that he moves rapidly to incorporate the laws of nature into the positive law of the state and to give the Sovereign (all but) entire authority over their content, it appears either that law has subsumed morality or that morality has been "legalized."

This characterization does capture much of what Hobbes says under the rubric of morality. And there are conceptions (persuasive definitions) of morality (of "moral") that, if accepted, would require us to draw the stronger conclusion that it captures everything that he says *deserves* a place under that rubric. If we mean by a morality a system of categorical imperatives or a set of norms that override any and all considerations that conflict with them, then the laws of nature-cum-the-Sovereign's laws encompass the entirety of his morality.[13]

As regards his own conceptual or linguistic practice, what Hobbes regarded as his moral theory included a diverse array of elements only a subset of which he formulated as laws. Even his most severely reductive statement concerning the virtues appropriate to life in commonwealths insists upon equity (later charity) as well as justice (*De Homine*, Ch. 13, pp. 69, 70), he more characteristically identifies virtues specific to the several laws of nature,[14] he has a different list of the virtues and vices (or *virtus* and weaknesses) in the state of war,[15] and he promotes a variety of qualities of character and disposition that he sometimes calls virtues, sometimes not.[16]

These aspects of Hobbes's thinking at least supplement and qualify his deontic or law and obligation morality (metaethical purists may think they betray or contradict it), clearly align him with the tradition of philosophy that privileges the good among the moral notions and treats the virtues as dispositions or qualities of character that must be cultivated if people are to act steadily in pursuit of the good or goods appropriate to them. In at least one respect Hobbes is explicit—albeit grudging—in recognizing his kinship with this way of thinking. "[T]he writers of moral philosophy," he admits, "acknowledge the same virtues and vices" as he (*Lev.*, Ch. 15, p. 124). He never entirely gives up his view that the possibility of peace sufficient to mutual self-preservation depends first and foremost on fear, on the "caution" that overtakes human beings upon recognition of their rude vulnerability to one another.[17] Even this realization, certainly the capacity to act effectively upon it, comes from education and not from nature.

Nor will it suffice to codify the lessons of experience into laws and commands. Philosophy will effect improvements in human affairs only if civil philosophers also acquire and teach concerning the "dispositions, affections, and manners of men" (*De Corpore*, Ch. 1, p. 30). "Forasmuch as will to do is appetite, and will to omit, fear; the cause of appetite and fear is the cause also of our will; but the propounding of the benefits and of harms, that is to say, of reward and punishment, is the cause of our appetite, and of our fears, and therefore also of our wills, *so far forth as we believe* that such rewards and benefits as are propounded, shall arrive unto us; and consequently, our wills follow our opinions, as our actions follow our wills; in which sense they say truly . . . that . . . the world is governed by opinion" (*Elements,* I, Ch. 12, p. 238, italics added). "[M]an is made fit for society not by nature, but by education. Furthermore, although man were born in such a condition as to desire it, it follows not, that he therefore were born fit to enter into it. For it is one thing to desire, another to be in capacity fit for what we desire; for even they, who through their [false] pride, will not stoop to equal conditions, without which there can be no society, do yet desire it" (*DC,* Ch. I, p. 110).

Aristotle and the other theorists of good and virtue were therefore on the right track. They went astray, and Hobbes "tractates" them and us, for reasons and in ways that are by now familiar. "[Y]et not seeing wherein consisted . . . [the] goodness [of the virtues that for the most part they correctly identified], nor that they come to be praised, as the means of peaceable, sociable, and comfortable living, [they] place them in a mediocrity of passions: as if not the cause, but the degree of daring, made fortitude; or not the cause, but the quantity of a gift, made liberality" (*Lev.,* Ch. 15, p. 124). The end of moral and political laws and virtues is not some supposititious good or excellence that is called "moral." Their immediate or instrumental end is "peaceable, sociable, and comfortable living" and their final end or telos is not and cannot be any single condition or state of affairs. Rather, it is the felicity of individual human beings as each of them sees or imagines it.

V

(C) Hobbes's reference to "the mediocrity of the passions" is meant to put down Aristotle's view that the "mean" between two "extreme" forms of conduct is often the virtuous act. Despite Hobbes's derisive tone, this remark can serve to remind us of important points of agreement between the two thinkers and to bring us to the conclusion of our consideration of prudence and morality.

Notwithstanding the self-confident, often dogmatic character of his discussions of the laws of nature, Hobbes knew as well as Aristotle that so much as middling success in the day-to-day conduct of affairs requires much more than knowledge of and dispositions to abide by those laws. It also requires a nice discernment among possibilities, good practical judgment regarding what others will and will not do, foresight of consequences, and like capacities that Aristotle described as involving practical as opposed to theoretical reasoning (and that his discussion of the "golden mean" is primarily intended to exemplify and recommend).

The strongest support for this claim about Hobbes may be his argument for the absolute authority of the Sovereign. Although necessary in part to legitimate the use of power against those recalcitrant subjects who refuse to do what they know they ought, sovereign authority is also essential to settle issues about which subjects, however good their educations and characters, are unable to agree. Hobbes thinks that attention to his own civil philosophy will greatly assist sovereigns in this activity. If his or anyone else's general reasonings were dispositive concerning very many moral and political issues sovereign authority would be largely redundant.

Further and more direct evidence comes from his many diatribes against the religious and political fanatics that he sometimes calls *"dogmatici"* and from his enthusiasm for the quality that he usually terms prudence, sometimes "sagacity." *Dogmatici* are identified by contrast with "mathematici." The latter proceed "from humble principles" to indisputable conclusions concerning matters that permit of such and hence "are absolved of the crime of breeding controversy." In Aristotelian parlance they make proper use of theoretical reasoning. In the same language *dogmatici* attempt to use such reasoning where practical reasoning is required. Making matters worse by confusing passion with reason and *oratio* with *ratio,* they "press to have their opinions pass everywhere for the truth, without any evident demonstration either from experience, or from places of Scripture of uncontroverted interpretation" (*Elements,* I, Ch. 13, p. 242). Those of sagacity prudently avoid these errors. Moved by a particular "appetite" that "maketh him think upon the next means of attaining, and that again of the next, &c," the "assurance" of such persons "is more or less; but **never full** and **evident**" and involves "taking of signs from experience warily" out of recognition that often "cases are not alike that seem so" (*Elements,* I, Ch. 4, pp. 194, 195).

If the admonition to take signs warily is not quite an endorsement of "mediocre" intellectual passions, a less captious reader than Hobbes might agree that Aristotle himself could have penned the encomium to *practicality* with which Hobbes all but ends his own most mature treatment of natural reason and the prudence of daily experience: "There is no action of man in this life, that is not the beginning of so long a chain of consequences, as no human providence is high enough, to give a man a prospect to the end. And in this chain, there are linked together both pleasing and unpleasing events; in such manner, as he that will do any thing for his pleasure, must engage himself to suffer all the pains annexed to it; and these pains, are the natural punishments of those actions, which are the beginning of more harm than good. And hereby it comes to pass, that intemperance is naturally punished with diseases; rashness, with mischances; injustice, with the violence of enemies; [false] pride, with ruin; cowardice, with oppression; negligent government of princes, with rebellion; and rebellion, with slaughter" (*Lev.*, Ch. 31, pp. 269-70. This is the penultimate paragraph of Part Two).

Temperance rather than gluttony or asceticism; moderation in preference to reckless abandon or timidity; justice and equity not self-aggrandizement or self-sacrifice; modesty in place of arrogance or humility; a certain persevering but not grandiosely heroic mettle; diligence and rectitude but neither zeal nor dereliction; complaisance instead of docility or asperity. For or to "most" human beings, Hobbes's counsel is that these Aristotelian-sounding virtues are the appropriate prudential/moral analogues and complements to the prudential/intellectual disposition to cautious, circumspect, experimentalist thinking that he thinks essential throughout the practical domains of life. What the rest of us do with his advice is of course for us to decide.[18]

For or to *most* human beings.

For the most part claiming to speak of and to all of humankind, there are scattered through Hobbes's writings references to types of human beings whose characteristics and capacities give them, in fact or in possibility, a particular interest and importance. These several "genres" of persons are not such "by nature" in Aristotle's sense and neither Hobbes's descriptions of nor his prescriptions concerning them qualify his doctrine of natural equality.[19] But he does single them out for certain kinds of special attention, does offer distinctive counsel to them or to the rest of us about them.

The three most prominent such categories of people are (1) those of false pride and overweening ambition and given to vain-glory; (2) persons who are genuinely "temperate"; (3) those few who are of "a certain nobleness or gallantness of courage" (*Lev.,* Ch. 15, pp. 116-17).

In respect to (1), we might say that the preponderance of his prudential/moral admonitions are against false pride and excessive ambition and hence are addressed specifically to those who display these characteristics. But Hobbes seems to think that there are some considerable number of human beings on whom such advice and instruction are simply wasted. Whether by nature or (more likely) by bad nurture,[20] they are incessant in their quest for wealth and glory, for dominance over and "precellence" in comparison with everyone they encounter. Hobbes's *special* advice is that the rest of us take particular precautions in relating to them, maintain a singular wariness concerning them. It is arguable that the existence of women and men of this character are at once the main reason for absolute government and the greatest obstacle to establishing and maintaining it. However this may be, he urges all of us, but above all sovereigns, to employ an intricate combination of force and guile, threat and promise in order to keep the excessively ambitious under some degree of control.[21]

The character of the "temperate man" is delineated primarily by contrast with that of the excessively ambitious, in part with the noble or gallant one. "All men in the state of nature have a desire and will to hurt, but not proceeding from the same cause, neither equally to be condemned. For one man, according to that natural equality which is among us, permits as much to others as he assumes to himself; which is an argument of a temperate man, and one that rightly values his power. Another, supposing himself above others, will have a license to do what he lists, and challenges respect and honour, as due to him before others; which is an argument of a fiery spirit. This man's will to hurt ariseth from vain glory, and the false esteem he hath of his own strength; the other's from the necessity of defending himself, his liberty, and his goods, against this man's violence."[22]

The temperate are those who have assimilated or internalized Hobbes's prudence/morality; who, with wary and otherwise intelligent attention to the changing particulars of their circumstances, have cultivated in themselves dispositions to pursue their desires and interests under the

guidance of his prescriptions and counsels. Adopting a later but conge-
nial idiom, the temperate are those who pursue self-interest rightly
understood. If we add the importance that Hobbes attaches to "temperateness"[23] in Sovereigns, we can say that it is on this "type" of person that
peace and hence the felicity of the great preponderance of human beings
primarily depends. In this perspective, the making of ourselves into such
persons is the most important kind of self-enactment.

As will become clear in the next chapters, my addendum concerning
sovereigns speaks importantly to Hobbes's estimation of the prospects
that human beings could actually sustain peace and enjoy a measure of
felicity. In addition to giving us plenty of reason to doubt that any
substantial number of people will become temperate, he deliberately
leaves the selection of sovereigns to the happenstances of heredity and
argues strenuously that we should abide whomever we happen to get in
this office. I entered the further qualifier "in this perspective" in part
with this same question in mind, in part as transition to the third
category in Hobbes's prudential/moral characterology.

Nobility and gallantness of courage being "rarely found," if very
much depends upon them the outlook for human affairs is bleak. Hobbes
sometimes writes as if much does depend upon them and draws the
pessimistic inference. In the perilous and prudentially/morally distracting
and debilitating state of nature, the noble are those who nevertheless
disdain cruelty and maintain the courage to act effectively. Out of a sense
of their own powers, particularly out of a self-esteem that "scorns to be
beholden for the contentment of . . . life to fraud or breech of promise"
(*Lev.*, Ch. 15, p. 117), they make the laws of nature the rule of much of
their conduct in respect to others. By "gallantly" performing their part of
agreements without assurance that others will do so, they cancel the latter's
justification for nonperformance and just might introduce an element of
stability and predictability into otherwise chaotic interactions. In commonwealths they could in principle make a yet more important contribution.
"Of all passions, that which inclineth men least to break the laws, is fear.
Nay, *excepting some generous natures,* it is the only thing, when there is
appearance of profit or pleasure by breaking the laws, that makes men keep
them" (*Lev.*, Ch. 27, p. 221, italics added). Such "appearances" being
everywhere and the Sovereign's *power* being limited, noble character
may be the only reliable sources of support for authority.

Those of nobility and honor, then, go beyond prudence, dutifulness, and even temperateness to a blend of superogatory qualities such as wisdom and courage, gallantry and especially magnanimity. "[F]ear can hardly be made manifest, but by some action dishonorable, that bewrayeth the conscience of one's own weakness;" accordingly, "all men, in whom the passion of courage or magnanimity hath been predominant, have abstained from cruelty" (*Elements,* II, A, Ch. 6, p. 307); "**Magnanimity** is . . . **glory well grounded** upon certain experience of a power sufficient to attain his end in open manner" (ibid., I, Ch. 9, p. 223). "A. If craft be wisdom they [the members of the Long Parliament] were wise enough. But **wise** . . . is he that knows how to bring his business to pass (without assistance of knavery and ignoble shifts) by the sole strength of his good contrivance. A fool may win from a better gamester, by the advantage of false dice, and packing of cards. B. According to your definition, there be few wise men now-a-days. Such wisdom is a kind of gallantry, that few are brought up to and most think folly" (*Behemoth,* p. 38).

Hobbes's estimation of the potential instrumental value of these qualities is evident from the *Behemoth* passage. He thought that the presence of a small number of persons of this character diminished somewhat the horrors of the English civil war and was vital to the success of the Restoration. He yet more clearly and emphatically thought that the scarcity of such people was a main reason for the protracted tumult through which he had lived and the devastation it had wrought.

Hobbes's psychology and philosophical anthropology make it impossible for him to expect any very large number of persons with these qualities, forbid him to make the achievement or even the cultivation of such characteristics a matter of duty or obligation. For the great purpose of achieving felicity and commodious living among the preponderance of human beings, he places his primary reliance on that disciplined or moderated wariness that he often calls prudence, calls temperateness when it is at its best, and makes the fundament of the "morality" that is to guide us as we pursue our felicity.

His discussions of the *virtus* of magnanimity, gallantry, and generosity are more than laments, are certainly not ways of expressing his disdain for those who do not raise themselves to these heights. Those discussions delineate, largely in formal or adverbial terms, what we might call the modalities of human self-making and individuality that

Hobbes himself most admires. The ends or objectives to which the noble or gallant aspire are of course for them to determine. Whatever they may be, in pursuing them they will scorn "fraud or breech of promise," "craft, knavery and ignoble shifts," above all cruelty. They will proceed in an "open" manner and rely as fully as possible on resources and powers that are "acquired [not] by necessity, or affected upon occasion, but inherent, and shining in" the selves they are or are in the way of making themselves to be.[24] As with all human beings and all human actions, felicity is their end, their only intrinsic good. As distinct from the prudent and the temperate, in their case that end and good are not merely served but partly constituted by the *virtu* with which they pursue them.[25]

Notes

1. The judgment is manifestly incorrect as regards the promises, agreements and contracts made between or among subjects in the course of their private affairs and interactions. So long as these do not violate the law or otherwise threaten the authority of the Sovereign, Hobbes makes the voluntarist conditions necessary to obligation and construes them in a quite ordinary way.

2. In terminology more salient in moral philosophy than that I have used above, Hobbes's insistence on consent or subscription can be regarded as a version of the view that the primary objective of a normative theory is to guide conduct conjoined with the doctrine that reason itself is never sufficient to move human beings to act. Believing that reason is no more than a "scout" for passions that are the primary motive forces in human conduct, in his own judgment Hobbes would necessarily fail to achieve the purposes of his civil philosophy if he grounded obligations in reason alone. Consent proceeding from the agent's conception of her own desires and purposes effects the requisite connection back to the passions and hence forward to action.

In foregrounding his commitment to individuality in the discussion above I am in effect repeating my earlier claim that Hobbes thought his philosophical psychology "good" as well as true, that he welcomed and even celebrated the fact that human beings act first and foremost from passions that are their own, only secondarily and derivatively on the basis of reasons that are everyone's or anyone's. In this perspective, his readiness to license refusal of obligations on the basis of the right of nature, and to let the latter excuse nonperformance of obligations to which consent has been given, may manifest a certain regret concerning some of the realities on which his own arguments for obligations heavily depend. Would it be better if the passions and desires of yet more human beings were as diverse and fluctuating as those of the persons who refuse the obligations that Hobbes himself most avidly promotes?

3. "**Good**, and **evil**, are names that signify our appetites, and aversions; which in different tempers, customs, and doctrines of men, are different: and divers men, differ not

only in their judgment, on the senses of what is pleasant, and unpleasant to the taste, smell, hearing, touch, and sight; but also of what is conformable, or disagreeable to reason, in the actions of common life. Nay, the same man, in divers times, differs from himself; and one time praiseth, that is, calleth good, what another time he dispraiseth, and calleth evil: from whence arise disputes, controversies, and at last war" (*Lev.*, Ch. 15, p. 123). It is striking that Hobbes reasserts this deeply skeptical doctrine literally in the midst of advancing two of the strongest versions of his claim to have banished all reasonable doubts concerning the obligations entailed by the laws of nature. I discuss what seem to be his practical political reasons for doing so in the next paragraphs below.

4. *Lev.*, Ch. 15, p. 122. It is also striking that in this passage Hobbes begins by allowing that his derivation of the laws of nature "may seem too subtle a deduction . . . to be taken notice of by all men; whereof the most part are too busy in getting food, and the rest too negligent to understand." Thus in order "to leave all men inexcusable" he shifts from the geometric to a traditional sermonizing or didactic mode and "contracts" the laws into "one easy sum, intelligible even to the meanest capacity; and that is, **Do not that to another, which thou wouldest not have done to thyself**; which sheweth him, that he had no more to do in learning the laws of nature, but, when weighing the actions of other men with his own, they seem too heavy, to put them into the other part of the balance, and his own into their place, that his own passions, and self-love, may add nothing to the weight; and then there is none of these laws of nature that will not appear unto him very reasonable" (ibid). However "reasonable" they may find these counsels, on Hobbes's psychology very few human beings will be able to act steadily upon them. "By an inbred custom" human beings behold "their own actions in the persons of other men, wherein, as in a mirror, all things on the left side appear to be on the right, and all things on the right side to be as plainly on the left" (*DC,* Epistle Dedicatory, p. 90). More important in the present context, Hobbes knows full well that (a) his version of the Golden Rule is but one of several sharply disputed formulations of that nostrum and (b) that applying it can hardly be the mechanical process that he here suggests. (*Elements* contains a closely comparable passage [II, A, Ch. 4, p. 298], but later he says that the "foundation of natural law" is stated by a different scriptural injunction, namely "**Thou shalt love thy neighbor as thyself**" [ibid., Ch. 5, p. 303].) His first gloss on this rule of life seems intended to make it consonant with his psychology: "which is not so to be understood, as that a man should study so much his neighbor's profit as his own, or that he should divide his goods among his neighbors; but that he should esteem his neighbor worthy of all rights and privileges that he himself enjoyeth; and attribute unto him whatsoever he looketh should be attributed unto himself." He goes on to say that this means "that he should be humble, meek, and content with equality," advice that, unless humility and meekness are equivalent to being content with equality, he is no longer giving in *Leviathan.*

5. Of course authority is also necessary in order to legitimate the power by which laws are enforced against those who are unfaithful to their covenants. But it is the "perspicuity" of the Sovereign's laws that, by comparison with the laws of nature, allows ready identification of cases of fidelity or infidelity. In this respect the legitimacy of enforcement and hence power is dependent on the perspicuity of the laws that are enforced.

From yet another perspective that we must keep before us, the availability of a fully reliable but nongovernmental procedure for achieving clarity and agreement concerning our obligations might engender failures by other standards, failings of the kinds earlier discussed under the headings of merely conventional or habitual conduct, of behaviors that are rote, mechanical and unthinking.

6. Ch. XI, pp. 48-49. Even the "non compos mentis" passage goes on to say, "And therefore, methinks, that if he kill himself, it is to be presumed that he is . . . by some inward Torment or Apprehension of somewhat worse than Death, Distracted" (*Dialogue,* pp. 116-17).

7. Peace, security, and the various actions and arrangements that are conducive thereto are not goods or ends in themselves, they are conditions that are generally favorable to most of the myriad conceptions of felicity that individual human beings have formed or might form for themselves. It is because Hobbes knows that there are circumstances under which peace does not favor familiar, indeed prominent, conceptions of felicity that he licenses circumstantial disobedience and other war-engendering conduct in the passages just discussed. It is because he knows that there are conceptions of felicity that are seldom or never favored by peace that he begins with the right of nature and then qualifies it with reasoning that is itself hypothetical and that is further qualified by his contractarian or voluntarist theory of obligation.

It is true that Hobbes says that in commonwealths the "rule of good and evil, [is] to be taken . . . from the person that representeth it," that is the Sovereign (*Lev.,* Ch. 6, pp. 48-49). But the structure or logic of his argument for accepting this conclusion is the one I have just described and the conclusion is qualified in all and more of the ways we are now considering.

8. *Lev.,* Ch. 14, p. 105. In this place he identifies the end for which alienable rights are renounced or transferred as "the security of a man's person, in his life, and in the means of so preserving life, as not to be weary of it," the last clause being the analogue to "living well" in the passage discussed above.

We might say that it is not suicide but the apparent attempt to alienate inalienable rights that shows a person to be non compos mentis. Recurring to Hobbes's epistemology, it is tempting to say that the statements enunciating inalienable rights are the "primary propositions" of Hobbes's civil philosophy, the propositions that he reasons *from* but that themselves "are not to be demonstrated" (*De Corpore,* Ch. 3, p. 50). This interpretation, which puts Hobbes's civil philosophy in the company of natural rights thinkers such as Robert Nozick, seems to me to be mistaken. *If* there are primary propositions in Hobbes's civil philosophy they are the propositions concerning "desirable," "good" and "felicity." Indulging partly anachronistic language once again, Hobbes is first and foremost an axiological and teleological thinker, secondarily and derivatively a theorist of rights, tertiarily and yet more derivatively of obligations.

9. The laws forbidding cruelty and revenge, and some other laws that concern primarily self-regarding conduct that I discuss below, are exceptions. This seems to be because Hobbes, for all of his remarkable openness to a grand diversity of experiments in living, simply could not envisage or perhaps comprehend a conception of good to which these actions would contribute.

10. The graphological device of putting a slash between "prudence" and "morality" is meant to abbreviate and underline the significance of much of the discussion in this and the previous chapter. It signals the ways in which Hobbes at once employs and conflates two related distinctions, his epistemic distinction between prudence and philosophy and the more familiar one between prudence as enlightened self-interest and morality as a set of principles or requirements that might conflict with self-interest.

In calling his basic conduct-guiding norm a rule of reason, Hobbes claims that it is philosophical not prudential. Setting aside other difficulties with this claim, the bifurcated character of this rule makes prudence necessary to acting on "it," to deciding whether to exercise the natural right accorded by its one branch or to discharge the obligations created by its other one. In its application to this distinction, my slash is intended to signal the at once inseparable and antagonistic relationship between the two.

It is less clear that the second distinction has a place in Hobbes's thinking. His predominantly egoistic psychology and his insistently voluntarist theory of obligation both suggest that morality can only mean something like self-interest rightly understood or intelligently pursued. Hobbes can endorse various principles and rules traditionally regarded as moral, but only on the ground and to the extent that living by them contributes to the felicity of those who do so. On this interpretation, which is the one I predominantly give, we would either drop the word *morality* altogether or perhaps conjoin it to "prudence" with a hyphen.

I instead sustain both terms and put a slash between them because I think that Hobbes's position is more complex and interestingly dissonant than the one just described. It is evident from his constant use of conventional moral vocabulary and his invocation of the golden rule and other proverbial moral formulae that he wanted some parts of his readership to think that he offered a morality not merely a prudence. If or to the extent that this is rhetorical or tactical, it is a strategy fraught with the various risks I have discussed and manifests Hobbes's belief that they were risks he had to take in order to pursue all of the complexly related objectives he had set for himself.

But there are also elements in Hobbes's doctrine that resist this interpretation. His categorical prohibition on cruelty and his unqualified insistence that "every man acknowledge" all others as "his equal by nature" seem to be conditions or side-constraints on his prudence rather than or at least as well as parts of that prudence. If so, if in his view there are or could be circumstances in which prudence would require violating these principles, he has both a prudence and a morality and, as with prudence/philosophy, they are at once inseparable and antagonistic. It is not obviously a defect that he recognized this feature of his thinking and left it that way.

11. As William Connolly has emphasized to me, Hobbes's condemnations of pride, excessive ambition and vain-glory at least appear to him put in company with thinkers, for example Augustine, of a very different tendency of thought than I attribute to him. In at least one respect this is more than appearance. Hobbes clearly thought that there are certain human characteristics or tendencies that, if not controlled (he saw no possibility of eliminating them), make felicity impossible. At least for this instrumental reason, and perhaps on noninstrumental moral grounds in the case of that form of false pride that is the denial that others are by nature my equal, he wanted to restrict various forms of conduct and to alter prevalent modes of thinking. His is not the view that "anything goes." As I read him, the far more remarkable feature of his thinking, and not only circumstantially, is how little he wanted to control and alter thought and action, how much he was prepared not only to accept but to celebrate in humankind. Can anyone imagine the passages quoted just above in a book by Augustine? Would Augustine not think that Hobbes himself *epitomized* the sin of pride?

12. "I cannot enter into other men's thoughts, farther than I am led by the consideration of human nature in general." "It is a hard matter, or rather impossible, to know what other men mean, especially if they be crafty." "Hypocrisy hath indeed this great prerogative above other sins, that it cannot be accused" (*Behemoth,* pp. 29, 37, 48). It is an error of the clergy of his time to attempt to "extend the power of the law, which is the rule of actions only, to the very thoughts and consciences of men, by examination, and **inquisition** of speech and actions. By which, men are either punished for answering the truth of their thoughts, or constrained to answer an untruth for fear of punishment" (*Lev.,* Ch. 46,

p. 491. Cf. *Behemoth,* pp. 125-26). In Chapter 7 we see Hobbes's application of these views to the difficult matter of religious toleration.

13. There is of course the much deeper point that, if Hobbes accepted this conception of morality he had no moral theory at all, only a theory of prudence that he chose to dress up in moral language. (And indeed that if he accepted the analogous jurisprudential view concerning "law," he had no theory of law.) We must return, yet again, to this point below.

14. "**Justice, gratitude, modesty, equity, mercy** and the rest of the laws of nature are good; that is to say **moral virtues**; and their contrary; **vices**, evil" (*Lev.,* Ch. 15, p. 124).

15. "The sum of virtue is to be sociable with them that will be sociable, and formidable to them that will not. And the same is the sum of the law of nature: for in being sociable, the law of nature taketh place by way of peace and society; and to be formidable, is the law of nature in war, where to be feared is a protection a man hath from his own power: and as the former consisteth in actions of equity and justice, the latter consisteth in action of honor. And equity, justice, and honor, contain all virtues whatsoever" (*Elements,* II, A, Ch. 4, p. 301).

16. "[T]here are other precepts of **rational** nature, from whence spring other virtues; for temperance, also, is a precept of reason, because intemperance tends to sickness and death. And so fortitude, too, that is, that same faculty of resisting stoutly in present dangers, and which are more hardly declined than overcome; because it is a means tending to the preservation of him that resists" (*DC,* Ch. III, p. 152). "However, the other three virtues (except for justice) that are called cardinal—**courage, prudence,** and **temperance**—are not virtues of citizens as citizens, but as men, for these virtues are useful not so much to the state as they are to those individual men who have them. For just as the state is not preserved save by the courage, prudence and temperance of good citizens, so is it not destroyed save by the courage, prudence and temperance of its enemies. For courage, like prudence, is more a strength of the mind than a goodness of manners; and temperance is more a privation of those vices that arise from the greedy dispositions of those that harm not the state, but themselves, than it is a moral virtue. For just as every citizen hath his own private good, so hath the state its own public good. Nor, in truth, should one demand that the courage and prudence of the private man, if useful only to himself, be praised or held as a virtue by state or by any other men whatsoever to whom these same are not useful" (*De Homine.,* Ch. XII, pp. 69-70).

17. "[T]he original of all great and lasting societies consisted not in the mutual good will men had towards each other, but in the mutual fear they had of each other" (*DC,* Ch. I, pp. 113-14).

18. The admonitory passage quoted above is a digest of the harms and sufferings with which Hobbes threatens imprudent/immoral thought and action in the course of the rest of *Leviathan* and his other works. The oppositions and calibrations I have just used appear, if not always in the exact terms I have used, in the various discussions of the intellectual and moral virtues and vices in *Leviathan* and the other works. If they are reminiscent of Aristotle, they are yet more characteristic of skeptical thinkers from Sextus Empiricus to Montaigne to Hume to Nietzsche to Oakeshott.

19. Nor do his types constitute classes in a Marxist or any other sociological or socioeconomic sense. In fact the "types" that most concern him are most likely to be encountered among the wealthy and leisured, but in principle any human being can have or acquire the characteristics that set them apart.

20. Hobbes's most extensive discussion of the formation of dispositions and character is in Ch. XIII of *DC.*

21. When he moves beyond the source and extent of sovereign authority to give advice as to how those who have authority should exercise it, large parts of his discussions concern how to keep the ambitious in check. Chapters 19 and 22-29 of *Leviathan* and the comparable chapters of *Elements of Law* and *De Cive* return frequently to this issue and it is Hobbes's pervasive concern in *Behemoth*—a book that is predominantly a history of the evils produced by the inordinately ambitious together with the failure of the temperate members of English society to take the measures necessary to control them.

The intensity of Hobbes's concern with this problem is revealed by his willingness to entertain the use of inhumane and perhaps cruel methods to deal with it. At one point in the "dialogue" of which *Behemoth* consists, "B" (who is usually the interlocutor or foil in the "conversation") suggests that King Charles should have taken an early preemptive strike against the rebellion and simply slaughtered all of its instigators. "A," who for the most part speaks Hobbes's own thoughts, responds as follows: "God forbid that so horrible, unchristian, and inhuman a design should ever enter the King's heart. I would have him to have money enough readily to raise an army to suppress any rebellion, and to take from his enemies all hope of success . . .; but to put none to death without actually committing such crimes as are already made capital by the laws" (p. 58). A little later, however, "A" himself considers whether "Had it not been much better that those seditious ministers, which were not perhaps 1000, had been all killed before they had preached? It had been (I confess) a great massacre; but the killing of 100,000 is a greater" (p. 95).

22. *DC,* Ch. I, p. 114. To the extent that commonwealths succeed in reducing the incidence of violence by the ambitious there will presumably be less need for that part of the temperate character that enables effective self-defense. But no human being is ever entirely without need for this capacity and the other elements of the temperate character are at least as valuable in commonwealths as in the state of nature.

We might expect a further contrast as well, namely between the temperate character and those who are excessively modest, self-diminishing or timid. Hobbes does attack religious doctrines that promote humility, self-abnegation and -disdain and the like, and he is certainly no admirer of cowardice or pusillanimity. But his psychology disposes him to doubt that proponents of the former will have any very wide success, inclines him to be tolerant of cowards, and leads him to treat pusillanimity as an aspect or function of the misestimation of self that is basic to excessive ambition and vain-glory.

23. We cannot say "temperance" because the qualities Hobbes attributes to those of temperate character only partly overlap with those usually associated with the virtue of temperance. If temperance means abstinence from pleasures, low or high, Hobbes is against it.

24. The quotation is from the epistle dedicatory of *Leviathan* (p. 5) and is an encomium to the character of Hobbes's patron but above all friend Sidney Godolphin (see also, ibid., p. 504.) This and his other—always brief—discussions of persons Hobbes greatly admired give somewhat greater substance to his conception of noble character. We will have occasion to consider some of these (especially his remarks about Thucydides) in dealing with his views concerning participation in politics. His remarks about Sidney Godolphin are characteristic in emphasizing the qualities of the person's character not the particular objectives or purposes that she or he pursued.

25. "Great persons that have their mindes employed on great designes . . . are pleased with the contemplation of their own power and virtues, so as they need not the infirmities and vices of other men to recommend themselves to their own favour by comparison . . ." (*Gondibert,* pp. 84-85). "[M]uch laughter at the defects of others, is a sign of pusillanimity. For of great minds, one of the proper works is, to help and free others from scorn; and compare themselves only with the most able" (*Lev.,* Ch. 6, p. 52).

6

Of Liberty, Authority and Power

There is no mistaking Hobbes's admiration for distinctive individualities. Along with the exquisite intellectual constructs devised by geometers, self-enactment of the kind exemplified by Sidney Godolphin may well have been the form of human making that he treasured most deeply. Unlike numerous other thinkers of this sensibility, Hobbes was never tempted by the view that the bulk of humankind exists for the sake of the gallant, noble or merely uncommon few. He never entertained the idea that the no-more-than temperate, the imprudent or even the vain-glorious (all of whom engage in the making, mismaking, and unmaking of their own lives and selves) can justifiably be subordinated to the rule or sacrificed to the needs or wants of those of superior character or accomplishment. The most noble or cultivated of humankind must acknowledge natural equality and must accommodate themselves to arrangements necessary if naturally equal human beings are to keep company with one another. Those capable of enacting a distinctive individuality are to do it within these constraints. (Those who reject this imperative thereby show themselves to be arrogant and vain-glorious rather than noble.)

Hobbes's egalitarianism is manifest in his argument for the right of nature and for a single set of laws of nature to which all human beings should in prudence/morality subscribe. He clearly and rightly thinks this argument consistent with his commitment to individuality. The right of nature and the voluntarist theory of obligation that is one of its corollaries are at once egalitarian and individualistic. Peace and self-preservation are conditions of a diversity of felicities, not ends in themselves. The further laws of nature consist primarily of formal or adverbial considerations that individuals consult and adapt as each of them pursues their felicity as they see it. A society whose members act steadily on Hobbes's prudence/morality would feature both common-alities or uniformities of kinds associated with egalitarianism and a diversity of ends and purposes, dispositions and temperaments. It was Hobbes's purpose to theorize the possibility of this combination and perhaps his aspiration to bring into being societies that actually achieve and maintain it.

On my reading, Hobbes intended his treatment of commonwealth, sovereign authority and power, and the other most specifically political aspects of his theory to further this project, to serve his dual but complementary egalitarian and individualistic objectives. This is by no means a usual reading and Hobbes puts difficulties in the way of sustaining it. In arguing for absolute and preferably monarchical gov-ernment he appears to favor sharply defined hierarchy and strictly imposed uniformity and conformity. He proposes collective political makings by which everyone in a particular territory submits to a single person who thenceforth controls and directs their lives.

There are respects in which this arrangement maintains or even extends equality. Hobbes never claims that those who become sover-eigns are or thereby become morally or intellectually superior to their subjects. Subjects submit to an "artificial" not a natural person, to the holder of an office that in one way or another they have invested with authority that is by nature their own. Because they submit in common and uniformly, in political and jural respects they thereafter stand in a strictly equal relationship to one another. But this appears to be the equality of the dungeon not of free, self-esteeming and self-enacting human beings. The arrangement might enhance the estate of the person who becomes sovereign, but it marks the end of the individualities of those who have made themselves subjects.

Just as there is textual evidence for reading Hobbes as a deontic natural law thinker who promotes strict adherence to the laws of nature, so there is much in his work that supports a collectivist, conformity- and uniformity-seeking interpretation of his political thinking. Hobbes himself links these two aspects of his thinking quite closely. Political governance is necessary primarily because human beings who govern themselves do not do what they know the laws of nature require of them, secondarily to eliminate real or perceived indeterminacies in the laws of nature. If the first duty of the Sovereign is to protect the common- wealth against foreign enemies, her foremost domestic or municipal function is to promulgate as positive laws the laws of nature and to assign punishments for violations of those laws. By doing so she gives imprudent and vain-glorious subjects new and powerful motivations to discharge obligations they know they already have, annuls the justifi- cation that the temperate otherwise have for "obeying" the laws of nature only *in foro interno,* and eliminates uncertainties as to what the laws of nature actually require.

The tightness of this linkage lies behind Hobbes's tendency to treat his argument for political association and sovereign authority as a deduction or derivation from his natural law theory. Although not warranted by criteria of logical inference, Hobbes's affection for this "deduction" underlines the deontic, regularian, and authoritarian tenden- cies of his thinking, foregrounds the extent to which he thought human conduct can and should be controlled by agent-neutral rules and by sover- eigns who are the enforcers and importantly the makers of those rules. It is a main source of Hobbes's widely received reputation as a thinker who, finding himself "in a way beset with those that contend, on one side for too great liberty, and on the other side for too much authority" (*Lev.,* Epistle Dedicatory, p. 5), sided enthusiastically with the latter.

Hobbes's own expectation, amply confirmed by events, was that he would not "pass . . . unwounded" (ibid.) by any of the contending forces he identified, that he would be attacked as savagely by the self-appointed champions of existing authority and order as by the enthusiasts for liberty. He was hated by the established clergy for his

materialism and reputed atheism and the more so for his argument that
the Sovereign must control the clergy and religious doctrines and
practices; the lawyers and judges despised him for his rejection of
custom in general and common law and constitutionalism in particular;
the parliamentarians regarded him as their enemy because he attacked
both rule by assembly and mixed or divided government; his contractarianism and rejection of the divine right theory of kingship made
him persona non grata among the courtiers and for a time with the king.
The more philosophically disposed of these critics, agreeing with his
own judgment that these positions were grounded in his materialism,
skepticism and nominalism, his primarily egoistic psychology, and his
egalitarian and individualist prudence/morality, concluded that his civil
philosophy would undermine authority of all kinds, make effective
government impossible, guarantee that very war of all against all that
he himself had so vividly described.

Hobbes disdained all of these assessments. As against the "too much"
liberty and "too great" authority for which his various critics severally
contended, he was convinced that he had shown "the way" to commonwealths that could be accepted by human beings as they are because
these political associations would promote and enhance freedom, felicity, and individuality. His claim that his argument for sovereign authority is derived from his theory of natural law, if read in the light of our
previous explorations of the latter and the larger philosophy of which
it is part, is key to understanding and assessing this conviction.

I

If we take the laws of nature as our starting point, Hobbes's argument
for government, its authority, and the obligation to obey its laws and
commands, is quite straightforward. Grounded in our human nature and
our natural condition, the laws of nature tell us what we ought and ought
not to do over a considerable range of our conduct. Owing to the
diversity of our passions compounded by diverse and wayward uses of
language and reason, the scarcity of some of the goods that satisfy our
desires, and particularly to the presence of persons of false pride and
ambition, if left to our own individual devices the number of us who

act temperately on the basis of the laws of nature is far too few to assure peace. Recognizing this, and realizing that peace is essential to felicity, we devise and establish government to enforce the laws of nature and otherwise to prevent war among us. Because of the pervasive possibility and destructive character of violent conflict, we cannot know in advance what laws and commands will be necessary to prevent it. Therefore the authority of government cannot be limited. Because the proclivity to disagreement and conflict extends to those who govern, it is best if authority is concentrated in a single person. There are disadvantages to this arrangement, but these are due to human nature and the human condition themselves and in any case are far less serious than the disadvantages of the known or otherwise available alternatives.[1]

There are a number of complexities in this argument that would require further attention even if we concluded that it accurately represents the main lines of Hobbes's political thinking. These include Hobbes's account of liberty and the ways it is and is not qualified by political consent or covenant, his theory of authorization and representation and hence of authority, and certain aspects of his theory of positive law and of the uses to which it should and should not be put. Most importantly, they include his account of how the Sovereign obtains power sufficient to enforce as well the authority to promulgate laws and commands. But if the main propositions of the argument are those outlined in the previous paragraph, they ought to permit us either to resolve the puzzles or to see them as exhibiting defects in Hobbes's theory.

As with the account of Hobbes as a strongly deontic natural law theorist, the political argument I have sketched is easily discernible in Hobbes's texts. It is an argument of enduring and perhaps particularly of contemporary interest. It is of enduring interest because it directly confronts the fundamental issue of specifically political theory, the question of how the *rule* of one or some over others can be justified. Hobbes largely eschews various comforting but in his view delusive evasions of the true character of rule. All commonwealths have and must have all but absolute authority. Subjects cannot have reliable legal or other institutional protections against the excesses of their rulers, cannot have continuously or even generally effective influence on the laws and policies of their governments, certainly cannot rule themselves through the instrument of government. (Thus he rejects as evasions and harmful confusions such notions as the rule of law, constitutionalism, checks and balances, representative or direct democracy.) With brutal and perhaps reckless candor he argues that a political society is a form of association in which one or some have the entire right to rule all the others. The argument is of particular interest in our time because it proceeds from egalitarian premises that are by now widely accepted, makes little or no reliance on by now largely discredited assumptions concerning divinely, naturally or otherwise given wisdom or other forms of authority-warranting superiority.

For these reasons together with the fact that the argument I have sketched is clearly present in Hobbes's texts, it would be a serious mistake to dismiss these features of Hobbes's thinking. The account I have thus far given is nevertheless seriously misleading as an interpretation of his thought as well as an impediment to further political thinking provoked by his formulations. It has the first of these defects because it fails to appreciate the ways in which his political argument is influenced by the larger set of ideas of which it is a part, particularly the skeptical and the individuality-affirming elements in his thinking. Because these elements are importantly responsible for his admirable estimation of the limits of what can and should actually be attempted through government and politics, this same failing is the chief source of the second defect as well.

With a few notable exceptions, students of Hobbes who accept the above account of his political argument but also recognize his sense of the limitations on human knowing and acting have tended to find an inconsistency between the two. (This tendency is especially pronounced among commentators who themselves have experienced and perhaps look with favor on the enormously powerful states of the twentieth century.) They read his argument for political absolutism as expressing a desire for an active, wide-ranging government that will not only control much of the conduct of its subjects but will use its authority and power to effect a transformation in human beings and their affairs. Seeing that Hobbes's own wider premises exclude the possibility of either the knowledge or the power necessary to this project, they argue that his thinking is at odds with itself.

Not entirely without warrant, this is neither the most perspicuous account of nor the most productive response to his political philosophy.

Hobbes's desire for government at all derives more from his sense of the limitations on the human capacity for cooperative activity than from a favorable estimation thereof. Equally, his preference for governments of the particular kind he promoted manifests his belief that such governments would do best what can and should be done by political and legal means while being the least likely to undertake grandiose collectivist objectives, objectives that cannot be achieved but the pursuit of which diminishes if it does not destroy the equality, liberty and individuality that Hobbes cherished.

II

We have seen some of the respects in which Hobbes begins his moral and political argument with propositions concerning the "natural" condition or estate of human beings. In part presented as if they are true statements concerning actual or actually possible characteristics of human beings and their circumstances, these propositions serve as criteria that are to be satisfied by the argumentation that follows them and as norms any departure from which requires justification. The most important of these criteria/norms are those concerning natural freedom.

Famously, Hobbes adopted an exceedingly spare concept of liberty or freedom and unfreedom. In its most general sense, "**Liberty** . . . is nothing else but **an absence of lets and hindrances of motion**; as water shut up in a vessel is therefore not at liberty, because the vessel hinders it from running out; which, the vessel being broken, is made **free**. And every man hath more or less **liberty**, as he hath more or less space in which he employs himself" (*DC*, Ch. IX, p. 216). Recalling that motion is the natural condition of all the matter of which the universe consists, we see that Hobbes is prepared to attribute freedom and unfreedom to all bodies whatsoever.[2] Motion being the "natural" condition of all bodies, it is almost as if movements occur by a kind of right or propriety and that every unfreedom needs to be justified.

But Hobbes the civil philosopher is primarily interested in the special class of freedoms and unfreedoms that involve "voluntary" motions. While all movements are caused as distinct from occurring by chance or randomly, in the case of some of the movements of animate creatures the causes are partly in the creatures themselves, cannot be fully explained by reference to forces that impinge on them from outside of their bodies. In the further case of the voluntary (as distinct from "vital") movements of human beings, the causal forces include the creature's own beliefs, passions, desires, and so forth. The agent moves *because* she has an appetite that she seeks to satisfy or an aversion to something that she wants to avoid.[3] Howsoever it may be with the motions of inanimate bodies and the vital motions of animate ones, it is clear that all actions that hinder the voluntary motions of human beings need to be justified, that you must justify any and every action of yours that prevents or deflects me from the movements (actions) I am voluntarily attempting. Such actions of mine are "natural" not only in the metaphysical or descriptive sense that as a body I am naturally in motion, but also in the evaluatively charged sense that it is only by taking them that I can acquire the goods that I desire and avoid the evils to which I am averse. A person without desires and aversions that move her is dead; a person without freedom to act on her desires might as well be dead.

Freedom of action is always a good, unfreedom always an evil. It is an instrumental not an intrinsic good, but it is instrumental to virtually all other human goods. Human beings can give up freedom to do this or that, submit to unfreedom in this or that respect, *only* to obtain or preserve freedom to do something else that they judge more important to their felicity.[4] Insofar as entering a commonwealth and submitting to the authority of the Sovereign involves a loss of freedoms of action, human beings can agree to do so only in the expectation that they will thereby acquire or secure other freedoms that they value more highly.[5]

Hobbes's thinking about the value of natural freedom is given its most explicit formulation in his doctrine concerning the right of nature. By nature all human beings have and can never entirely relinquish this prudential/moral and proto-jural license to take any action (save those that are cruel or vengeful) they judge necessary to their self-preservation and well-being. If respected by others this right protects each person against a particular and particularly insidious kind of intrusion or interference, namely attempts to dissuade them from action by convincing them that the actions they are contemplating are morally wrong. Awareness that she has this right reinforces the agent's sense of what we might call *standing,* of the value or worth of herself and her desires and purposes. She cannot be shamed into sacrificing or subordinating herself and her freedom of action to others. Or rather, she has, in advance and almost unqualifiedly, justification for preferring her desires and purposes to those of any and everyone else, for acting in ways that diminish their freedom to pursue their interests in order to protect and expand her own.

The right of nature does not directly protect freedom itself. The assurance and self-esteem that it enhances are powers not freedoms, and moralistic intrusions of the kinds that it disqualifies may weaken such powers but do not constitute the physical impediments to action that are the exclusive sources of unfreedom. Just as Hobbes will not allow the Sovereign or anyone else to make us free by enhancing our powers or abilities, so he will not allow us to claim that we have been made unfree by their obnoxious ministrations. Moreover, the condition in which human conduct is guided primarily by the right of nature is in fact a condition of very little freedom and of little or no felicity. Perhaps emboldened by the right of nature, human beings so regularly come into physical conflict with one another that they seldom succeed in carrying out their actions, rarely achieve the objectives that lead them to act.

III

It is to achieve protections of freedom of action that the right of nature does not and cannot provide, to make our natural freedom effective as a means to our felicity, that we are to agree to the creation of a politically organized society and to submit to the authority of its Sovereign. Political society and its authority are not for their own sake or for the sake of some good or value superior to or independent of the freedom and felicity of its individual members; rather, they are precisely for the sake of the latter.[6] If it were impossible for political society to diminish the unfreedoms of the state of nature there would be no reason to institute it or submit to it. If this or that political society fails to protect its members against those disorders that threaten the conditions essential to freedom and felicity—life itself plus those things necessary to "living well"—then the obligation to submit to it ends with the only reason for such submission.[7]

How then are we to construct and sustain a political society that will serve these purposes as reliably as our nature and circumstances permit? How should and should not Sovereigns and their subjects go about pursuing these objectives?

Recall that Hobbes recognizes two basic processes of constructing commonwealth, by "institution" or mutual covenant and by "acquisition" or submission to life-threatening power. Of these two, the former is apparently most favorable to legitimacy and hence to stable and effective governance. Acting on the basis of the prudential reasoning I have been discussing, each of us makes the following covenant with all of the others (except the Sovereign) who will thereafter form the political association: "**I authorize and give up my right of governing myself, to this man, or this assembly of men, on this condition, that thou give up thy right to him, and authorize all his actions in like manner.**" This procedure, Hobbes says, produces not mere "concord" but "a real unity of them all, in one and the same person" and "is the generation of that great LEVIATHAN . . . to which we owe . . . our peace and defence" (*Lev.,* Ch. 17, p. 132).

Hobbes does not think that this procedure has ever been or ever would be followed, this formula enacted, in exactly these terms. He says it is "as if every man should say" these words to every other, indicating that he is identifying the requirements that commonwealths by institution should satisfy as best they can. If there are commonwealths that can be placed in this apparently favored category, they deserve that standing because their members testify, over time and through a variety of doings and forgoings, that they subscribe to their authority. To repeat, "state of nature" and "commonwealth" are analytic not historical or otherwise descriptive concepts and Hobbes never seriously entertained the idea of an abrupt and decisive movement from one of these "states of affairs" to the other. He is a contractarian thinker, but only in that he insists that there can be political authority and obligation exclusively where there is some meaningful sense in which subjects have voluntarily subscribed to them.

Hobbes nevertheless does much to encourage the conclusion that commonwealth by institution is neither a possible nor a prudentially desirable state of affairs for human beings as he describes them. Oddly given the views I have just attributed to him, he frequently writes as if such a commonwealth could only be constructed by the deliberate, self-conscious decision of some number of assignable persons who assemble specifically for this purpose. He gives us numerous and carefully articulated paragraphs concerning the decision procedures of such assemblies, meticulously elaborates the formula that the covenant must take and the speech-acts by which consent must be given, painstakingly distinguishes between the covenant among subjects and the authorization each subject gives to the Sovereign (see, e.g., *Lev.,* Ch. 18, pp. 134-36; DC, Ch. VI, pp. 174-76). At the same time, he gives us an abundance of reasons for thinking that it would be grossly imprudent for any person to enter into such an assembly, to make such covenants and authorizations. Given his account of human nature and the human condition, we have little reason to expect the establishment of commonwealths by institution. If political societies that take their beginnings in this way are the only ones that are fully legitimate, we cannot be surprised by Hobbes's own concluding judgment that "there is scarce a commonwealth in the world, whose beginnings can in conscience be justified" or even by his sometimes nostalgia for the ancient time in which "the duties of men . . . as subjects" were "delivered . . . either curiously adorned with verse, or clouded with allegories, as a most beautiful and hallowed mystery of royal authority; lest by the disputations of private men it might be defiled" (*Lev.,* "A Review and a Conclusion," p. 506; *DC,* "The Author's Preface To The Reader," p. 95).

Hobbes never wavered in his view that human affairs are untenable without the discipline of political authority. Because he also anticipated Hegel's judgment that Socrates had destroyed forever the possibility of a "happy" or enchanted acceptance of such discipline, it would appear from these and related passages that he in effect gave up on the possibility of commonwealth by institution, looked instead to the less attractive but pragmatically more realistic commonwealth by acquisition. If human beings cannot successfully operate the complex, rationality- and trust-demanding procedures necessary to construct and sustain the former, they do and in prudence should submit when confronted with the life-threatening power that is the origin of the latter. As Rousseau and numerous other critics have complained, Hobbes is in fact a theorist of the ugly proposition that might makes right. His talk of science and reason, equality and liberty, covenant and consent, rights and duties, authority and obligation, is no better than camouflage for the despotism of the strong or the cunning over the weak or credulous.

As a historical matter Hobbes clearly thought that most if not all known political societies took their origins from force or fraud. Nor is there any doubting his conviction that these and other repugnant devices and methods are necessary to effective rule. Even if a commonwealth by institution somehow developed, its sovereign would be distinguished from its subjects primarily by the fact that he "hath the use of so much power and strength . . . that by terror thereof, he is enabled to form the wills of them all, to peace at home, and mutual aid against their enemies abroad" (*Lev.,* Ch. 17, p. 132).

Rousseau's critique, however, overlooks the fact that Hobbes's thinking provides even greater reasons for pessimism concerning the prospects of stable or lasting commonwealths by acquisition than for the likelihood of commonwealths by institution. It is believable that Hobbesian human beings will voluntarily and prudently submit, here and now, to the power another or others have temporarily acquired. His theory of natural equality, artfully elaborated in his several quite detailed and insightful accounts of sedition and rebellion, makes it very difficult to believe that power sufficient to compel continued obedience can be sustained for long and even more difficult to believe that very many human beings will or in prudence/morality should choose to remain faithful to the agreement by which they initially submitted. His movement from commonwealth by institution to commonwealth by acquisition compounds rather than abates the difficulties of his specifically political theory.

We might, then, adopt the familiar view that Hobbes is simply confused. He wants active, forceful government but fails to see that his own theory makes such government impossible. More plausibly, we might say that he is clear-headed but deeply pessimistic. He thinks human affairs would go better if there were such government but is convinced that the very characteristics of human beings that make it desirable also make it highly unlikely. Scorning as he does the delusive notion that a miraculous transformation of human nature can be effected by his own theorizing or by the happenstance emergence of something like a government, those parts of his thinking that show the desirability of wide-ranging and effective governance also and necessarily provide reasons for doubting that it can be established and sustained.

There is an additional possibility, one that acknowledges Hobbes's deep skepticism and considerable pessimism but also makes greater sense of the care that he lavished on commonwealth by institution and on the entire elaborate array of liberties and rights, obligations and duties, proprieties and improprieties of which his civil philosophy largely consists. On this third view, Hobbes did want to convince us that commonwealths can be valuable additions to God's creation, can make worthy contributions to individual freedom of action and felicity. He also wanted to persuade us that they are best able to make such contributions if they are quite simple in form or structure, if the authority-cum-right of action of those who rule is closely akin to the right of action that every human being has by nature. But he thought extensive, expansive, ambitious government neither feasible nor desirable, no more likely to achieve its objectives than ambitious and vain-glorious individuals, as likely to do harm to itself and others as are the latter. Perhaps not significantly more optimistic concerning the probability of "temperate" government than of conduct of this sort on the part of private persons, his constant insistence on the difficulties of establishing and sustaining governmental authority and power is counsel not of despair but to a more substantially political version of the kind of prudence represented by his notion of temperateness. Some of this guidance, concerning appropriate objectives and how and how not to pursue them, is explicitly addressed to sovereigns and constitutes Hobbes's theory of temperate rule or statesmanship. He also has many words for those who, by whatever process, have become subject to a politically organized and governed association.

IV

The best known of Hobbes's words to sovereigns urge them to insist on and otherwise act to protect their absolute authority. Equally, the most widely discussed aspect of his advice to subjects concerns their obligation to obey their rulers and thereby make efficacious governance possible. But much of his advice to rulers urges temperateness in the use of their authority and many of his counsels to subjects are admonitions to confine and delimit their specifically political commitments and relationships. They are to understand political association as instrumental to their individual and hence non- or extra-political purposes and they are to act in ways that, because temperate, help to temper the conduct of their fellow subjects and their rulers. In the admittedly unlikely event that these several counsels were widely and steadily heeded, the distinctive and inherently dangerous mode of keeping company that is political association might ameliorate somewhat the difficulties of the human estate.

In order to be effective the Sovereign must be invested with all but absolute authority. As Hobbes understands absolutism, this means that there can be no law that the Sovereign cannot rightfully promulgate, no command that she cannot properly issue. There are laws and commands that it would be morally wrong for her to issue (for example those that would be cruel or vengeful), but the duty not to do so is owed to God not to her subjects and the latter have no political or legal right to enforce it. In strict jural terms we should eliminate the qualifier "all but" from the statement that the Sovereign must have absolute authority. Properly speaking, this qualifier speaks not to the Sovereign's authority but to the obligations of subjects that ordinarily correlate with it. There are commands that subjects are not obligated to obey, or rather that they have a natural right to disobey; but in Hobbes's view this natural right, while it may reduce the Sovereign's power, does not diminish her de jure authority.

It is important to notice a distinction Hobbes makes between two senses of or moments in absolutism and the quite different arguments he gives for each of them.

When a number of people covenant with one another to create a political association they necessarily claim entire right or authority to do so. (Equally, when a number of people simultaneously or successively submit to the power of the same person, they each claim the right or authority to do so.) How they exercise that authority, for example whether they make that government absolute or qualify its authority in certain ways, is a question they must regard as within their authority to decide. They may decide to make the government absolute or to limit, divide, or otherwise qualify the authority of government in certain ways; in either case it is they who make the decision and who therefore claim the right or authority to do so. (Again, as a matter of right the same is true of those who negotiate an agreement with someone who is threatening their lives.) This is nothing other than the prepolitical right each of us has by nature. As Hobbes incisively puts it: "This device therefore of them that will make civil laws first, and then a civil body afterwards (as if policy made a body politic, and not a body politic made policy), is of no effect" (*Elements,* II, B, Ch. 1, p. 318).

In this its founding moment, political authority is necessarily absolute. The alternative to absolutism is not limited authority, it is anarchism. However it is exercised or implemented, absolute authority is the basis of all systems of rule. This is a truth of reason, an indisputable deduction from the meanings of the words "authority," "rule," and "government" (see esp. *DC,* Ch. VI and *Lev.,* Ch. 20). I wouldn't put it quite as Hobbes does, but his point is well taken and should not be pretended or wished away.

Hobbes makes the further argument that those who covenant to create authority ought to invest it with the entirety of their natural authority. This further argument is not and cannot be a deduction in Hobbes's or any other useful sense of that word. Rather, it is an experiential or prudential judgment, a prediction or wager as to how best to achieve the purposes for which the political society is instituted. Hobbes argues repeatedly and vigorously for this judgment, but he is evidently aware that his own account of absolutism in the first sense is reason for wariness concerning absolutism in the second and indeed concerning government of any sort. He insists that the commonwealth must have entire formal or jural authority but he also sustains the individual's natural right to disobey laws and commands that she thinks contrary to her purposes in submitting to political rule. When a subject reaches this conclusion, she and her Sovereign are in the state of nature in respect to the disagreement between them.

Thus Hobbes's first political counsel only appears to be absolutism in both senses, in fact privileges absolutism in a sense that is individuating because it depends on the willingness of each and every potential subject to enter into and sustain the covenant with some number of others.

Later I assess the effects of this qualification on the power of the Sovereign and hence on the prudence of her provoking, and of individual subjects engaging in, acts of disobedience. Consideration of other aspects of Hobbes's advice to sovereigns will prepare the way for this discussion.

Hobbes argues that those human rulers invested with absolute authority should nevertheless exercise that authority only to the extent necessary (of which they must be the judges) to maintain the peace and defense essential to the felicity of their individual subjects. Perhaps more important, his skepticism leads him to the view that Sovereigns who pursue objectives significantly beyond peace and defense will almost certainly fail to achieve them and are very likely to lose their authority in the process.

Let us begin with the question of peace and war among common-wealths. Once political authority has been instituted, the first duty of the Sovereign is to protect her subjects against attacks from abroad. Owing to the incessant possibility of such assaults, the Sovereign must be constantly vigilant and always adequately prepared to fight effectively. But Hobbes is far from a supporter of bellicose or expansionist policies. Because no preparation can assure victory, "such commonwealths, or such monarchs, as affect war for itself . . . out of ambition, or of vain-glory, or that make account to revenge every little injury, or disgrace done by their neighbors, if they ruin not themselves, their fortune must be better than they have reason to expect" (*Elements,* II, B, Ch. 9, p. 384). "The subjects of those Kings who affect the Glory, and imitate the Actions of **Alexander** the Great, have not always the most comfortable lives, nor do such Kings usually very long enjoy their Conquests. They March to and fro perpetually, as upon a Plank sustained only in the midst, and when one end rises, down goes the other" (*Dialogue,* p. 60).

Temperate conduct and comfortable living not the teeter-totter existence of those who, hybristically and vain-gloriously, overestimate their knowledge and power. These same themes reverberate through Hobbes treatment of domestic governance.

Hobbes thinks that we can have partial and for some purposes serviceable knowledge of one another's desires and thoughts. Setting aside doubts whether his theory actually warrants this possibility, it is plain that on that theory the Sovereign's knowledge of and capacity to govern her subjects (as with their knowledge of and ability to influence or control one another) can be no more than partial and can never be secure into the future. Like his brief but chastening advice concerning war and peace, his theory of jurally absolute but practically limited domestic government elaborates these skeptical views.

"[O]f the voluntary acts of every man, the object is some good to himself" (*Lev.,* Ch. 14, p. 105). For this reason alone, it is *possible* for the natural person whom I make my sovereign to pursue my ends if and only if her ends and mine happen to coincide. What is more, not actually being a god, my sovereign can know my ends, and hence can know whether our ends coincide, only to the limited extent that she as one human being can know and understand the passions, deliberations, stipulations and so forth of me, another such being. For all of her formal *authority* to act, the sovereign's *abilities* to do so are as severely limited as those of any other person.

Why then should we create sovereigns and submit to their rule?

Perhaps we should answer, as in consistency Hobbes himself must and does answer in part, that we should do so on the wager that the sovereign's ends and our own will coincide often enough that the advantages outweigh the disadvantages.

This is only part of Hobbes's answer. For the most part writing of the office of the Sovereign and its formal authority, only rarely discussing the personal qualities appropriate to holding that office, Hobbes recognizes that ruling is a distinctive activity, he distinguishes good and bad ruling, and he counsels sovereigns—primarily in the name of their own self-interest—to rule well rather than badly. Ruling well does not require the impossibility of pursuing the ends of someone other than the ruler or the near impossibility of acting only if the ends of the ruler and those of the ruler's subjects coincide. It requires, rather, that rulers be especially attentive to a distinction that reason urges on all human beings, namely between the ends of our actions and the conditions under which we are most likely to be successful in pursuing whatever ends we have. Necessarily pursuing their own ends, and *urged* to consider that due to their position their ends will more often than is usual coincide with the ends of those others who are their subjects, sovereigns have a special responsibility to attend to the conditions necessary to the successful pursuit of the kinds or classes of ends that experience and reason have shown to be most common among humankind. (As such, Hobbes argues that the sovereign's personal ends will very likely be encompassed within these classes.)

It is a signal advantage of this view that on it the inherently uncertain business of "searching hearts" is largely irrelevant to ruling. To repeat a passage quoted above, "let one man read another by his actions never so perfectly, it serves him only with his acquaintances, which are but few," while "[h]e that is to govern a whole nation, must read in himself, not this or that particular man; but mankind." To discharge their offices well (and hence to keep them), rulers must discern "the similitudes of **passions**, which are the same in all men, **desire, fear, hope, &c.**; not the similitude of the **objects** of the passions."

Relieved of, or rather largely excluded by incapacity from, the duty to know and advance the particular ends of their individual subjects, the Sovereign is nevertheless confronted with the arguably greater difficulty of "reading mankind" and pursuing what has traditionally been called the common good. Recognizing that from Plato forward the daunting character of these tasks had been taken as reason for pessimism concerning government and everything that has been thought (however absurdly) to depend on it, Hobbes continues the lines of thought I am tracing in ways that permit him to "recover some hope" that "the disorders of state" can be "taken away" (*Lev.*, Ch. 31, p. 270).

Concerned with the conditions of felicity not felicity itself (and not even *the conditions* of the integration of self or self and community, moral perfection, perfect freedom, and like repugnant fantasies), the deep and transcendental truths that Plato and his successors thought good rulers must know are in fact irrelevant to governance. The "only science necessary for sovereigns and their principal ministers" is the "science of natural justice" (ibid). Hobbes convinced himself that he had so well "read mankind" that it would largely suffice for sovereigns to read Hobbes. Apparently eschewing the skepticism that I have attributed to him, he modestly claimed to have "put into order, and sufficiently or probably proved all the theorems of moral doctrine, that men may learn thereby, both how to govern, and how to obey." Almost all that is necessary for good government is that "this writing of mine may fall into the hands of a sovereign, who will . . . by the exercise of entire sovereignty . . . convert this truth of speculation, into the utility of practice." (ibid. Note that even this ill-considered remark recognizes the need for a "converting" that Hobbes has no reason to think so much as possible.)

Hobbes's "hope," however, the success of his project of employing absolute government to increase the prospects of human felicity, requires sovereigns and subjects to draw and act on several further inferences from the arguments thus far considered. The most general of these, from which Hobbes draws at least three subordinate inferences, is that sovereigns will limit themselves to governing primarily by law and that subjects (as such) will relate to one another and to their sovereigns first and foremost as obeyers of the civil law. (Hobbes is a theorist who urges rule primarily by law, but not a theorist of the "rule of law" when that phrase means that rule contrary to or by any means other than law is illegitimate.)

The "skill of making, and maintaining commonwealths consisteth in certain rules, as doth arithmetic and geometry; not, as tennis-play, on practice only" (ibid., Ch. 20, p. 158).[8] The rules of arithmetic and geometry are "certain" in the sense of beyond dispute. Their certainty in this sense depends on another, namely the clarity or "perspicuity" of the definitions that mathematicians have stipulated and from which their further reasoning and their conclusions proceed. Analogously, by promulgating positive laws sovereigns define the terms in which thereafter their subjects (again as such as distinct from persons acting and interacting in ways not covered by law) make their "calculations." Perspicuous laws provide a settled basis on which the members of a commonwealth can maintain a modus vivendi despite the mutual antagonisms, misunderstandings, and unintelligibilities that result from their individuating characteristics.

The first of the inferences subordinate to the proposition that sovereigns should rule by law is that it "belongeth to . . . the office of a legislator" to make the laws as perspicuous as possible (*Lev.,* Ch. 30, pp. 255-57). The second and third such inferences can be viewed as elaborations on differences between positive laws and their model, the stipulations of mathematicians. The former of these is simply a deduction from one such difference already noted, that the Sovereign's definitions are invested with authority and hence binding. Viewed in comparison with geometry, the point here is that law is not a system in the rigorous sense of a mathematics and hence sovereigns are advised but not obliged to maintain consistency between their new or altered laws and those they have previously promulgated. Subjects should not be punished for obeying only one of two or more laws that make mutually incompatible demands upon them (as also they are excused from "obedience" if a "law" is so lacking in perspicuity that it is impossible for them to know what would count as obeying it), but conflicts among laws or between them and other desiderata do not invalidate or justify disobedience to any law. Hobbes refines this proposition in various ways, but in its fundamentals it is simply a corollary of his absolutism.

Together with his absolutism, the first subordinate inference might lead us to expect Hobbes to recommend extensive and encompassing legislation, to urge the sovereign to promulgate numerous laws governing many aspects of life in the commonwealth. If law eliminates or obviates the consequences of disagreement and mutual unintelligibility, why shouldn't the Sovereign use it freely and widely?

In fact, while reiterating that the Sovereign must have complete discretion concerning the number and scope of the laws promulgated, Hobbes proposes two criteria of "good laws," namely perspicuity and "needful," and interprets them in ways that imply (albeit Hobbes is not invariably faithful to the implication) the desirability of narrowly limited legislation.

"Unnecessary laws are not good laws; but traps for money: which where the right of sovereign power is acknowledged, are superfluous; and where it is not acknowledged, insufficient to defend the people" (*Lev.*, Ch. 30, p. 256). What does Hobbes mean by "needful" and its contrary "unnecessary"? Consistent with his view that freedom of action is necessary to felicity, his answer is that the "use of laws . . . is not to bind the people from all voluntary actions; but to direct and keep them in such a motion, as not to hurt themselves by their own impetuous desires, rashness or indiscretion; as hedges are set, not to stop travellers, but keep them in *their* way. And therefore a law that is not needful, having not the true end of a law, is not good" (ibid. Italics added).

Still, the presence of words such as *direct, hurt* and *impetuous desires* in this passage might be construed as recommending a highly active legislator, a paternalistic or even a moralistic governance. Hobbes does not rejoin directly to this interpretation but his rejection of an inference that might seem to be licensed by his absolutism is instructive concerning it. It might be thought, Hobbes considers, that "a law may be . . . good, when it is for the benefit of the sovereign; though it be not necessary for the people; but it is not so. For the good of the sovereign and people, cannot be separated" (ibid.). Knowing as we do that the good of the Sovereign qua natural person is in all likelihood different from the good of her subjects, and taken together with his revealing use of the metaphor of travelers and hedges, this caveat makes it sufficiently clear that by needful and unnecessary Hobbes means what we have by now been led to expect. Generically, those laws are needful that are essential to reduce the incidence of conditions adverse to the felicity of the individual members of the commonwealth. Equally, laws that have any other objective are "unnecessary" and should not be adopted.

We also know that for Hobbes the condition most generally destructive of felicity is death and that the condition most likely to result in premature death and otherwise most adverse to felicity is civil war and violent conflict generally. We can therefore infer that the most needful laws are those that prevent or (more sóberly) diminish the frequency of the former and the severity of the latter, the least needful are those that restrict activities that do not or are unlikely to lead to war and violence. Prudence and reason in the conduct of private individuals are defined by reference to felicity, needfulness and unneedfulness in law (hence prudence or temperateness in the conduct of sovereigns) by reference to the conditions essential to the pursuit of felicity by those composing the commonwealth.

We do not yet have a complete account of good and bad law and rule. To complete our account, and to see its place in the highly estimable civil philosophy with which Hobbes has gifted us, we need to understand how and why the two criteria of good laws are complementary.

The perspicuity of a law "consisteth not so much in the words of the law itself, as in a declaration of the causes, and motives for which it was made. This is it, that shows us the meaning of the legislator . . ." (ibid.). Good laws must have "preambles" that explain how they are to be understood. Assuming that the legislator has succeeded in making "the reason perspicuous, why the law was made," the law itself "is more easily understood by few, than many words." Why is this? Why would the clarity of the law not be enhanced by elaboration and explication within as well as without it? Hobbes's answer is consonant with if not required by his larger philosophy, but it at least appears to confound the argument he is here advancing: "For all words, are subject to ambiguity; and therefore multiplication of words in the body of the law, is multiplication of ambiguity: besides it seems to imply, by too much diligence, that whosoever can evade the words, is without the compass of the law. And this is a cause of many unnecessary processes. For when I consider how short were the laws of ancient times; and how they grew by degrees still longer; methinks I see a contention between the penners, and pleaders of the law; . . . and that the pleaders have got the victory" (ibid.).

These remarks are less than encouraging concerning the prospects of good law. Words being necessary to the formulation and promulgation of laws, all words being subject to ambiguity and the multiplication of words therefore compounding ambiguity, the legislator's prospects of achieving perspicuity in laws are less than bright. However well the legislator has "read mankind" and mastered the science of natural justice, however satisfied she may be (in her own mind as we might put it) with her reasons for thinking a law needful, she can have no assurance of making those reasons or the law itself clear to her subjects and hence no assurance of enhancing the prospects of felicity by promulgating it. A perfect law is an impossibility, a good law and hence a good system of laws extraordinarily hard to achieve.

V

These deep-going complications in Hobbes's theory of governance are rooted in the fundaments of his thinking. The problematic character of *making* good law dramatizes and compounds difficulties faced by all those who must keep company with others. Placed by God in a universe that is largely devoid of meaning and in close association with other creatures who are naturally intelligible to them only in the limited respects in which they were severally created alike, each of them must *make,* largely if not entirely for herself and primarily by the device of arbitrary stipulation, sense of the universe and of those others she encounters. To the extent that she and some number of others succeed in doing these things, they must then find means, again by artifice, to communicate with one another and to order their affairs in terms of the meanings they have respectively devised.

Nothing in Hobbes's analysis suggests that these things will be done easily or with steady success and Hobbes could not have been unaware that his argument for the farfetched device of Leviathan magnifies his own conception of the difficulties.

For reasons suggested earlier, we might stop here. We might read Hobbes's civil philosophy as ironic if not a *reductio,* as an argument or even a demonstration that government, if possible at all, is far more likely to compound than to ameliorate the ineliminable "inconveniences" of keeping company.

Insofar as "reading" means "appropriating to my or our own purposes," something close to this response will be hard to avoid—harder, I hope, after what follows in this text. But even this understanding of reading is incoherent apart from some notion (however resistant to generalizable articulation) of grasping the intentions of the author and thus the senses of the text under consideration. We are, I think, obliged to recognize that Hobbes's was the more complicated intention of conveying *both* the possibilities *and* the limitations of Leviathan, the at least possible gains as well as the probable losses of my submitting to the rule of another who by my own lights is far more likely to be worse than better than myself.

Hobbes was a proud and buoyant man inclined to regard the human predicament as a bracing challenge, not a circumstance sickly to lament. Reflecting as they do the difficulties of all human endeavor, to take the problems of governance as reasons for forgoing its possible advantages would be tantamount to forgoing the pursuit of felicity.[9] If barely possible for those of the species who have the least "worthiness,"[10] this was not a course Hobbes was prepared to accept for himself or recommend to others.

As with his treatment of the language of natural science, Hobbes's discussions of political and legal language and their limitations are meant to encourage sovereigns to make their laws as clear and readily followed as possible. Every law, nevertheless, increases the number of words that must be perspicuous to large numbers of persons few of whom can be personally known to the sovereign. In part for this reason, and because laws that are unneedful or inperspicuous advantage the enemies not the friends of the law, good sovereigns "sometimes forbear the exercise of their right; and prudently remit somewhat of the act, but nothing of their right" (*DC,* Ch. VI, p. 181).

VI

Sovereigns who respect the forgoing counsels of prudence, especially the last of those counsels, greatly advantage the liberty and hence the possibility of felicity on the part of their subjects. "The greatest liberty of subjects dependeth on the silence of the law" (*Lev.,* Ch. 21, pp. 165-66). "In cases where the sovereign has prescribed no rule, there the subject hath the liberty to do, or forbear, according to his own discretion," that is by exercise of her right of nature. Such cases are *necessarily* very numerous: "all the motions and actions of subjects are never circumscribed by laws, nor can be, by reason of their variety; it is [therefore] necessary that there be *infinite* cases which are neither commanded nor prohibited, but every man may either do or not do them as he lists himself" (*DC,* Ch. XIII, p. 268, italics added).[11]

These as it were natural or ontological limits on governance do not provide a liberty wide enough for human beings as Hobbes understands them. Metaphor, hyperbole, periphrasis, and rhetorically convenient borrowings of the languages of his opponents are concatenated in underlining this point: "As water inclosed on all hands with banks, stands still and corrupts; . . . so subjects, if they might do nothing without the commands of the law, would grow dull and unwieldy; . . . Wherefore . . . it is against the charge of those who command and have the authority of making laws, that there should be more laws than necessarily serve for good of the magistrate and his subjects. For since men are wont commonly to debate what to do or not to do, by natural reason rather than any knowledge of the laws, where there are more laws than can easily be remembered, and whereby such things are forbidden as reason of itself prohibits not of necessity, they must through ignorance, without the least evil intention, fall within the compass of laws, as gins laid to entrap their harmless liberty; which supreme commanders are bound to preserve for their subjects by the laws of nature."[12]

The hortatory quality of this passage, while no doubt conveying the genuineness of the sentiments it expresses, also foregrounds the fact that it and Hobbes's other counsels to sovereigns are just that, advice that, as a matter of authority, of justice and of right, sovereigns are entirely at liberty to reject. Having authorized all of the Sovereign's actions, subjects may be "harmed" but cannot be "injured" by any of them, have no constitutional, legal, or other institutionalized right to or means of redress against any of them. Whether members of a common-wealth by institution or by acquisition, subjects can do little more than "hope" that their sovereigns conduct themselves in a temperate manner (see esp. *Lev,* Ch. 20, pp. 150ff).

Subjects have no such rights, can only hope for prudence in their Sovereign. But just as sovereigns are also natural persons with the usual complement of desires and aversions, strengths and weaknesses—and hence persons to whom counsels of prudence/morality can be ad-dressed—so no human being is merely or exclusively a political subject the entirety of whose conduct is or should be governed by her political obligations. Keen to disqualify (almost) all purported agent-neutral and hence generalizable claims against the Sovereign (and hence to do what he can to eliminate or weaken group or collective as distinct from individual disobedience),[13] Hobbes insists that our "true liberties" consist not of those freedoms of action left to us by the grace or prudence of the Sovereign but rather of those "things, which though commanded by the sovereign, . . . [we] may nevertheless, without in-justice, refuse to do" (*Lev.,* Ch. 21, p. 163).

These "true liberties" consist of those aspects of our right of nature that each of us must retain. They explicitly include "the liberty to disobey" commands "to kill, wound or maim himself; or not to resist those that assault him; or to abstain from the use of food, air, medicine, or any other thing, without which he cannot live" and to refuse "to accuse himself" of a crime without assurance of pardon (ibid., p. 164). Consistently if nevertheless surprisingly given his general animus against group resistance, while in general I cannot "resist the sword of the com-monwealth, in defence of another man, guilty or innocent," "in case a great many men together, have already resisted the sovereign power unjustly, or committed some capital crime, for which every one of them expecteth death, whether have they not the liberty then to join together, and assist and defend one another? Certainly they have: for they but defend their lives, which the guilty man may as well do, as the innocent" (ibid., p. 165).

Remembering that Hobbes is thinking not of mere life but of "living well," this catalog of true liberties can hardly be regarded as inconsequen-tial. Much more important is the reasoning that leads to it, reasoning that will readily support additions to the liberties that Hobbes explicitly lists. As if to counterbalance his (too) ready imputation of tacit consent, Hobbes says that authorizations of the Sovereign's actions, and the obligations thereby undertaken, "must either be drawn from the express words . . . or from the intention of him that submitteth himself to his power, which intention is to be understood by the end for which he so submitteth; . . . namely, the peace of the subjects within themselves and their defence against the common enemy." In what we have reason to regard as the most consequential class of cases, words that we may have spoken are to be set aside in favor of intentions and ends. "[T]he obligation a man may sometimes have, upon the command of the sovereign to execute any dangerous, or dishonourable office, dependeth not on the words of our submission; but on the intention, which is to be understood by the end thereof. When therefore our refusal to obey, frustrates the end for which the sovereignty was ordained; then there is no liberty to refuse: otherwise there is" (ibid., pp. 164-65).

The Sovereign will by right make and act on her own judgments concerning these matters. In these as in all other respects, the Sovereign's right to do so is simply the right of nature that she has done nothing to relinquish or transfer. Those persons who are or have theretofore been her subjects will by natural right make their own judgments. If one or more of them decides, contrary to the Sovereign's judgment, that the end for which they submitted is served by refusal to obey, their obligation to obey is annulled and they join the Sovereign in the state of nature, return to that condition in which they as well as she have the right to do all they judge necessary to their preservation and well-being. From this moment, they have as much right to resist, attack, and if necessary to kill the Sovereign as the Sovereign has right to attack and if necessary to kill them.

Who will win the fights that are likely to ensue? Does Hobbes accord a natural right to disobedience confident that subjects will rarely if ever successfully exercise it?; confident even that he will have convinced subjects that it is manifestly imprudent to attempt to exercise it? Before trying to answer these questions, we should underline the significance of the fact that they arise so prominently and urgently in Hobbes's thinking. Let us emphasize again that, because the rights in question in effect cancel one another, civil *philosophy* as such cannot answer the questions. Both the Sovereign and the subject confront prudential questions in both of the senses Hobbes uses. Neither of them can have certain knowledge of the answer to them and in answering them as best they can they must gather and assess the pertinent facts in the light of their personal desires and aversions. This feature of the situation underscores Hobbes's distinction between persons and subjects, perhaps also his related distinction between the artificial and the natural persona of the Sovereign. The obligations that define and govern the performance of the role of subject do not answer the question. When confronting it, those persons who are also subjects must think themselves out of that role and instead consult the considerations appropriate to their conduct as natural persons. If Hobbes's sovereigns are more deeply politicized creatures than their subjects, if artificial and natural or private and public considerations are harder to differentiate in their cases, not a little of Hobbes's advice to them appeals to their personal interests.

Further and more general aspects of these distinctions will emerge as we proceed. But let us address the question of who is likely to win if and when push comes to shove between sovereigns and subjects.

It is a question of power; and Hobbes has made it clear that no individual person has or can hope to keep for long power sufficient to assure triumph in conflicts with others. If it follows that prudent subjects will avoid these confrontations wherever possible, the aspects of the situation thus far considered would seem to recommend the same inference to sovereigns. Taken together with Hobbes's other counsels to sovereigns, his doctrine of the true liberties of subjects suggests that prudent rulers will "sometimes forbear" the use of their authority rather than provoke uncertain trials of strength by commands that threaten the life or well-being of their subjects. If the Sovereign has as much, or more, at stake in the preservation of commonwealth as her subjects, she no more than they will put it unnecessarily at risk.

Perhaps these trials are not uncertain or are so little uncertain of outcome that sovereigns have no reason to avoid them. Granted that the Sovereign cannot have scientific knowledge that she will be the winner in all such confrontations, perhaps she is furnished with such an abundance, such an overwhelming superiority, of power that she has no practical reason for hesitation. Is not the whole objective in creating a commonwealth to provide its Sovereign with "the use of so much power and strength . . . that by terror thereof, he is enabled to form the wills of them all, to peace at home, and mutual aid against their enemies abroad"?

Of what power and strength does the Sovereign have "the use"? Her own personal or natural capacities being insufficient, how does she augment them sufficiently to "terrorize" the throng of individuals, whose congenital unruliness can hardly have been diminished by the teaching that they have a right to resist her, who she is to govern?

As a metaphysical individualist and nominalist Hobbes insists that collectivities are and can be nothing but aggregations of their individual members gathered under a single name. A commonwealth is a "real unity," but only in the sense that a "multitude of men, are made **one** person, when they are by one man, or one person, represented; so that it be done with the consent of every one of that multitude in particular. For it is the **unity** of the representer, not the **unity** of the represented, that maketh the person **one**. . . . and **unity**, cannot otherwise be understood in multitude" (*Lev.*, Ch. 16, p. 127).[14] If the artificial person who is the Sovereign is to have greater power than the natural person who she also is, it must consist "in the power and the strength, that every of the members have transferred to him from themselves by covenant."

On the same radically individualistic doctrine, "it is impossible for any man really to transfer his own strength to another, or for another to receive it." Therefore, "it is to be understood, that to transfer a man's power and strength, is no more but to lay by, or relinquish his own right of resisting him to whom he so transferreth it" (*Elements,* II, A, Ch. 6, p. 310).

Quite obviously, on this account the Sovereign, in particular that monarchical Sovereign that Hobbes strongly prefers, will be advised to "forbear" issuing commands that any but the feeblest of her subjects are likely to have reason to resist. If her other subjects do no more than "lay by" as she does combat with those who exercise their natural right to defend themselves against her, her chances of defeating any single opponent are no better than even. And if, perchance, her commands provoke the combined resistance of several subjects, her chances of victory are manifestly nil. If the "essence" of the power of "a body politic . . . is the not-resistance of the members" (ibid., II, B, Ch. 1, p. 320), we are out of the equality of the state of nature, if at all, only to the extent that subjects do not find the Sovereign's commands threatening to their preservation or well-being.

If this is a difficulty in Hobbes's thinking, he was evidently aware of it and made various gestures toward diminishing it. The passage just quoted first says that the Sovereign "ought . . . in all actions to be assisted by the members," albeit it immediately goes on to say "at least not resisted by them" and finishes with the words about essence quoted above. With one exception this pattern is repeated in the discussion of this topic in the several works. In *De Cive* he first says "not resist." He then construes this to mean "that is, . . . refuse him not the use of his wealth and strength against any others whatsoever" and "conveys to [the Sovereign] . . . the right of his strength and faculties." But he ends the discussion by repeating the *Elements* formulation that "because no man can transfer his power in a natural manner" the authorization involves "nothing else than to have parted with his right of resisting" together with the commitment "not to assist him who is to be punished" by the Sovereign (Ch. V, pp. 170-71, 176).

The first statement that addresses this issue in *Leviathan* claims that commonwealths are the greatest of human powers because "compounded of the powers of most men, united by consent, in one person . . . that hath the use of all their powers depending on his will" (Ch. 10, p. 72). The accounts of "laying down," "renouncing" and "transferring" a right, however, as well as the later discussion of the basis of the Sovereign's right to punish her subjects, revert to the language of "standing aside." "To **lay down** a man's **right** to any thing, is to **divest** himself of the **liberty**, of hindering another of the benefit of his own right to the same. For he that renounceth, or passeth away his right, giveth not to any other man a right which he had not before; because there is nothing to which every man had not right by nature: but only standeth out of his way, that he may enjoy his own original right, without hindrance from him; not without hindrance from another. So that the effect which redoundeth to one man, by another man's defect of right, is but so much diminution of impediments to the use of his own right original" (ibid., Ch. 14, p. 104). The Sovereign's right to punish "is not grounded on any concession, or gift of the subjects" but simply in her own right of nature now "strengthened" because "left to him alone" by the covenants and authorizations of her subjects (ibid., Ch. 28, p. 229).

In this last passage Hobbes once again speaks of the obligation of subjects to "assist him that hath the sovereignty, in the punishing of another; but of himself not" (ibid). Despite the vacillations that I have just followed, the recurrence of this notion, together with the manifest weakness of the Sovereign's position on the "stand aside" view, may be sufficient reason to think that some version of this view represents his most considered position. Exactly which version? We have seen his doctrine that individual subjects have an obligation to undertake "dangerous and dishonorable offices" only if they themselves judge that their refusal to do so will directly jeopardize the purposes or ends for which they entered into the commonwealth. Given that the in any case powerful urge to the preservation of life and well-being has been enhanced by the natural right to protect them against all threats, we have to assume that most subjects will be disposed to resist the Sovereign's attempts to inflict any very severe punishments on them. Thus there is excellent reason for other subjects to expect that assisting the Sovereign in this activity will be a dangerous business that they will undertake only at their own discretion and in most cases with a good deal of hesitation. It looks as if the obligation to assist the Sovereign, despite being a feature of civil society, is *in foro interno*. It also looks as if, for all of her authority, the Sovereign's power is mainly on paper, that the Leviathan is indeed a paper tiger.

There is one substantial but by no means entire qualification to this conclusion. The character of the qualification, together with the fact that it is the only one, tells us a good deal concerning Hobbes's thinking about government and politics. In "A Review, and Conclusion" that Hobbes appended to later editions of *Leviathan,* he proposed a twentieth law of nature that reads as follows: "**that every man is bound by nature, as much as in him lieth, to protect *in war* the authority, by which he is himself protected in time of peace**" (italics added).[15] As we are led to expect by the phrases "by nature" and "as much as in him lieth," Hobbes allows important exceptions to this obligation. "[A] man that is commanded as a soldier to fight against the enemy, though his sovereign have right enough to punish his refusal with death, may nevertheless in many cases refuse, without injustice; as when he substituteth a sufficient soldier in his place" (ibid., Ch. 21, p. 165). This particular excusing condition, and the more general one provided by having "a timorous nature," are taken away from "he that enrolleth himself a soldier or taketh imprest money." More important, "when the defence of the commonwealth, requireth at once the help of all that are able to bear arms, every one is obliged; because otherwise the institution of the commonwealth, which they have not the purpose, or courage to preserve, was in vain" (ibid).

Viewed as a kind of culmination of Hobbes's overall theory of political obligation, more particularly viewed in the light of the internally dissonant discussion of which it is immediately a part, there is a strained, unconvincing quality to this the least qualified of his exhortations to support the Sovereign. The final sentence concedes that the Sovereign lacks the power to compel her subjects to fight on her behalf, makes it clear that the preservation of commonwealth depends upon the self-chosen and largely self-sustained allegiance of subjects. Because Hobbes himself has made such fidelity appear unlikely if not ill advised, his argument is about as likely to encourage Sovereigns to expect active assistance from their subjects as it is to inspire fear of Sovereign power in subjects.

Notes

1. Once again, Hobbes's texts contain a parallel argument that he presents as a deduction from his *Christian* natural law theory. God, who made human beings as they are and who enunciated the laws of nature to govern their conduct, also commanded that earthly governments be created and endowed with (all but) absolute authority. This and that government are of human making (Hobbes is not a divine right theorist and he favors erastianism or the rule of the Sovereign over both the church and the state, not theocracy or the rule of the church), but the institution of government is of divine origin and the obligation to obey it is owed to God as well as to the Sovereign.

2. But only to bodies. "But when the words **free** and **liberty** are applied to any thing but **bodies**, they are abused; for that which is not subject to motion, is not subject to impediment: and therefore, when it is said, for example, the way is free, no liberty of the way is signified, but of those that walk in it without stop" (*Lev.*, Ch. 21, p. 159).

3. It is important to underline Hobbes's insistence that unfreedom is always and only due to external lets and hindrances. "But when the impediment of motion, is in the constitution of the thing itself, we use not to say; it wants the liberty; but the power to move; as when a stone lieth still, or a man is fastened to his bed by sickness." (*Lev.*, Ch. 21, p. 159). Hobbes will have none of the "positive freedom" view that I am made unfree by my own fears, weaknesses, or irrationality and hence none of the view that you, my priest, psychotherapist or Sovereign can "force me to be free" by making me into a better person. Freedom and unfreedom presume power or ability to act and are not to be confused with them or with conditions or relationships that enhance them.

4. Leaving aside religion, *if* there is an intrinsic good for Hobbes, it is the felicity of individual human beings. As Jerome Schneewind has pointed out to me, this is a good only in a formal sense because there is nothing such that in desiring it or not one makes a mistake. As to the instrumental good of freedom and the instrumental evil of unfreedom, we might call them "primary" goods and evils.

5. We might say that a person who agreed to commonwealth and its authority for any other reason would be irrational or that she would be acting in a manner inconsistent with her nature; we can certainly say that she would be deeply imprudent.

6. This is true of all association with other people. "We do not . . . seek society for its own sake, but that we may receive some honour or profit from it; these we desire primarily, that secondarily" (*DC,* Ch. I, p. 111).

7. In saying "the only reason for doing so" I am setting to the side Hobbes's argument that God commanded us to create and submit to political society. If we tried to harmonize the two arguments we might say that God issued this command out of benevolent concern for the earthly freedom and felicity of the human beings She had created. Presumably She would command disobedience to political societies that did not achieve this goal or at least conscientiously pursue this purpose. Officially, Hobbes himself cannot claim to know God's intentions in this or any other regard and ought not to speculate concerning them. God's commands are simply God's commands and it is not for us to wonder why. It is for this reason that Hobbes's "Christian" arguments are the most unqualifiedly deontic aspects of his thinking (and loom largest in those interpretations of his work that construe him as a strictly deontic moralist and political/jural theorist.)

It is for the same reason that there is considerable tension between Hobbes's secular and his religious or theological argument for obedience to government. Hobbes's secular argument not only licenses a good deal of disobedience but encourages withdrawal from and the destruction of political societies under a considerable and by no means improbable array of circumstances. But his Christian argument relies almost entirely on the Pauline doctrine of strict obedience to all earthly authorities and makes justified disobedience nearly impossible. As a speculation, this may be because his Christian argument was addressed primarily to people who would disobey and disrupt political society for reasons other than to protect their earthly freedom and felicity. I discuss this issue in the next chapter.

8. In saying "not . . . on practice only" Hobbes allows that skills learned by practice and not embodied or embodiable in rules do play a role in making and sustaining commonwealths. The most important of such skills are those that he discusses (for example in *Lev.,* Ch. 30) under the heading of public "instruction" as distinct from law. On the reading I am presenting these parts of Hobbes's argument have a problematic place in his civil philosophy. I return to the topic of public instruction in the next chapter.

9. In theological terms, if Hobbes did not permit himself the conceit of judging the human condition to be a manifestation of God's benevolence, neither was he prepared for the impiety of imputing to God the cruelty of having altogether withheld from humankind the wherewithal of activities that She had made unavoidable for them and of arrangements necessary to tolerable success in those activities.

10. In Chapter 10 of *Leviathan* Hobbes distinguishes the "worthiness" of a person from the "worth or value; and also from his merit, or desert." Whereas all of the latter depend in one way or another "on the need and judgment of another," "worthiness . . . consisteth

in a particular power, or ability for that, whereof he is said to be worthy: which particular ability is usually named FITNESS or **aptitude**" (p. 79). My suggestion, broached in the previous chapter and to which I return below, is that he thinks some persons have more, some less, worthiness to pursue felicity under the less than propitious circumstances in which human beings find themselves.

11. Although Hobbes does not here mention his views about the limitations of language and what might be called the rule-skepticism that it implies, his emphasis on the variety of actions can be read as saying that actions are too diverse to be encompassed, "perspicuously" or perhaps at all, by the general and prospective rules through which sovereigns are urged to govern.

12. *De Cive,* Ch. XIII, pp. 268-69. Together with his admiration for the brevity of the ancient laws, the last sentences of this admirable paragraph dramatize the enormous gulf between Hobbes's thinking about law and governance and the assumptions and practices that have become commonplace in the centuries that divide him from us. The idea that a citizen or subject of a modern state could "easily remember" all of their laws, and that each and every of the plethora of legal prohibitions are dictated by reason, is simply comic. Or rather it is tragi-comic because, in the words of his next sentence, nothing is now so familiar as citizens entrapped by and losing their harmless liberties to the laws and regulations of the modern state.

13. Hobbes underlines this point by arguing that the Sovereign ought to accord individual subjects something approximating rights against her in various respects. "If a subject have a controversy with his sovereign, of debt, or of right of possession of lands or goods, or concerning any service required at his hands, or concerning any penalty . . . grounded on a precedent law; he hath the same liberty to sue for his rights, as if it were against a[nother] subject" (*Lev.,* Ch. 21, p. 166). Because such matters are personal or even private to the individual in question, they are not likely to become a basis for group or collective action that threatens the Sovereign's authority or power.

14. Cf. his distinction between a "multitude" and a "people" in *DC,* Ch. XII, pp. 250-51.

Hobbes's use of an organic analogy to represent Leviathan, and the famous Frontispiece to *Leviathan* that appears literally to "embody" all of the subjects in the single body of the Sovereign, have misled his readers on this point. The "animal" that is Leviathan is "artificial" not natural, is a machine, engine, or "automaton" not an organism and Hobbes carefully distinguishes its several parts (*Lev.,* "Author's Introduction," p. 19). The "body" depicted in the Frontispiece, the drawing of which Hobbes closely supervised, meticulously maintains the separate identities of the numerous individual bodies (persons) of which it is composed. Hobbes's most extended treatment of identity, in *De Corpore,* Ch. 11, strongly underlines these points.

15. P. 504 (underlining added). We should interpret this law to hold for civil as well as international wars. Equally, the law would deserve the degree of special attention Hobbes gives it only if war is taken to mean actual fighting against an armed and organized force, not that "known disposition to" conflict that is pervasive in human affairs and not the Sovereign's attempts to prevent and punish the disobedience of individual subjects. It is clear from his numerous discussions of sedition that Hobbes thinks that the first two types of conflict are the chief threats to commonwealth and its purposes.

7

Of Liberty, Politics and Political Education

In the perspective of Hobbes's larger philosophy, the results thus far obtained are not notably surprising, comport well enough with the major tendencies of his reflections. Hobbes has analyzed the thinking, knowing and doing of human beings in ways that lead us to expect conflict and disorder in relations among them. He wants to diminish somewhat the strife and discord, but he believes that it is neither possible nor desirable to do so by eliminating the human characteristics that produce them. He turns instead to impersonal status and role concepts such as sovereign and subject, authority and obligation, concepts that invite each of us to abstract from our most personal, individuating and conflict-generating characteristics. If we think about and conduct some of our activities and relationships in these more subsuming, stable, and orderly terms, our lives will go better. In particular, those larger and more gratifying parts of our lives in which we act upon and vigorously enact our individualities will go better.

Many of the tensions and dissonances in Hobbes's theory of authority and obligation are due to the fact that relationships conducted in these terms are nevertheless among persons with the full array of human characteristics and for whom—with Hobbes's full approval—personal or individual purposes are what matter most. Hobbes urges us to subscribe to a single authority and to undertake and discharge uniform obligations; he repeatedly, one might almost say compulsively, qualifies and even contradicts that advice in order to protect freedom of action and to serve individuality.

It is not surprising that these tensions are at their sharpest, these dissonances at their most pronounced, in his theory of sovereign power. Convinced by his own analysis of human nature and the human condition that few human beings will reliably respect authority and discharge their obligations, he must buttress the latter with power. Because power is something that only individual persons can have, in discussing it he is obliged to descend to the unruly particulars of office holders, subjects, and their activities, to the very features of human affairs that the abstractions of his civil philosophy are intended to subsume and to order.[1] Because every successful exercise of power diminishes the freedom of action of one or more others, Hobbes's most general convictions and values lead him to the conclusion that every attempt to exercise it will and should be viewed with suspicion. He values and promotes authority and power, obligation and obedience; he also and at least equally values and promotes freedom, felicity and individuality. It is an instructive advantage not a regrettable or remediable difficulty of his thinking that he shows that—and in important measure why— these two sets of desiderata are incessantly in tension and recurrently in conflict one with the other.

We can enlarge these thoughts, can see something of how Hobbes hoped he and we could live with these ineliminable tensions and conflicts, by considering three further topics that, like power (and otherwise intimately related to it), are less abstract, formal, or properly philosophical than authority and obligation. The first of these concerns what might be called the emotional stance or attitude that Hobbes urges subjects to take toward their political associations, the significance subjects should and should not accord to government and politics. Here we must discuss issues that for some time have been dealt with in categories largely absent from Hobbes's writings, categories such as allegiance, patriotism and nationalism. The second and closely related topic involves Hobbes's sparse but savory remarks about politics as distinct from government, about political participation, democracy, and what before and after Hobbes has been called citizenship. Lastly, we must give attention to features of Hobbes's thinking that pose the greatest difficulties for the interpretation I have for the most part been offering. This discussion primarily concerns the Sovereign as educator or indoctrinator of her subjects, as properly instilling and otherwise controlling many of their political, moral, religious and even scientific beliefs and practices.

I

Consistent with his predominately egoistic psychology, as a matter of prudential/moral and jural reasoning Hobbes rarely urges anything but an instrumental stance toward commonwealth. Hobbesian subjects enter and undertake obligations to political associations exclusively in order to satisfy their desire for peace, defence, and the possibility of commodious living to which peace and defence are necessary. A subject's obligations end if her life or bodily well-being are jeopardized by the Sovereign or by others against whom the Sovereign should protect the subject. The same consequence ensues if a monarch fails, on abdication or before her death, to designate a successor and if the Sovereign banishes a subject or permits her to migrate to another commonwealth.[2] In these respects, subjects relate to commonwealth in a cool, calculated, rather distant manner. It seems that the relationship has little depth and an uncertain durability. If it persists, it will do so because the Sovereign takes care not to provoke disobedience or rebellion by arousing fears greater than fear of her, because the subjects fear one another more than they fear the Sovereign, or because of a combination of these factors or considerations.

Perhaps Hobbes hopes to bolster the power and stability of commonwealths by encouraging subjects to cultivate among themselves dispositions or sentiments that counter or somewhat qualify this predominately self-serving attitude. Not a strict egoist, Hobbes acknowledges a human capacity for altruism, benevolence, and fellow feeling, certainly for love and friendship. Perhaps subjects are to identify their good with that of their commonwealth, to love or cherish their monarch, to make their country or their fellow subjects the objects of their affections. Given Hobbes's reputation as a major theorist and progenitor of the modern nation-state, and given that sentiments of this sort—patriotism and nationalism as they are usually called in our political discourse—are widely thought to be essential to such a state, we might expect him to encourage them.

Happily, this expectation is largely disappointed. As preparation for showing and more particularly appreciating that this is the case, let us consider some of the ways in which Hobbes himself engenders the expectation.

Famously, Hobbes himself says that the "passion to be reckoned upon" to create and sustain commonwealth "is fear" (*Lev.,* Ch. 14, p. 111)—fear guided by reasoning of the calculating kind just discussed. Fear of what? He goes on to identify two "very general objects" of fear, namely "the power of objects invisible" and "the power of those men they shall . . . offend" if subjects violate their covenants. Because the former of these is "the greater power" one would think that fear of it would also be the greater fear and hence would be the emotion or passion to be reckoned on to bring about obedience and mutual accommodation. This inference is confuted by experience. Although by nature all human beings believe in and are affrighted by gods and other invisible spirits, in the state of nature they seldom obey the divine command to keep their covenants. (Hobbes nevertheless appeals to fear of divine punishments in order to bolster obedience, but he seems to have, or at any rate to be entitled to, little confidence in this tactic.) Hobbes therefore concludes that "fear of the latter" of the two kinds of power "is commonly the greater fear."

If "those men who they shall therein offend" are the other denizens of the state of nature, experience shows this fear to be as inefficacious as the fear of spirits invisible. The usual inference, frequently encouraged by Hobbes, is that the fear to be reckoned on is of the power of the Sovereign. The Sovereign and her supporters are those who will be offended when covenants are broken and laws disobeyed.

Taken together with our previous discussions of sovereign power, this conclusion gives us several more definite reasons for anticipating an argument, or for inculcating, some warmer or more affirmative basis for fidelity and obedience. If neither fear of God nor of one another generally will get us out of the state of nature, commonwealth can get started only through the highly uncertain process of "acquisition" by one or more powerful individuals. Should that miracle take place and a commonwealth with a substantial number of subjects emerge and stabilize, its sovereign will be that less than terrifying creature we have been discussing, its subjects narrowly calculating egoists. If Hobbes wants a powerful modern state, he had better take some further steps to get it.

It has been widely and not implausibly thought that Hobbes takes such a step when he introduces his fifth law of nature. This law requires "COMPLAISANCE" or "**that every man strive to accommodate himself to the rest**" by avoiding an "asperity" of nature that "will strive to retain those things which to himself are superfluous, and to others necessary" (*Lev.,* Ch. 15, pp. 118-19; *DC,* Ch. III, p. 141). In explaining and justifying this "law" Hobbes employs a figure that appears to be collectivist and quite ferocious. Likening the diversity of persons that make up a commonwealth to the "stones brought together for building an edifice," he suggests that those who make a commonwealth should imitate builders and "cast away as unprofitable, and troublesome" any person who, like a hard and irregular stone, "cannot be corrected." (Hobbes is thinking of fieldstones, not the uniform concrete blocks that [like the members of mass society?] came later.)

In company with his analysis of personal "worth," this law does diminish Hobbes's otherwise robust commitment to individuality. On his account of the law itself, however, subscription to and enforcement of it will do little or nothing to alter a subject's thinking about or feelings toward the commonwealth or its sovereign.

Immediately prior to introducing this law in *De Cive,* Hobbes says the following: If one person deprives or otherwise harms another and the latter "should expostulate the mischief," "he that did it should answer thus: **what art thou to me; why should I rather do according to your than mine own will, since I do not hinder but you may do your own, and not my mind**? In which speech, where there hath no manner of pre-contract passed, I see not, I confess, what is reprehensible" (*DC,* Ch. III, p. 138). Accordingly, "that we may rightly understand" this fifth law of nature, "we must remember that there is in men a diversity of dispositions to enter into society, arising from the diversity of their affections" and that "each one not by right only, but even by natural necessity, is supposed with all his main might to intend the procurement of those things which are necessary to his own preservation." When account has been taken of these facts about our species, the most self-serving among us will understand *why* they should conform to the requirements of this law. They will be obliged, that is, to acknowledge (the "pre-contract" that is political covenant having been made) that to go on contending for superfluities at the expense of the necessities of others will renew that very "war" in which they themselves are all but certain to be among the losers.[3] Here at least the prudence element in the prudence/morality relationship is clearly dominant.

The duty that this law imposes is not to direct concern for the well-being of my fellow subjects or the good of the collectivity as such. I am to subordinate some of my desires or purposes for the quite different reason that doing so serves other of my interests that I judge more important to me. In short, Hobbes's argument for the fifth law of nature reinforces rather than qualifies the fractionating implications of his egoistic psychology and prudence.

The same effect is produced, in ways that speak powerfully to the question of identification with or affection for one's commonwealth and indeed one's country, when Hobbes considers the case of those who—for whatever reason—are "cast out" of a commonwealth of which they have been subjects. "**Exile** (banishment) is when a man is for a crime, condemned to depart out of the dominion of the commonwealth." Although writing before the advent of nationalist theories according to which this is a fate worse than death, Hobbes is of course aware of the Socratic and Aristotelian view that a person is what she is, has the character and hence the possibility of a virtuous and hence a happy life, owing to her membership in a political society. So far from agreeing with this view, Hobbes thinks that banishment "seemeth not in its own nature, without other circumstances, to be a punishment." Rather, it is "an escape, or a public commandment to avoid punishment by flight," indeed "a refuge of men in danger." "For if a man banished, be nevertheless permitted to enjoy his goods, and the revenue of his lands, the *mere change of air* is no punishment" (*Lev.*, Ch. 28, p. 233, italics added). And if deprived of his goods or revenues, "the punishment lieth not in the exile, but is to be reckoned amongst punishments pecuniary" (ibid., p. 234).[4]

It might be argued that this passage is no more than a glorification of Hobbes's own narrowly personal preferences. Forced by the civil war to spend an extended period on the continent, Hobbes was distressed and angered by the events and regretted the rupture or suspension of friendships and activities that he enjoyed in England. He nevertheless found "the change of air" more than acceptable. Fortunate enough to have "goods and revenues" sufficient to satisfy his modest material desires, he was able to continue the intellectual endeavors that mattered most to him and he quickly established agreeable relationships with persons of similar interests. Almost entirely excluded from the political and in that sense the public life of the commonwealths to which he was now subject, the "quiet" private life—which of course was highly public and indeed turbulent in respects other than political—that he treasured went on much as before.

Hobbes clearly means to generalize his point of view, has no hesitation in recommending the same outlook to everyone else. He never entertained the thought that everyone should (or could) undertake the intellectual pursuits that were his primary pleasure, but he thought most lives go best if they are politically "quiet."

Isn't this a departure from, even a betrayal of, the commitment to individuality that I attribute to him? What business does Hobbes have instructing others how they should and should not live their lives? If there are those whose felicity, as they conceive it, is enhanced by active involvement in political affairs, on what grounds can Hobbes deny them this possibility?

II

I begin to address these questions by examining his response to those who promote political participation and democracy out of egoistic psychological and prudential assumptions that are close to Hobbes's own. We will find that in Hobbes's judgment views of this sort, even when remaining egoistic, become entangled with misbegotten thinking influenced by the likes of Socrates and Aristotle. We will also find that he opposes such views because they end up by dangerously increasing the power of political society.

"[S]ome will say that a **popular** state is much to be preferred before a **monarchical**; because that where all men have a hand in public businesses, there all have an opportunity to show their wisdom, knowledge, and eloquence . . . which by reason of that desire of praise which is bred in human nature, is to them who excel in such-like faculties, and seem to themselves to exceed others, the most delightful of all things. But in a monarchy, this same way to obtain praise and honor is shut up to the greatest part of subjects; and what is a grievance if this be none?" (*DC,* Ch. X, p. 229).

Although hardly the only reasons for egoists to enter the political hurly-burly, Hobbes's own analysis of human nature obliges him to acknowledge the incidence and appeal of the thinking manifested in this objection. Perhaps for this very reason, he is unrelenting in his opposition to it. His first response is given by the very manner in which he poses his rhetorical question. The unnamed objectors to whom he entrusts the position are presented as "ambitious" in the worst Hobbesian sense of the term, are clearly afflicted with the disease called vain-glory. As with all who are vain-glorious, they are deeply, self-destructively, imprudent. "I will tell you," Hobbes answers: "to see his opinion, whom we scorn, preferred before ours; to have our wisdom undervalued before our own faces; by an uncertain trial of a little vain glory, to undergo most certain enmities (for this cannot be avoided, whether we have the better or the worse); to hate and to be hated, by reason of the disagreement of opinions; to lay open our secret councils and advices to all, to no purpose and without any benefit; to neglect the affairs of our own family: these, I say, are grievances" (ibid., pp. 229-30).

Thus far, those who are prudent in the pursuit of their interests have potent reasons to avoid involvement in political life. The activities politics requires of them maximize their exposure to and dependence on the estimations of others. Such satisfactions as these activities yield are the least reliable and otherwise make the smallest contributions to felicity. Politics distracts or deflects them from other concerns that are far more rewarding.

Worse, an active politics, in particular an active democratic politics, breeds that most destructive of human characteristics, proclivity to the profitless contentions that vain-glory engenders. Worst of all, when coupled with confusions of thought and misbegotten aspirations that descend from Aristotle and that are now compounded by forms of religiosity from which Aristotle was spared, such a politics greatly enhances the power of government and puts it at the disposal of the vain-glorious.

The imprudent confuse liberty with that species of "dominion" that consists in "the equal participation of command and public places. For where the authority is in the people, single subjects do so far forth share in it, as they are parts of the people ruling; and they equally partake in public offices, so far forth as they have equal voices in choosing magistrates and public ministers. And this is that which Aristotle aimed at, himself also through the custom of the time miscalling dominion liberty" (ibid., pp. 228-29). Properly understood, liberty is greatest where "there be few laws, few prohibitions, and those too such, that except they were forbidden, there could be no peace." Thus in the liberty-dominion pair as Hobbes is here using it, liberty is greatest where dominion is the least possible, where the authority and power of government are in fact used sparingly. In part staying with this usage, Hobbes goes on to argue that the ambitious among us, in addition to failing to gain or to keep for long the glory they crave, compound their imprudence by enhancing the dominion of the state at the expense of their own liberties. But first he recurs to his analysis of absolutism in order to dispel a related confusion that afflicts the thinking of his democratic opponents. If by "dominion" we mean the possession of authority, there is nothing to choose among forms of government. All political societies do and must have absolute authority and in each and every of them the "true liberties of subjects" are the same. In this sense of the liberty-dominion pair there is no "more liberty in **democracy** than **monarchy**; for the one as truly consisteth with such a liberty as the other" (ibid., p. 228).

This misunderstanding corrected, prudent thinkers ask which form of government and mode of political practice will minimize dominion in the other sense, are most likely to make temperate use of their authority and power. Hobbes has not the slightest doubt that by this criterion the combination of temperate monarchy and a politically "quiet" populace is preferable to democracy and a politically active one.

Because "whosoever . . . expecteth pleasure to come, must conceive withal some power . . . by which the same may be attained," and "because the power of one man resisteth and hindereth the effects of the power of another" (*Elements*, I, Ch. 8, p. 212), Hobbes puts "for a general inclination of all mankind, a perpetual and restless desire of power after power, that ceaseth only in death" (*Lev.*, Ch. 11, p. 80). Power is essential to me. But my having it is dangerous for everyone other than me, anyone else having it is dangerous to me. Political office (including the "office" of citizen in a democracy) being a source of power, as the number of officeholders increases the number of people with this power to pursue their ends increases with it.

In this perspective the advantage of monarchy is that it keeps the number of such persons to the minimum. Let the monarch be as greedy as may be, let him "through his lust" enrich not only himself but "his sons, kindred, favourites, and flatterers too," he "may in great part satisfy" his passions without "robbing" his subjects "of those treasures given in for the maintenance of war and peace." Let it be that "some Nero or Caligula reigning, no men can undeservedly suffer but such as are known to him, namely courtiers, and such as are remarkable for some eminent charge; and not all neither, but they only who are possessed of what he desires to enjoy. . . . Whosoever therefore in a **monarchy** will lead a retired life, let him be what he will that reigns, he is out of danger. For the ambitious only suffer; the rest are protected from the injuries of the more potent" (*DC*, Ch. X, pp. 226-27). Restricting political power to a single person at once maximizes its efficacy in doing the job that it alone can do and minimizes the danger that it will be put to harmful uses.

Remaining for the moment with the narrow egoism of this discussion, Hobbes finds that the matters just discussed are very different in a democracy. "Look how many demagogues, that is, how many powerful orators there are with the people (which ever are many, and daily new ones growing), so many children, kinsmen, friends, and flatterers are to be rewarded. For every of them desire not only to make their families as potent, as illustrious in wealth, as may be, but also oblige others to them by benefits, for the better strengthening of themselves. . . . Though a **monarch** may promote unworthy persons, yet oft times he will not do it; but in a **democracy**, all the popular men are therefore supposed [expected, obliged] to do it, because it is necessary; for else the power of them who did it, would so increase, as it would not only become dreadful to those others, but even to the whole city also."

As to the safety against government and one another that the prudent above all hope for in submitting to political rule, "subjects are less often undeservedly condemned under **one ruler**, than under the **people**. . . . [I]n a popular dominion, there may be as many Neros as there are orators who soothe the **people**, and they mutually give way to each other's appetites, as it were by this secret pact, **spare me to-day and I'll spare thee tomorrow**, while they exempt those from punishments, who to satisfy their lust and private hatred have undeservedly slain their fellow subjects" (ibid).

To this juncture, Hobbes's analysis anticipates later critiques that emphasize the narrowly self-serving but also conspiratorial character of democratic governance and politics. The personally ambitious, particularly those few who have the oratorical skills necessary to manipulate the more passive many, appropriate to their own purposes the authority of "popular" government. Inherently in competition and conflict with one another, the members of this "elite" have the diabolical wit to cooperate to the extent necessary to maintain the acquiescence of the "mass." In this regard Hobbes's appraisal is distinctive primarily in his insistence that the members of this elite are merely vain-glorious not truly powerful or accomplished; they destroy themselves as they harm others.

Hobbes has a further and more strongly felt objection to democracy and the politics of active citizenship, one that he formed early in his life by reading Thucydides' analysis of the turbulent democracies of ancient Greece and that was intensified by his experience of the religious sects and other seditious groups of his own time. The brunt of this objection is that democracy begets collective aspirations far in excess of human capacities, breeds fanaticism and frenzy, and generates vastly more dominion than is needful or can be controlled.[5]

The main elements of this assessment are already present in the introduction to Hobbes's first published work, his translation of Thucydides' *History*. A master of those oratorical skills already encountered, it "need not be doubted" that Thucydides could have been "a great demagogue," could have achieved "great authority with the people" of Athens. He realized that such activities would be worse than futile. "[I]n those days it was impossible for any man to give good and profitable counsel for the commonwealth, and not incur the displeasure of the people. For their opinion was such of their own power, and of the facility of achieving whatsoever action they undertook, that such men only swayed the assemblies, and were esteemed wise and good commonwealth's men, as did put them upon the most dangerous and desperate enterprises. Whereas he that gave them temperate and discreet advice, was thought a coward, or not to understand, or else to malign their power."

Partly due to the arrogance of individual Athenian citizens, these difficulties "holdeth much more in a multitude, than in one man. For a man that reasoneth with himself, will not be ashamed to admit of timorous suggestions in his business, that he may the stronglier provide; but in public deliberations before a multitude, fear (which for the most part adviseth well, though it not execute so) seldom or never sheweth itself or is admitted. By this means it came to pass amongst the Athenians, who thought they were able to do anything, that wicked men and flatterers drave them headlong into those actions that were to ruin them; and the good men either durst not oppose, of if they did, undid themselves" (*Thucydides,* pp. 12-13).

Democratic institutions and procedures empower mob behavior. As distinct from an "aggregate" of persons each of whom "reasoneth with himself," the "multitudes" who form decision-making assemblies become as one, unite in passion or opinion and hence in action. As is clear from his preoccupation with this phenomenon in his later works, there was nothing that Hobbes, the admirer and proponent of individuality, feared and despised more.

He discusses what he seems to regard as a pathetic more than a dangerous form of such behavior under the heading "panic-terror." "**Fear**, without the apprehension of why, or what, PANIC TERROR, called so from the fables, that make Pan the author of them; whereas, in truth, there is always in him that so feareth, first, some apprehension of the cause, though the rest run away by example, every one supposing his fellow to know why. And therefore this passion happens to none but in a throng, or multitude of people" (*Lev.,* Ch. 6, p. 51). Panic-terror has the excuse that it takes its origin from a real danger. Because it brings about a running away from the thing feared rather than the fanatical pursuit of an unattainable objective, its harmful consequences may be confined primarily to those who are part of the throng.

Hobbes thinks that something like panic-terror is engendered by the essential dynamics of decision making in assemblies. Assemblies "cannot move but by the plurality of consenting opinions" (ibid., Ch. 25, p. 196). Monarchs who augment their own reasoning by hearing several counsellors apart from one another may "examine, when there is need, the truth, or probability of his reasons, and of the grounds of the advice he gives, by frequent interruptions, and objections." These things cannot be done in assemblies, many of the members of which "deliver their advice with **aye** or **no**, or with their hands, or feet, not moved by their own sense, but by the eloquence of another, or for fear of displeasing some that have spoken, or the whole assembly, by contradiction; or for fear of appearing duller in apprehension, than those that have applauded the contrary opinion." Thus, "the passions of men, which asunder are moderate, as the heat of one brand; in an assembly are like many brands, that inflame one another" and those seeking good advice from it are more "astoni[sh]ed, and dazzled . . . than informed of the course [they] ought to take" (*Lev.,* Ch. 25, pp. 195, 196).

Here Hobbes begins to move beyond panic-terror to behaviors that he regards as no less than madness of a kind that has wide and horrific consequences. With the religious sects and their preachers-orators of his day foremost in his mind, he writes that "though the effects of folly, in them that are possessed of an opinion of being inspired, be not visible always in one man, by any very extravagant actions . . . yet, when many of them conspire together, the rage of the whole multitude is visible enough. For what argument of madness can there be greater, than to clamour, strike, and throw stones at our best friends? Yet this is somewhat less than such a multitude will do" (ibid., Ch. 8, p. 63).

Panic-terror spreads by contagious effect from the justified fears of one individual. The fires of the kinds of folly just described are deliberately set and fanned into consuming conflagrations by those who are personally ambitious and vain-glorious; who command the "eloquence" necessary to move multitudes but are utterly lacking the "wisdom" to guide them to prudent conduct. Enabled by institutions that have the authority of the commonwealth, this form of mutually destructive misbehavior is all but inevitable in democracies. "In an assembly of many, there cannot choose but be some whose interests are contrary to that of the public; and these their interests make passionate, and passion eloquent, and eloquence draws others into the same advice . . . to the setting of commonwealth on fire, under pretence of counselling it" (*Lev.*, Ch. 25, p. 196).[6]

A democracy, then, is a mob ruled by that worst kind of aristocracy, an "aristocracy of orators."[7] Incapable of ruling itself, the "mass" that is the people is used and abused by the ambitious "elite." To the extent and for as long as a "faction" of the elite holds together sufficiently to keep power in their hands, its members "oppress the commonwealth" by putting the authority and power of government to their own narrow and ill-considered purposes. Sooner rather than later, they fall out and "rend" the political association into civil war (*DC*, Ch. XII, p. 255).

In making and structuring a commonwealth, the temperate will cleave to the prudence that serves them best in their personal affairs. "[W]ho is there that so far approves the taking of counsel from a great assembly . . . that wisheth for, or would accept of their pains, when there is a question of marrying his children, disposing of his lands, governing his household, or managing his private estate, especially if there be amongst [the assembly] such as wish not his prosperity? A man that doth his business by the help of many and prudent counsellors, with every one consulting apart in his proper element, does it best. . . . He does next best, that useth his own judgment only; . . . But he that is carried up and down by the plurality of consenting opinions, the execution whereof is commonly, out of envy or interest, retarded by the part dissenting, does it worst of all" (*Lev.*, Ch. 25, p. 196). In conducting themselves within their commonwealths (especially if they have the misfortune of finding themselves in a democracy) they will follow, "as far as" possible, the excellent example set by Thucydides himself. "[T]hat he might not be either of them that committed or of them that suffered the evil," Thucydides "forbore to come into the assemblies; and propounded to himself a private life, as far as the eminency of so wealthy a person, and the writing of the history he had undertaken, would permit" (*Thucydides*, p. 13).

Hobbes's words "as far as . . . would permit" will require further consideration in the final chapter when I offer an assessment of the value, to us, of his caustic and sardonic reflections about democracy and political participation. At this juncture the important point is the resounding negative that these aspects of his thinking return to the question we have been considering. So far from reasons for encouraging active involvement in and affirmative identification with politics and the government that gives politics much of its life and power, the tendency of democracy and participatory politics to produce these effects, and hence to extend the activities and increase the power of government, is the very reason Hobbes opposes them. Everything considered in this and the previous sections indicates that Hobbes favored an authoritarian but neither an active nor very powerful government; promoted a minimal, reserved and disaggregating politics.

III

Hobbes's views concerning government and politics are rooted in his commitment to liberty and individuality, in his belief that the kind of artificing that matters most is the making of individual selves and their lives. Authoritarian government is necessary in order to maintain conditions necessary to self-enactment, but animated politics and the energetic government that it spawns impede and disrupt that activity.

The difficulties with this reading do not reside in what Hobbes regards as the fundaments of his civil philosophy, do not arise out of the stipulative-deductive or deontic-jural elements in his thinking. The most serious of them, which are defects in Hobbes's meditations as much as with my reading of him, trace finally to his anomalous notion of individual "worth" and what must be done to sustain it. More immediately and prominently, they are due to his often frightening and anything but liberty-enhancing counsels concerning the control sovereigns should exercise over the thoughts and beliefs, and through them the actions, of their subjects. Here too we simply have to recognize that Hobbes sometimes strays from the most persistent, distinctive and estimable of his views, that he is at odds with himself in ways that prevent a single, unified interpretation and certainly forbid an unqualified appropriation of his thinking. But the difficulties in this regard are less severe and deep-going than those concerning "worth." There are important respects in which his theory of sovereign-controlled "civic education" strengthens the tendencies in his thought that I have for the most part emphasized.

Despite his own remarks about "reckoning on" the passion of fear and particularly fear of the sovereign's power, Hobbes's experience and the most basic elements of the theory he devised to make sense out of it are against the likelihood of maintaining a commonwealth by terror of punishment. Convinced that an "enchanted" allegiance had long since ceased to be a possibility, and totally opposed to an "enthusiastic" or "patriotic" one, he was forced to the conclusion that the prospects for stable and effective government depend heavily on education, on instilling the belief that the sovereign has a right to rule.

It is against the Sovereign's "duty, to let the people be ignorant, or misinformed of the grounds, and reasons of those his essential rights; because thereby men are easy to be seduced, and drawn to resist him when the commonwealth shall require their use and exercise. And the grounds of these rights, have the rather need to be diligently, and truly taught; because they cannot be maintained by any civil law, or terror of legal punishment. For a civil law, that shall forbid rebellion (and such is all resistance to the essential rights of the sovereignty), is not, as a civil law, any obligation, but by virtue only of the law of nature, that forbiddeth the violation of faith; which natural obligation, if men know not, they cannot know the right of any law the sovereign maketh. And for the punishment, they take it but for an act of hostility; which when they think they have strength enough, they will endeavour by acts of hostility, to avoid" (*Lev.*, Ch. 30, p. 248. Cf. *Behemoth*, p. 62: "[I]f men know not their duty, what is there that can force them to obey the laws? An army, you will say. But what shall force the army?").

Living as most of us do in societies that have long since turned over to the state the task of teaching or at least supervising the teaching of "civics," it is at best awkward for us to object to what Hobbes here tells us. Given that the "grounds" of the duties are to be "diligently, and truly taught," if we agree with Hobbes that there are reasons good and true for civic duties—whether the grounds Hobbes gives or some other, it seems that Hobbes means what he says when he speaks of education, does not mean indoctrination or some other process of inculcating beliefs that advantage the ruler because or despite being false. To reject his view of the Sovereign as educator would seem to involve us in promoting some less rational or reasoned basis for legitimacy and obedience—or in opting for anarchism.

Hobbes develops and deploys this view in ways that reflect some of the least attractive elements in his thinking. The difficulties do not lie with his argument that, formally, the authority of the commonwealth extends to control of speech and doctrine and to thinking and believing insofar as effective access to them can be gained. They stem, rather, from his consuming fear of the disruptive and destructive power of ideas and doctrines, beliefs and opinions. Whereas for the most part he urges sparing and temperate, honorable and even lenient use of authority,[8] in respect to the beliefs and opinions that subjects should and must not hold, ought to be taught and must never be allowed to consider, he often exhorts the Sovereign to wide-ranging, energetic and intrusive activity, not only licenses but encourages deception, scheming, and certainly severity.

"There is scarce any principle, neither in the worship of God nor human sciences, from whence there may not spring dissensions, discords, reproaches, and by degrees war itself. Neither doth this happen by reason of the falsehood of the principle, but of the disposition of men, who, seeming wise to themselves, will needs appear such to all others" (*DC*, Ch. VI, pp. 179-80). Accordingly, "civic education" must encompass large parts of the thinking and believing of the members of the commonwealth, may in principle reach to virtually any subject matter. Convinced that religious doctrines and beliefs are the single most potent source of disobedience and civil disorder, the content of religious dogma and the character of religious practice are to be determined and inculcated by the Sovereign, all contrary professions and practices forbidden and all teaching of them severely punished. Moral and political philosophy being a major source of seditious doctrines and disruptive activity, the Sovereign must take control of "the universities" and see to it that they teach the truth and nothing but the truth (that is Hobbes's own doctrines!) on these subjects. Because sexual behavior, marriage, divorce, and the procreation and raising of children have important political consequences, the state should instruct its subjects concerning these matters and will properly regulate numerous aspects of them. Sobriety, a moderate and otherwise healthful diet, and industry are to be encouraged by law and public policy; drunkenness, gluttony, and sloth forbidden and punished.[9]

Under the heading of teaching beliefs and opinions supportive of civic duties and the preservation of the commonwealth, then, Hobbes sometimes insists that sovereigns control the bases on which individual action occurs and felicity is achieved, often encourages them to do so.

Hobbes clearly hopes that sovereigns will teach nothing but truth and wisdom, but "disobedience may lawfully be punished in them, that against the laws teach even true philosophy" (*Lev.,* Ch. 46, p. 493). In general counseling against "cruelty" and even "severity," "fraud" and "cunning" on the part of sovereigns (*DC,* Ch. VI, p. 185), we have seen him entertain the first of these in dealing with seditious preachers, he extols the chilling effects of severity toward the "leaders and teachers in a commotion" (*Lev.,* Ch. 30, p. 257) and he encourages subjects to spy and inform on the seditious and rebellious (*DC,* "Author's Preface to the Reader," p. 104).

A very different picture than the one I have been painting.

IV

In these passages and generally toward the end of Part II of *Leviathan,* Hobbes takes almost literally the term *common*wealth and appears to favor the kind of political society that that name was then widely thought to imply. There are goods that are common, interests that are public; although in some respects compatible with and complementary to the goods and interests of groups and individuals, the former cannot be reduced to and must be preferred against the latter; public authority and power are created to advance the goods and interests specific to the commonwealth and to protect them against foreign powers and against the narrow and self-serving activities of private associations and individuals; it is the duty of the sovereign to use public authority and power to pursue these purposes.

These ideas are clearly present in Hobbes's works, do play a role in his thinking. He did believe that advances in natural philosophy would afford power sufficient to effect previously unattainable improvements in the human estate. Thinking that his civil philosophy had put government on an equally secure scientific foundation, he did not altogether resist the temptation to use its scientifically warranted authority to further this improving process. His discussions of sovereigns as educators are the chief locus and most potent expression of these dimensions of his thinking. As with the natural philosopher, the Sovereign translates "his" (i.e., Hobbes's!) science into power by teaching it to others, by getting them to believe and to act on its principles.

In this perspective, which may be made difficult for us to resist by the fact that, religion partly excepted, the sovereigns of our time do all and more of the "teaching" that Hobbes recommends, Hobbes does indeed appear to be a theorist and a proponent not only of commonwealth in a sense current in the seventeenth century but of "the modern state."

An exegetically required qualification to or complication of my reading, this perspective nevertheless profoundly misleads us concerning Hobbes's thinking, distracts and deflects us from what is distinctive in his philosophy. As a basis on which to enhance our own thinking by attention to his, it is no less than a disaster.

One means of supporting these claims is to note some of the ways in which positions discussed earlier lead Hobbes to qualify and even to confound his advice to sovereigns taken as educators. The case of the Sovereign as religious teacher will be especially instructive in this regard. But let us first correct the partly mistaken comparison between natural philosophers and sovereigns in the next to the last paragraph and use doing so to remind ourselves of some of Hobbes's doctrines from which we are distracted by the perspective just sketched.

Because geometers work with concepts that are entirely of their own making, those skilled at this science can arrive at and teach principles and propositions that are entirely certain, truths that one needs only to understand in order to accept. Hobbes claims that sovereigns provided with his writings are in the same position in respect to those concepts in his civil philosophy that have a comparable provenance, concepts such as authority and obligation, right, liberty and law. Largely invulnerable to the fluctuating contingencies of the empirical world, once the meanings of these concepts have been stipulated and the implications of those stipulations deduced, to understand them is to know the truth of propositions they are used to enunciate. In respect to the chief rights and duties of sovereigns and subjects, sovereigns are in a position "diligently, and truly" to teach the grounds thereof. Accordingly, Hobbes speaks of the "ignorance" of those who have not been taught and the "absurdity" of those who have been taught but have not understood or believed.

To this extent my comparison between natural philosophy and sovereigns is apt enough. But the comparison does bring a number of questions to mind, one of which leads us to respects in which the comparison is at least misleading. That question is why *sovereigns* need to teach these truths, why subjects can't invent the truths for themselves or at least learn them directly from civil philosophers. It is Hobbes's answer to this question that leads him to urge sovereigns to "teach" concerning the many further subjects just canvassed.

The basic principles of civil philosophy are demonstrably true. It does not follow that all human beings, even all those to whom they are diligently taught, will believe them. Truth produces belief only in minds not inflamed by passion or distracted by false opinions. It is also true (albeit not indisputably so) that human action proceeds from beliefs and opinions. But there is no inference from A's belief X to the conclusion or even the reliable expectation that A will act on X in all circumstances in which it is relevant. Human beings form and hold a great and typically conflicting variety of beliefs; the question of which among them they act on is influenced by their characters, their passions and many other forces and considerations.

Reminding us yet again of the bootstrap problem of how to get from the state of nature to a political society in which sovereign authority is established, civil duties must be taught by sovereigns not merely by civil philosophers because subjects have no duty to obey or even listen to the latter. (Matters would of course be eased if the Sovereign were also a civil philosopher. We can appreciate Hobbes's admiration for Plato.) The Sovereign's success in teaching the demonstrable civil duties will not suffice to assure peace and order. She must eradicate all other beliefs that lead subjects to disobedience, replace them with beliefs that are supportive of their civil duties. It is here that my comparison between political rule and natural philosophy misleads. The further beliefs that sovereigns must teach are beliefs about matters concerning which, at best, "probable truths" are possible, that are questions for prudence not science. They also concern issues about which passions run high and a great diversity of conflicting opinions have already been formed. For the second reason, the Sovereign's teaching will meet with powerful resistance. For the first reason, sovereigns cannot combat this resistance by demonstrating the truth of what they teach. In instructing their subjects, they must rely on a kind of authority that, as shown by the very need to do the further teaching, is woefully insufficient to achieve success in effecting that further teaching. Hobbes's skeptical epistemology haunts his doctrine of the Sovereign as educator and everything that depends on it.[10]

That doctrine, especially if we think of sovereigns as educators to *common*wealths, is also haunted by the radical individualism of Hobbes's metaphysics and metaethics, psychology and sociology. As with all of the bodies of the natural world, human beings are radically particularized, stand in contingent and fluctuating relationships with one another, relationships that are never more than partly understood. By nature they are in constant competition with one another. Except in the sense of conditions necessary or contributive to the satisfaction of any desire whatever, the notion of a common good or public interest has at best a marginal and in any case a doubtful place among them. It is for these reasons that sovereigns cannot amass sufficient power to force them into unity. It is against these odds that sovereigns must conduct their educational campaigns.

We cannot be surprised to find Hobbes conditioning and tempering his counsel to sovereign educators, attenuating and even drawing back from what sometimes appears to be his desire for an encompassing fellowship or at least an overlapping consensus of belief. (We might experience disappointment at Hobbes's refusal of fanaticism, at his failure to demand that sovereigns or those they represent intensify their efforts as resistance mounts and failures multiply. If our own wish is for allies in our quest [open or secret, witting or unadmitted to ourselves] for a fellowship of belief, we might avert our glance from Hobbes's tempering conditions and qualifications.) As we might expect given his psychology and his theory of language, and in any case the conclusion to which Hobbes was brought by observing the war of words and doctrines that accompanied and intensified the sanguinary conflicts of his time, it is often easier to halt or deflect conduct than to bring about changes in thought and belief. The timorous, the prudent and even the excessively ambitious among humankind will sometimes adjust their course of action to avoid a threatened sanction or to acquire a proffered benefit; even they, and certainly the "inspired" and "fanatical," are often if not typically impervious to arguments against their cherished beliefs. "A. A state can constrain obedience, but convince no error, nor alter the minds of them that believe they have the better reason" (*Behemoth*, p. 62).

Rooted in human nature, the difficulties of reeducating the miseducated become all but insuperable when confronted with religious "inspiration," ideological fanaticism and violent self-interest. As to the first two of these: "[M]en, vehemently in love with their own new opinions, though never so absurd, and obstinately bent to maintain them," rather than yielding to diligent teaching or rational argument, give their own "opinions the reverenced name of conscience, as if they would have it seem unlawful, to change or speak against them" (*Lev.,* Ch. 7, p. 57). As to the third, "the profit" of most of these "dark doctrines," rarely if ever given up without struggle, "redoundeth manifestly to the setting up of an unlawful power . . . or for the sustaining of the same . . . or to worldly riches, honour, and authority of those that sustain it" (ibid., Ch. 47, p. 497).

What then is Hobbes's counsel to sovereigns? Chastening his own sometimes zeal for homogeneity or uniformity, his advice is to cleave to the concern for peace, order, and the liberty and individual felicity that they serve, to teach and suppress only as needed for the former, to leave other beliefs and opinions to the individuals and groups to whom they matter most.

As with excessive punishment, "Suppression of doctrine does but unite and exasperate, that is, increase both the malice and power [of those who] . . . have already believed them" (*Behemoth,* p. 62). Where a people had already been "possessed" by self-serving spiritual or otherwise fanatical preachers or orators, "there was no human remedy to be applied, that any man could invent" and the "impatience of those, that strive to resist such encroachment, before their subjects' eyes were opened, did but increase the power they resisted" (*Lev.,* Ch. 47, p. 498). (As "for the remedies that God should provide," we are "to attend his good pleasure.") While there "is scarce any principle" that might not foment dissension, in many cases "yet may they be restrained by the exercise of the supreme power, that they prove no hindrance to the public peace. Of these kinds of opinions, therefore," Hobbes has "not spoken" in his counsel to sovereigns as educators (*DC,* Ch. VI, pp. 179–80.)

These comments address the doctrines and beliefs that Hobbes and his contemporaries feared most and tried hardest to control. As such the comments are circumstantially remarkable in their recognition that, faute de mieux, sovereigns must abide a diversity of religious doctrines and beliefs. Hobbes entertains, ruefully, the possibility that a succession of truly skillful sovereigns might have averted the religious fractionation that had come to afflict most of the nations of Christendom. That opportunity having been wasted, present sovereigns should not make matters worse by pretending to power or other resources that in fact they lack. Given that these comments are a part of Hobbes's blistering assault on the presumptuous attempts of popes, bishops, presbyters and sects to do what sovereigns have failed to do, it is clear that he sees no realistic alternative to a considerable if no doubt vexatious religious diversity. Hobbes the absolutist and apparently uncompromising proponent of a state church is an early proponent of religious toleration.

V

This characterization of his position, basically correct as an account of his circumstantial judgments (as well as reflecting his deeper views concerning the potency of sovereign power), seriously misdescribes the fundaments of his thinking and his sensibility. The accommodation to religious diversity thus far described is itself an adjustment of views that Hobbes adopted for practical reasons not because those views accorded with his own deepest convictions. He did not favor a state church because he thought that there is or wished that there were an encompassing religious truth that all human beings should or would confess. He became an erastian because he saw no other way to respond to the lamentable fact that religion had become the chief source of destructive conflict.

Recall Hobbes's view that our beliefs, while subject to influence by ratiocination, argumentation, oratory, and the like, arise or form due to the workings of our sensations and passions. They are neither imposed on us by the force of impersonal truth nor chosen by us in any active or self-controlled sense of choice. Recall also that this aspect of his voluntarism is at its most pronounced in respect to religious belief. We infer or suppose *that* there is a God, but we can have no unmediated knowledge of *what* God is or what God wishes for us. God has chosen to reveal some things about Herself and Her wishes for us in Her holy word, but we have access to the light of that revelation only through the words of the prophets to whom it was accorded, words whose light has been refracted and dimmed by any number of translators, editors and interpreters (*Lev.,* esp. Ch. 43, pp. 426-27).

Our attention to these features of Hobbes's thinking (to his commitment to a version of "fideism" according to which religious faith, rather than being grounded or groundable in intersubjective reason or truth, is instead a profoundly personal matter) is deflected by his erastianism and more particularly by his detailed and dogmatic exegeses of scripture. He tells us in no uncertain terms what Christianity requires us to believe, and he refutes to his own satisfaction any number of conflicting interpretations.

Examination of these contentious and often tendentious discussions shows them to be for the most part consistent with his skepticism and fideism, to be more an expression of his political than his religious beliefs. He is most keen to refute views that require or license sedition on religious grounds, most ardent to establish that Christianity commands obedience to established political authority. Convinced that religious beliefs and actions are based on fear and especially the fear of eternal damnation, he is avid to reduce to the minimum the number of beliefs required to avoid this fate. The longer the list of required or forbidden beliefs, the greater the likelihood subjects will think that they are obliged to disobey sovereign commands that conflict with items on that list.

Hobbes argues that salvation or damnation are determined by the mysterious will of God, cannot be earned or merited by human action, in particular not by the actions of obedience or disobedience (*Lev.,* Ch. 31, pp. 263-64; Ch. 43, pp. 424-25). He concedes that faith is necessary to salvation and insists that it too is by the grace of God. Unfortunately, most human beings acquire the content of their faith primarily from "teachers" who tell them what they must and must not believe. Most teachers now being false and self-serving prophets, Hobbes undertakes to show "out of such places of" the Scriptures "as are without obscurity . . . what articles of faith are necessary, and only necessary for salvation." He proves to his own satisfaction that "the . . . *only* article of faith, which the Scripture maketh simply necessary to salvation, is this, that JESUS IS THE CHRIST" (ibid., p. 428, et seq., italics added). A distinctively if not uniquely consistent "protestant," he held that all other beliefs are at the discretion of believers.

In the cases that as a practical matter concern Hobbes, that is of Christians living under sovereigns who are Christians, this interpretation all but eliminates religious justifications for disobedience.[11] Let us notice, however, that it and the thinking with which Hobbes surrounds it has other and quite different implications and consequences. Insofar as sovereigns seek to insure the salvation of their subjects, those who accept Hobbes's reading of scripture will have no reason to establish and teach any very extensive or encompassing dogma. The number of "needful" religious laws will be minimal. Insisting as he does that subjects are at liberty to believe and teach as they see fit concerning all questions not regulated by law, in commonwealths ruled by sovereigns who are Hobbesian in this sense, subjects will have a considerable religious liberty. Hobbes also makes it the Sovereign's duty to protect this liberty against private persons and parties who infringe it. "If the state give me leave to preach, or teach; that is, if it forbid me not, no man can forbid me. . . . Therefore to deny these functions to those, to whom the civil sovereign hath not denied them, is a taking away of a lawful liberty, which is contrary to the doctrine of civil government" (*Lev.*, Ch. 46, p. 492).

Insofar as Hobbesian sovereigns are effective in maintaining peace, order, and the proper liberties of their subjects, the latter will be protected against main sources of religious intolerance and oppression. Much more important, any very widespread acceptance of Hobbes's minimal religious dogmatic (to say nothing of his pervasively skeptical stance toward religion and religious dogmatisms) would take much of the zeal and fanaticism out of religious controversy and religious life generally. Professed concern for the salvation of those entangled in erroneous belief is of course the main justification for intrusion and interference with their religious liberties. In a society convinced that one and only one belief is necessary to salvation, the reach of that justification would be greatly diminished.

Short of Hobbes himself ascending the throne, there can be no guarantee that the Sovereign or any appreciable number of subjects will be converted to Hobbes's views. Out of her own religious zeal, or because it is the only way of quelling or containing conflict and disorder, the Sovereign might use her authority to establish an encompassing and confining religious dogma.[12]

Although he would counsel strongly against the first and regret and seek to minimize the second of these possibilities, should they occur Hobbes would insist (albeit not with much optimism) that subjects conform to these laws. But what does he mean by conformity?

In answering this question, the Hobbes of *Leviathan,* instead of recommending martyrdom, first invokes his theories of belief generally and of faith in particular. "But what, may some object, if a king, or a senate, or other sovereign person forbid us to believe in Christ? To this I answer, that such forbidding is of no effect; because belief and unbelief never follow men's commands. Faith is a gift of God, which man can neither give, nor take away by promise of rewards or menaces of torture. And if it be further asked, what if we be commanded by our lawful prince to say with our tongue, we believe not; must we obey such command? Profession with the tongue is but an external thing, and no more than any other gesture whereby we signify our obedience."

Troubled by the apparent conflict between this response and Christ's saying "**Whosoever denieth me before men, I will deny him before my Father which is in heaven,**" Hobbes takes the occasion to clarify his theory of authority and law. In doing so, he further manifests one of the most admirable aspects of his commitment to individuality. "This we may say, that whatsoever a subject . . . is compelled to do in obedience to his sovereign, and doth it not in order to his own mind, but in order to the laws of his country, that action is not his, but his sovereign's; nor is it he that in this case denieth Christ before men, but his governor, and the law of his country" (*Lev.,* Ch. 42, pp. 363-64).

Sovereigns take their authority to enact laws and commands from the fact that subjects "author" the actions by which they do so. Sovereigns as such are "actors" only in the sense that derives from the theater and the law courts, the sense in which one person "plays," "represents" and, Hobbes wittingly says, "counterfeits" another (*Lev.,* Ch. 16, p. 125). There is always a difference, an appreciable and important distance, between sovereigns and subjects. Sovereigns do not *become* their subjects, do not literally *re-present* them as they actually are. Subjects may admire or disdain the "performances" of sovereigns, but they do not, should not, identify with them, do not and should not think of them as their alter egos.

The importance Hobbes attaches to this distance between subjects and sovereigns is at its most vivid in his statement that it is the sovereign not the subject who denies Christ. Having "authored" the Sovereign's action, the subject has an obligation to obey the law the Sovereign has promulgated. Because the law does not threaten the subject's worldly or eternal life or well-being, the escape hatch that is the subject's right of nature is closed. In her mind and before her God, the subject has not denied Christ. In this as in all respects, subjects are in and have obligations to their political societies. If they take Hobbes's advice they will be of their political societies only in a thin and attenuated sense.

The best of Hobbes's thoughts concerning religion and its relation to government and politics are gathered in his endorsement, at first sight surprising but in fact consonant with much of what is most admirable in his political philosophy, of the religious freedom and pluralism that obtained in the earliest days of Christianity. Queen Elizabeth "totally dissolved" the power of the Pope. The presbyterians put down the Anglican episcopacy. "And almost at the same time, the power was taken also from the presbyterians: and so we are reduced to the inde-pendency of the primitive Christians, to follow Paul, or Cephas, or Apollos [the freedom Hobbes admires was for more than just the Christians], every man as he liketh best: which, if it be without conten-tion, and without measuring the doctrine of Christ, by our affection to the person of his minister . . . is perhaps the best. First, because there ought to be no power over the consciences of men, but of the Word itself, working faith in every one, not always according to the purpose of them that plant and water, but of God himself, that giveth the increase. And secondly, because it is unreasonable in them who teach there is such danger in every little error, to require of a man endued with reason of his own, to follow the reason of any other man, or of the most voices of any other men, which is little better than to venture his salvation at cross and pile" (*Lev.,* Ch. 47, p. 499).

Going well beyond toleration, this is a celebration of freedom, of pluralism, above all of individuality and individual self-making.

* * *

It is for me to decide whether to enter and whether and when to leave political society.

The sovereign may do almost anything, has the power to do relatively little.

Of the actions that the Sovereign may and can take, prudence/morality teaches her to take very few.

Of the laws and commands the Sovereign does issue, I must and have the right to interpret and assess each of them for myself.

When I judge that a command of the Sovereign entails an obligation for me, I am at liberty to refuse to discharge it.

My various and fluctuating identities and identifications are with myself and those with whom I conduct my personal affairs, not with the Sovereign or the political society.

Notes

1. Hobbes's evident reluctance to make this descent, partly due to his conception of the proper tasks and methods of civil philosophy and philosophy more generally, may betray his awareness of and his attempt to avoid or diminish this difficulty. Whatever its sources, there is no doubt that it is partly responsible for the often quite arid quality of his treatment of sovereign power. Perhaps he did not want sovereigns to have very much power and hence was sparing in his advice as to how they could get it?

2. *DC,* Ch. VI, pp. 203-4; *Lev.,* Ch. 21, pp. 166-68. Given peace and defense, it falls primarily to individual subjects to provide themselves with the material and other goods necessary to their felicity as they see it; Hobbes strongly counsels sovereigns against interfering with their peaceful efforts to do these things. He also urges sovereigns to enhance productive activities by supporting useful arts such as agriculture and navigation, to penalize sloth, gluttony and drunkenness, and to provide, through public charity and related public policies, food and shelter to those who have genuinely tried but failed to acquire them for themselves (*DC,* Ch. XIII, pp. 266-68; *Lev.,* Ch. 30, pp. 254-55). But these are counsels, and the Sovereign's failure to heed or act effectively on them does not absolve subjects from obedience. (Consistent with his views concerning war, he strongly opposes attempts to enrich the commonwealth by "the spoils of war, foreign tribute, and the territories they have purchased by their arms. . . . For the militia . . . is like a die; wherewith many lose their estates, but few improve them" DC, Ch. XIII, p. 267.)

3. *DC*, Ch. III, p. 141. Although hardly an admirer of "possessive individuals," with two exceptions Hobbes has no moral objection to those who pursue "superfluities" when doing so does not deprive others of the necessities of life. Those others, their necessities provided and left at liberty to seek superfluities for themselves, have no reason to complain. More important in the present context: "nor is the commonwealth defrauded by the luxurious waste of private men" (*Lev.*, Ch. 30, p. 255). The first exception is to the accumulation of excessive riches by sovereigns, to whom Hobbes recommends "frugality" (*Behemoth*, p. 45), the second to self-damaging gluttony, drunkenness, and excessive sensuality (*DC*, Ch. III, pp. 147-48). See below for further discussion of the second exception.

4. See also *Dialogue,* p. 151, where Hobbes fulminates against Sir Edward Coke's view that "If a Man that is Innocent be accus'd of **Felony**, and for fear flieth for the same; albeit that he be judicially acquitted of the **Felony**, yet if it be found that he fled for the same, he shall (notwithstanding his Innocence) forfeit all his Goods and Chattels, Debts and Duties." Hobbes's response, reflecting doctrines that extend the response to those who flee when guilty, is "O unchristian, and abominable doctrine!"

5. It is tempting and not entirely mistaken to say that this aspect of Hobbes's thinking anticipates later critiques of "totalitarian" as distinct from "interest-group" democracy. But it must be remembered that the actual and proposed or theorized democracies with which Hobbes was familiar involved (permitted) the participation of no more than a very small percentage of their populations. In discussing his views I have occasionally permitted myself the use of terms such as *mass* and *elite.* This language, and certainly the language of "totalitarianism," has connotations for us that it did not and could not have had for Hobbes. But if concern for liberty and individuality led Hobbes to fear and to despise the to our eyes limited concentrations of political power he experienced, perhaps attention to his thinking about the sources of that power will help those of us who have the same concern to misgivings and a certain reserve concerning the vastly more powerful democratic states of our time.

6. "[T]hat this kind of powerful **eloquence**, separated from the true knowledge of things, that is to say, from wisdom, is the true character of them who solicit and stir up the people to innovations, may easily be gathered out of the work itself which they have to do. For they could not poison the people with those absurd opinions . . . unless they held them themselves; which sure is an ignorance greater than can well befall any wise man. . . . But that they can turn their auditors out of fools into madmen; that they can make things to them who are ill-affected, seem worse, to them who are well-affected, seem evil; that they can enlarge their hopes, lessen their dangers beyond reason: this they have from that sort of eloquence, not which explains things as they are, but from that other, which by moving their minds, makes all things appear to be such as they in their minds, had already conceived them" (*DC,* Ch. XII, p. 254).

Hobbes's distrust of language, and his view that *ratio* is now for the most part *oratio,* are at their most pronounced in his discussions of political speech in democracies.

7. "Insomuch, that a democracy, in effect, is no more than an aristocracy of orators, interrupted sometimes with the temporary monarchy of one orator" (*Elements,* II, B, Ch. 2, p. 324).

8. On leniency, see *Lev.,* Ch. 30, pp. 257-59; *Dialogue,* pp. 102-3.

9. Hobbes's often frenetic advocacy of the control of religious belief and practice is too frequent to require specific documentation. The sharply contrary tendencies in his

thinking are discussed below. On moral and political doctrines and the uses of the universities, see esp. *Lev.,* Ch. 30, pp. 252-53; Ch. 29, pp. 241-42. On sexual behavior, see *Elements,* II, B, Ch. 9, p. 380. On marriage and the family, see *DC,* Ch. VI, pp. 185-86 and Ch. X. On drunkenness, gluttony and idleness and laws and policies to discourage and prevent them, see *DC,* Ch. 13, pp. 266-67; *Lev.,* Ch. 30, p. 255.

10. Another and arguably more confounding question raised by my comparison is why Hobbes, despite claiming that the duty of obedience is grounded in demonstrable truth, accords subjects the natural right to disobey many, in principle any, of the Sovereign's commands. If subjects judge that a command threatens their life or well-being, their right of nature to disobey it stands against truth as well as the Sovereign's authority or right of command. The most basic truths are contestable.

11. The possibilities that seem to remain are those of Christians who have subscribed to the rule of an "infidel" who forbids, on pain of death, profession of this one necessary article of faith or commands profession of a contradictory article. In *Elements* (II, B, Ch. 6, pp. 359-60) and *DC* (Ch. XVIII, pp. 383-84) Hobbes's counsel is that Christians in this plight refuse to obey the command but submit quietly to the punishment. They should "Go to Christ by martyrdom." Should this "seem to any man to be a hard saying, most certain it is that he believes not with his whole heart, **that Jesus is the Christ, the Son of the living God**; for he would then desire to be dissolved, and to be with Christ; but he would by a feigned Christian faith elude that obedience, which he hath contracted to yield unto the city." Given his usual doctrine that subjects have a right to resist all commands that *they think* threaten their life or well-being, this wryly put but stubborn doctrine has to be read as manifesting either Hobbes's overweening fear of religiously justified disobedience or his inclination to think that most such justifications (and most professions of Christian faith?) are hypocritical. Or perhaps it manifests both.

In *Leviathan,* where in general he vigorously combats the doctrine of "passive disobedience" according to which one can refuse the command if one submits to the assigned punishment, he drastically narrows even this concession. Cleverly threatening proponents of Christian martyrdom with the possibility that Moslems would use their arguments to justify disobedience to Christian rulers (but also seeming to call into question the certainty of his own construal of Christian dogma), our doubting Thomas says that only those who actually saw and knew Christ before and after his resurrection are entitled to disobedience in these circumstances. Even these long since departed few were justified only if their sovereign forbade them to preach Christ to infidels as distinct from the already converted (Ch. 42, pp. 364-66).

12. On Hobbes's doctrine of absolutism (in the first of the two senses discussed earlier) this possibility is inherent in government as such. If we the people or we the members of the constituent assembly are sovereign we can as well revoke as adopt religious liberties. *Pace* Hobbes, it obviously does not follow that we should or might just as well embrace absolutism in his second sense. The truth that resides in his claim that all politically organized societies must and do claim sovereignty over their members, however, underlines the importance of his concern with what sovereigns and subjects believe regarding religion and particularly the ways in which they should and should not relate to one another in respect to religion. There has never been and can never be religious toleration or any substantial religious liberty in a society pervaded by religious intolerance and dogmatism.

8

Of Individuality and Democracy

I said early on that Hobbes is a spirited participant in debates that remain alive and urgent in our own time. If my engagement with his texts has made that claim good over a considerable range of his thinking, it has also shown that he speaks in a voice that will provoke opposition and hostility.

In our time, resistance to Hobbes is apt to be most immediate and visceral when we encounter his antagonism to democracy and active participation in politics, his strong preference not only for monarchy but for the long since discredited view that monarchs should rule not merely reign. If we tarry long enough with his thinking to comprehend its complexly interwoven character, our resistance may very well spread and intensify. Hobbes allows that his argument for monarchy was "not . . . demonstrated, but only probably stated" (DC, "The Author's Preface to the Reader," p. 104), a concession he might have made concerning other of his arguments as well. But there is no doubting his conviction that his antidemocratic conclusions are consonant with and take support from the positions he adopts on issues reaching from the authority and power of the state and the proper duties and liberties of subjects all the way to his metaphysics, epistemology and theory of language. For this reason, and because his thoughts concerning forms of government and modalities of political relationships put both Hobbes and ourselves to a severe test, those thoughts provide an appropriate focus for concluding reflections.

Why do we, why should we, resist his antidemocratic and anticitizenship views? Even if we do and should resist them, is there something of value to be found in or taken from them?

In thinking about these questions we might begin by reminding ourselves that many full-fledged citizens of present democracies conduct themselves in much the manner that Hobbes recommends. Numerous among them regularly neglect the minimal political act of voting in elections; substantially larger numbers eschew membership in or any contribution to political parties; only a small minority ever run for political office or actively involve themselves in the electoral campaigns of those few who do; even the mightily interested activity of lobbying governments is increasingly left to professionals who make their living by doing it. Overt hostility to democracy as a form of government is rarely encountered among us, but if Hobbes were teletransported to our time he would find many who share his estimation of politics and politicians, yet many more who agree with his assessment of the comparative gratifications of the more personal as distinct from the more public-political dimensions of life.

Hobbes would say, and would surely be partly correct, that we profess democracy because we have been taught to do so. The societies of our time have adopted his view that the sovereign authority must teach the grounds of its right to rule and of the duty of citizens to obey. Hobbes would regret the fact that democracy, which he would regard as an unfortunate collectivization of his doctrine of individual consent, has become a main element in our legitimating political faith or ideology. Given that it has attained this standing, he would neither be surprised by nor oppose the practice of our societies of instilling or inculcating it in us from our earliest days.

Let us carry these speculations concerning Hobbes's reactions to the political societies of our time a little further. We can easily imagine him envying the success that some of these societies have had in implanting a stabilizing political doctrine. He would surely admire the ways in which some citizens, while accepting democratic doctrine as the ground on which they for the most part obey the laws of their countries, have adapted that doctrine to their own personal proclivities and purposes. Nothing in Hobbes's psychology would lead him to expect that the "teaching" of a general political doctrine would yield uniform under-standings of or generally slavish conformity to its principles. The discrepancies between the participatory injunctions of the official "civ-ics" of contemporary democratic societies and the actual conduct of many citizens would, in part, meet with his approval. Numerous of our citizens, if for different and less estimable reasons than Hobbes attri-butes to Thucydides, follow the example set by the latter.

This is an appropriate moment to consider further the phrase "as far as the eminency of so wealthy a person, and the writing of the history he had undertaken, would permit" in Hobbes's account of Thucydides' stance toward the politics of Athens. Neither Hobbes himself nor figures he greatly admired such as Thucydides and Sidney Godolphin are properly described as apolitical; neither he nor they followed the Stoic counsel of withdrawing into themselves and cultivating indiffer-ence toward the politics of their societies. Thucydides could hardly have written his *History,* Hobbes could hardly have written *Behemoth* or indeed any of his political works, if they had not paid the closest attention to the politics of their own and neighboring societies. Their interest in those politics, while importantly intellectual, was not exclu-sively and certainly not narrowly so. Hobbes hints that Thucydides involved himself in Athenian politics to the extent necessary to protect his wealth and we know that Hobbes vigorously pursued his personal interests at the court and elsewhere. Sidney Godolphin was hardly a "patriot" if that means embued with the sentiments now called patriotism and nationalism, but the virtues "shining" in the "generous constitution" of his nature included those that dispose "to the service of his country" and his "civil society," prepared him for "courage" in necessary civil and foreign wars as well as "a fear for [not of] the laws" (*Lev.,* pp. 5, 504).

In ways that cohere well with his most general convictions, and that qualify his opposition to democracy, Hobbes wrote these views into his political theory. "The best counsel, in those things that concern . . . the ease and benefits the subjects may enjoy . . . is to be taken from the general informations, and complaints of the people of each province, who are best acquainted with their own wants, and ought therefore . . . to be diligently taken notice of" (*Lev.,* Ch. 30, p. 259). Along with urging subjects to represent their concerns to the Sovereign, Hobbes favors the formation of a variety of substate associations for the pursuit of the purposes that he valued most highly. Such enterprise associations, in addition to properly having constitutions that expressly limit the authority of their governing bodies (*Lev.,* Ch. 22, p. 170), ought to be ruled by assemblies to which all members are eligible. "The end of these bodies, being . . . but the particular gain of every adventurer, it is reason that . . . the representative of the body must be an assembly, where every member of the body may be present at the consultations, if he will" (ibid., p. 175). If we are prepared to think of these comparatively "quiet," less widely or flamboyantly public activities as political, Hobbes's "so far as" leads him to substantial qualifications of his advice to stay out of politics.

The far greater qualification of that advice, one that pervades Hobbes's writings, is his strongly felt recommendation that subjects scrutinize laws and commands and be prepared to exercise their right of nature to disobey those that threaten their life or well-being. This counsel, which is to a form of political activity that is as constant as are the activities of the state, signals a respect in which he would strongly disapprove the kinds of political apathy increasingly prevalent in the democracies of our time.[1]

Hobbes's opposition to democracy was grounded in his skepticism concerning the human capacity for knowledge and effective action, in his fear of power untempered by knowledge and prudence, and in his abiding concern for individuality and the self-enactment that begets it. He argued against democracy, and for more individualized forms of political activity directed toward the state, because he was convinced that democracy and the highly public and collective political conduct that it tends to induce generate untempered passion, overweening power and submission and conformity.

Hobbes would be tolerant of but would have little admiration for the narrowly material character of the "interests" that so dominate our politics; he would fear and quite possibly despise the fact that they are predominately the politics of interest groups. If we can imagine him nevertheless finding some comfort in the tendency of many citizens to put their affirmative or constructive efforts primarily to their personal affairs and concerns, he would fear the judgments and attitudes out of which they do so. However much they may feel or affect disdain for politicians, bureaucrats, and the like, too many of the politically indifferent and apathetic citizens share with them, may exceed them in, an unchastened and anything but skeptical enthusiasm for the state and its power. Those who are politically passive do little to contest that power, much to sustain and augment it by uncritically accepting its democratic legitimacy and by looking unhesitatingly to it when they think doing so serves their interests or gratifies their jingoistic passions. Due in no small part to them, we can imagine Hobbes thinking, we now have not a Leviathan but a Behemoth, a gargantuan and immensely dangerous state.

In assessing our resistance to his antidemocratic views, we have to consider the wider thinking that informs those views and our reactions to them.

Hobbes's skepticism was deep but not dogmatic, his fear of power genuine but not paralyzing, his commitment to individuality authentic and powerful but tempered.

For the most part he thought within rather than argued for his skepticism. Doctrinal or programmatic skepticism tends to fall into dissonance if not contradiction but reasons for or impulsions to skepticism are constantly with us. We cannot avoid the thought that there is a God, but we fail in every attempt to comprehend Her or Her purposes. We cannot think or act without positing order and predictability in nature and in human affairs but our experience incessantly exceeds and confutes our best generalizations, explanations and anticipations. Above all, we can make sense of ourselves and our world only in language, but our uses and abuses of it oblige us to acknowledge its arbitrariness, its equivocality, and the ways in which our unavoidable reliance on it deepens opacity and unintelligibility, confounds rather than facilitates understanding. Our noetic, predictive and communicative achievements buoy us up from despair and sustain our continuing efforts, but we can deny our failures and limitations only by losing ourselves in an enthusiasm that compounds our difficulties.

The rights and powers each of us have to act are necessary if we are to enact ourselves and extract a measure of felicity from recalcitrant circumstances and our often rebarbative fellow human beings. The concentrated authority and aggregated power of political association are essential to stabilize our interactions sufficiently to allow each of us some hope of success in pursuing our own objectives. But your power competes with mine, the state claims (must claim) that its authority supersedes mine, and every increase in the power of the state is actually or potentially an enhancement of the power of some other person or persons over me.

As Hobbes understands and promotes them, individuality and felicity are necessarily personal, at their occasional best they are deeply so. They are necessarily so for reasons fundamental to Hobbes's philosophy. God and nature, in addition to making each of us physically separate from one another, have not provided us with truths, understandings or languages that unite us, that are given in common to us. Because we share an environment and certain faculties for perceiving and responding to it, I can adopt language that others have invented and communicated to me, accept beliefs and values that others have acquired and taught to me, enter into various relationships and arrangements with others. Just as my thinking and acting are affected by the nonhuman environment that I inhabit, so they are influenced by the other human beings with whom I share that environment. It is nevertheless an illusion or delusion to think that my language, beliefs and commitments are entirely due to something other or apart from me, have the qualities or characteristics that they have wholly because persons or things other than me are what they are or have done what they have done. My senses and imagination, my passions and reason, play an ineliminable role in all the perceiving and feeling, thinking and acting by which I become what I am.

Thus far, individuality is guaranteed to us, it is our fate. As I read Hobbes, he does not regret this fate, does not lament the fact that for the most part we have to make ourselves and our worlds for ourselves. Insofar as he credited the Eden story, he is neither nostalgic for the human condition it describes nor desirous of creating an approximation to it. His aspiration, rather, is that we use our powers of thinking and

acting to augment and enhance our fated individuality with individualities that are of our making in a stronger, a more chosen and hence more
gratifying sense. Because we must keep company with one another,
such self-enactment requires that we learn to accommodate to one
another in ways that our fated individualities makes difficult for us. The
prudence/morality that Hobbes urges upon us is our single best resource
in attempting to do so, our best means of tempering the effects of our
fated individualities. As a prudence, this prudence/morality maintains
the tie to our senses, imaginations and passions, a connection that must
be sustained if we are to act steadily on its principles and rules. As a
refreshingly moraline-free morality, it encourages us to construe and
apply its principles and rules in ways that facilitate the enactment of
our imagined and chosen individualities.

Politically organized society is a necessary but inherently dangerous
supplement to prudence/morality. It is necessary because our fated
individuality makes it difficult for us to remain faithful to our pru-
dence/morality. It is dangerous because we can establish and maintain
it only by departing from what is arguably the fundamental premise and
principle of that prudence/morality, the premise that by nature we are
roughly equal and the principle that we should mutually acknowledge
and respect that equality. If the state is weak and inactive, it does not
protect us against those who violate prudence/morality. If it is weak but
active, it provokes resistance and destroys itself. If it is powerful and
ambitious, it impedes or prevents individual felicity and self-enactment.

Hardly demonstrated by Hobbes or subject to demonstration by
anyone else, these views constitute an intelligible and intelligent outlook or sensibility. Having a basis in continuing and salient aspects of
our experience, the several components of the ideational configuration
that they comprise, though not mutually entailed, enhance one another's
plausibility. As may be sufficiently indicated by complaints that reverberate among us, elements in the configuration have recognizable
standing in thinking that is already influential among us. Insofar as our
perfervid enemies of relativism, deconstructionism and postmodernism
accept my readings of Hobbes, they do or will come to regard his
skepticism as an early but potent source of the most regrettable of the
tendencies of our time. Avid proponents of participatory democracy and
communal moralism persistently argue that our liberal democracies are

already far too Hobbesian in their egoistic individualism. And since many of these critics, as well as others who—more appropriately in my view—object to the disfiguring inequalities that persist in liberal societies, are distressed by the unwillingness to use the state to remedy our defects, it might be argued that we are also too much influenced by Hobbes's apprehensions concerning political authority and power.

If we are already more Hobbesian than most of us have realized, and if there are good reasons to be so, should we go further and give up our resistance not only to his antidemocratic views but to his rejection of constitutionalism, the rule of law and other institutionalized limitations on state authority? The short answer to this question is no. Some of the reasons for returning this answer can be elucidated by seeing ways in which Hobbes's antidemocratic and authoritarian views, rather than supported by his skepticism and commitment to individuality, are manifestations of the most objectionably dogmatic and anti-individuality elements in his thinking. Equally, reasons for a more nuanced answer are partly provided by his estimation of the limitations on our knowing and acting, the anxiety concerning power to which that estimation led him, above all by his commitment to individuality.

The excessively ambitious and vain-glorious lust for "precellence" in all of their encounters with other persons. An effect of this craving, which Hobbes emphasizes most strongly in his acerbic account of the vain-glory engendered by democratic politics, is to make the vain-glorious deeply dependent on the judgments that others make of them. As with sovereigns who think they must start a war over every slight they receive from abroad, vain-glorious democratic politicians represent the extreme case of other-directed behavior. Having made their own self-estimations depend on comparisons between themselves and others, they must constantly attend to the thinking and acting of others. Rather than choosing their thoughts and actions out of desires and beliefs authentic to themselves, they do so in reaction to what they think others think about them.

Hobbes's disdain for this aspect of vain-glory is partly independent of his fear of the consequences it produces in the setting of democratic politics,[2] is a manifestation of main elements in his psychology, his notion of temperateness, and certainly of his ideal of gallant or magnanimous individuality. "Proper self-esteem . . . is not a perturbation, but a state of mind that ought to be. Those . . . who estimate their own worth correctly, do so on the basis of their past deeds, and so, what they have done, they dare to try again. Those who estimate their worth too highly, or who pretend to be what they are not, or who believe flatterers, become disheartened when dangers actually confront them" (*De Homine,* Ch. XII, pp. 60-61). Anything but a humble man, Hobbes was against pride only when it is false.

Unfortunately, another striking element in his thinking puts the possibility of such proper self-esteem in serious doubt. In a passage that partly compromises his own commitment to individuality, he says that "worth," "merit," "dignity," "desert," "honor," "glory," and the like, the most important components of our self-estimations and hence of our powers to enact ourselves and achieve felicity, are "not absolute; but . . . dependent on the need and judgment of another." Our "true value," accordingly, "is no more than it is esteemed by others" (*Lev.,* Ch. 10, p. 73).

On this view of "worth" and hence of all the self-other relationships in which it is at issue, the generality of people are so insidiously and pervasively dependent on others as to be all but defenseless against their merest whims. Hobbes's distinction between the prudent and the vain-glorious is largely evacuated, his voluntarism and enthusiasm for self-making seem little more than futile gestures.

It is true that Hobbes also attributes to "most men" a tendency to "rate themselves at the highest value they can" (ibid.). In consistency with his agent-relative or voluntarist doctrine concerning evaluation (indeed with his nominalism and theory of language) he could thus say that each of us adopts or decides to treat as "true" your evaluations of my worth, thereby remaining entitled to at least a simulacrum of his agent-centered, self-enactment-oriented philosophy. But even this compromised phrase is followed by the dismaying words already quoted: "yet their true value is no more than it is esteemed by others." Aside from those few noble souls who somehow remain confident of their own "worthiness,"[3] the "selves" Hobbes describes are no better than chameleons to one another, relations among them are what Emerson described (in "Self-Reliance") as a game of blind man's buff. Certainly the independence and individuality that I have claimed his theory otherwise establishes and promotes is put in serious jeopardy.

The sharp conflict between Hobbes's account of "worth" and much of the rest of his thinking, together with the fact that it is primarily in his discussions of democratic politics that he emphasizes the worth-craving and dependent character of the vain-glorious (who otherwise are more often presented as angular and disruptive figures), suggests that Hobbes's antipathy to democracy is importantly influenced by these aberrant elements in his thinking. If so, the appropriate response is to draw on his other ideas to correct his assessment of democracy, not to adopt the latter. Hobbes is not alone in thinking that democracy begets power-generating and individuality-diminishing conformism. Even if he and his fellow antidemocrats are correct that democratic government and politics have these tendencies, it may be that Hobbes's thinking would help us to find ways to diminish them. (Or, if we do not succeed in doing so, to reach the conclusion that, *pace* Hobbes, democracy is nevertheless the least bad form of government and politics.)

As Hobbes sees it, many and in any case the most remediable of the obstacles to felicity are of our own mismaking, in particular those mismakings that are the misconceptions that we have formed of ourselves and our own powers. If we underestimate those powers, "renounce our senses, and experience," fold our "reason . . . in the napkin of an implicit faith" (*Lev.*, Ch. 32, p. 271), we sink into "dejection" and "MELANCHOLY," become subject to "causeless fears" and lose our capacity to think and act (*Lev.*, Ch. 8, p. 63). As Hobbes has read humankind, these forms of madness are rare and—with something of an exception that is especially pertinent to thinking about democracy—are harmful primarily to those few who are afflicted by them. Impelled by their passions, most human beings are active and energetic, vigorous in their pursuit of their own good as they see it. These are the characteristics that Hobbes admires and wants to encourage in human affairs.

More common and far more dangerous is the vain-glorious exaggeration of what we can know and do, particularly those forms of false pride that lead philosophers and moralists to imagine that they know what is good for all of us, convince self-appointed prophets that they are possessed of and should be obeyed as if they were God, embolden rulers and politicians to undertake the transformation of their subjects.

Our greatest need is for changes in our thinking about ourselves, changes that temper our passions but do not deprive us of the energy and direction they impart to us. If we become duly appreciative and appropriately chastened concerning ourselves we will have done what is most important toward other desirable makings, remakings and dismantlings. Having more disdain for than confidence in established educative agencies such as the state, the church, and the universities, Hobbes sought by his own teaching to disabuse them and us of our accumulated misconceptions, to encourage each of us to a fecund self-esteem while doing what he could to tame the inordinate and destructive forms of arrogance to which we are given.

As will long since have become clear to readers of this book, in my estimation large parts of Hobbes's teaching repay our close and sympathetic attention. I would say the same concerning the chastening components in his teaching concerning democracy. As its name itself tells us, democracy is first and foremost a system of rule, a system in which some rule over others. If we share Hobbes's view that each of us would or should prefer to rule ourselves, can in most respects rule ourselves better than anyone else can rule us, we will look upon democracy and all other systems of rule with suspicion. Nor have events discredited Hobbes's view that democracy, with its various but invariably enlarging effect on the number of people who play a part in ruling, fosters the wide and active use of state authority and power.

We are indebted to Hobbes for his acute analysis of the very real difficulties here. Nor is his response to them without continuing merit. But that response, which displays a curious combination of confidence in and distrust of his own ability to teach, makes extreme demands on us who are his students.

Hobbes wants such but only such rule as is necessary to sustain the conditions necessary to the pursuit, by individuals, of felicity. In order to get this elusive combination he has to convince monarchs to accept and to act faithfully on his conception of their task. In order for their rule to be effective, he also has to persuade natively recalcitrant subjects to subscribe to a system of rule. Both rulers and subjects have to be teachable.

Given his predominately egoistic psychology, the arguments he gives have to be cast primarily in prudential terms. In the case of his argu- -ments to rulers, he has to appeal to their interest in maintaining their authority and power. To do so, he threatens them with the very thing that he teaches subjects to eschew, that is disobedience and resistance. To the extent that he succeeds in teaching subjects to obey, he unintentionally but very probably encourages rulers to make excessive use of their authority and power. When they do so, when they needlessly threaten the lives and restrict the liberties of their subjects, the latter do what comes naturally to them, do what they do not need to be taught to do.

For reasons highly relevant to his thinking about democracy, it turns out that by far the most important but also the most difficult part of Hobbes's political teaching is his teaching to subjects. On the one hand, they must learn to leave ruling primarily to their rulers, must restrict their involvement in ruling to representations of their personal interests and concerns. If they fail to learn and to act on this lesson, their activities either disrupt or dangerously expand the power of the state. On the other hand, they must make evident their willingness to engage in those most robust and dangerous forms of political activity that consist in disobeying and resisting the needless and excessive actions of their rulers. It is as if they must have two very different political selves plus a higher self that tells them which of the two they should be or act out of at this and the next moment.

As anyone who is reflective about government and politics, democratic or any other, will agree, Hobbes is right in thinking that they make conflicting and not finally or entirely reconcilable demands on us. Returning to the questions posed at the outset of this chapter, we should not let our resistance to his antidemocratic views impel us to utopian thinking or quixotic collective adventures. It is the hope—never to be fully realized—of a government and politics that has learned from Hobbes, but that is more democratic than Hobbes was prepared to countenance, that it might abate difficulties that are exacerbated by the most truculently antidemocratic aspects of his thinking.

In such a government and politics, citizens who authorize the rule of a government thereby also authorize and through various of the institutional devices that Hobbes rejected empower themselves to prevent government from taking needless and harmful actions. In the somewhat fanciful language I used just above, a politics of this kind enhances the possibility of continuities among the several selves into which Hobbes's thinking threatens to divide us. I may indeed live a politically quiet life, may concern myself primarily with matters that are personal to me and my intimates. I may do so in part because I do not want to lend the force of my thinking and acting to government. But the thinking that informs my acting in this way need not be severed from or antagonistic to my more overtly and specifically political conduct. I may engage in conduct of the latter sort precisely in order to protect the possibility and the integrity of my most personal involvements and activities.

Times may well come when these same Hobbesian concerns and convictions will oblige me to subordinate my preferred personal involvements to political activity. The use of governmental authority and power is sometimes the least objectionable way to combat unjustifiable inequalities and right accumulated wrongs. Where this is the case affirmative political activity may well be required. In the more likely event that government itself is misusing its authority and power, opposition and perhaps engrossing political activities such as disobedience, resistance and rebellion may become unavoidable. Thucydides and Godolphin lived private lives as far as events allowed them to do so consonant with their prudential/moral commitments and the magnanimity of their self-made characters. Wisely, Hobbes did not attempt a general and prospective answer to the question how far "as far as" is.

Just as on this understanding there can be continuities among the several dimensions of my life, so a duly chastened democratic politics might create intermediate and less consuming possibilities for effective political action. In these possibilities—and not in personal fulfillment through political activity itself—resides the hope that democracy can have a restraining and tempering effect on government and other forms of collective power, can be a servant not the master of individuality.

Notes

1. It is important to connect this feature of Hobbes's political thinking to his argument that subjects should not identify with the Sovereign's commands and other actions, particularly his view that it is the Sovereign not the subject who "denieth Christ," that the subject's commanded obedience to do so is no more than "profession with the tongue" and "but an external thing." If Hobbes did not urge critical attention to the Sovereign's activities, if he counseled receptivity or even passivity concerning the content of the laws, these views would have a hollow ring.

I am especially indebted to my adverbially contained but intense engagements with William Connolly on this and numerous closely related points.

2. The consequences he fears are presumably produced by the combination of the ambitions of a few and the gullibility and timorousness of the many. The actions of the former set in motion the forces that produce panic-terror and madness in the latter. In stressing the other-directed and dependent character of the vain-glorious, however, he makes difficulties for this analysis of the power-generating dynamics of democracy. It is not easy to credit the idea that the vain-glorious will take a lot of striking initiatives or will set many others in motion.

3. "WORTHINESS, is a thing different from the worth, or value of a man; and also from his merit, or desert, and consisteth in a particular power, or ability for that, whereof he is said to be worth: which particular ability, is usually named FITNESS, or **aptitude**" (Lev., Ch. 10, p. 79).

Annotated Bibliography

I. Works by Thomas Hobbes

The Answer of MR Hobbes to SR William D'Avenant's Preface before Gondibert. In William D'Avenant, *Gondibert 1651.* Menston, England: Scolar Press Limited, 1970.

Aristotle's Treatise on Rhetoric. Literally Translated [by Thomas Hobbes] with Hobbes's Analysis. London: George Bell & Sons.

The Autobiography of Thomas Hobbes. Translated by Benjamin Farrington. *The Rationalist Annual,* 1958.

Behemoth or The Long Parliament. Edited by Ferdinand Tonnies, with an Introduction by Stephen Holmes. Chicago: University of Chicago Press, 1990.

Decameron Physiologicum. The English Works of Thomas Hobbes of Malmesbury, Vol. VII. Edited by Sir William Molesworth. Reprint of the edition of 1845. Scientia Aalen, 1962.

De Cive or The Citizen. In *Man and Citizen: Thomas Hobbes.* Edited by Bernard Gert. Atlantic Highlands, NJ: Humanities Press, 1972.

De Corpore. In *Body, Man, and Citizen: Selections from Hobbes's Writings.* Edited by Richard S. Peters. London: Collier Books, 1962.

De Homine. In *Man and Citizen: Thomas Hobbes.* Edited by Bernard Gert. Atlantic Highlands, NJ: Humanities Press, 1972.

A Dialogue between a Philosopher and a Student of the Common Laws of England. Edited and with an Introduction by Joseph Cropsey. Chicago: University of Chicago Press, 1971.

Elements of Law. In *Body, Man, and Citizen: Selections from Hobbes's Writings.* Edited by Richard S. Peters. London: Collier Books, 1962.

The Iliads and Odysses of Homer. Translated . . . by Thomas Hobbes. . . . With a large PREFACE concerning the Vertues of an Heroick Poem; written by the Translator. 2nd ed. New York: AMS Press, 1979.

Leviathan. Edited by Michael Oakeshott, with an Introduction by Richard S. Peters. London: Collier Books, 1962.

Of Liberty and Necessity. In *Body, Man, and Citizen: Selections from Hobbes's Writings.* Edited by Richard S. Peters. London: Collier Books, 1962.

A Physical Dialogue of the Nature of the Air. "Appendix" in *Leviathan and the Air-Pump: Hobbes, Boyle, and the Experimental Life.* Edited by Steven Shapin and Simon Schaffer. Princeton, NJ: Princeton University Press, 1985.

Six Lessons to the Professor of the Mathematics. In *The English Works of Thomas Hobbes of Malmesbury.* Edited by Sir William Molesworth. Reprint of the edition of 1845. Scientia Aalen, 1962.

Thomas White's De Mundo Examined. Translated by Harold Whitmore Jones. London: Bradford University Press, 1976.

"Third Set of Objections [to Descartes's *Meditations*] With the Author's [Descartes's] Replies." Vol. II, pp. 121-37, *The Philosophical Writings of Descartes.* Translated by John Cottingham, Robert Stoothoff, and Dugald Murdoch. Cambridge: Cambridge University Press, 1984.

Hobbes's Thucydides. Edited and with an Introduction by Richard Schlatter. New Brunswick, NJ: Rutgers University Press, 1975.

II. Other Works Cited

Aubrey, John. *Aubrey's Brief Lives.* Edited by Oliver Lawson Dick. Ann Arbor: University of Michigan Press, 1957.

Kavka, Gregory S. *Hobbesian Moral and Political Theory.* Princeton, NJ: Princeton University Press, 1986.

Nietzsche, Friedrich. *Thus Spoke Zarathustra.* Translated by Walter Kaufman. New York: Penguin, 1966.

Nietzsche, Friedrich. *Will to Power.* Translated by Walter Kaufman and R. J. Hollingdale. New York: Vintage, 1967.

Wittgenstein, Ludwig. *Philosophical Investigations.* Translated by G.E.M. Anscombe. New York: Macmillan, 1953.

III. Works Concerning Hobbes

There is a vast and rapidly growing literature concerning Hobbes. The single most encompassing listing, which runs to more than 1,500 items, is William Sacksteder, *Hobbes Studies (1879-1979: A Bibliography* (Bowling Green, OH: Bowling Green State University, Philosophy Documentation Center, 1982). In addition to thoroughly covering its chosen period, this work includes an introductory essay that usefully sketches the shifting tendencies in Hobbes scholarship and commentary.

A large portion of the writing that has appeared since 1979 is acutely discussed in Perez Zagorin, "Hobbes on Our Mind," *Journal of the History of Ideas,* Vol. 51 (1990) pp. 317-35. *The International Hobbes Association Newsletter* closely monitors and provides valuable commentary concerning the continuing flow of publications relating to Hobbes.

Beyond listing these readily available resources, I restrict this Bibliography to the works that I have had most in mind in writing this book plus a sampling of further works relevant to the issues discussed in my several chapters.

My greatest affirmative debt is to the construals-cum-appropriations of Hobbes's thought by Michael Oakeshott, especially his foregrounding of will and artifice, of individuality and of skepticism in Hobbes's thinking. See Michael Oakeshott, *Hobbes on Civil Association* (Oxford: Basil Blackwell, 1975). The first of these is also effectively emphasized in Martin A. Bertram, *Hobbes: The Natural and the Artifacted Good* (Bern: Peter Lange, 1981). Hobbes's commitment to individuality has recently been emphasized by George Kateb ("Hobbes and the Irrationality of Politics," *Political Theory,* Vol. 17, No. 3 [August 1989], pp. 355-91) and by Alan Ryan ("Hobbes on Individualism" in G.A.J. Rogers and Alan Ryan, eds., *Perspectives on Thomas Hobbes* [Oxford: Clarendon, 1988]; "A More Tolerant Hobbes?" in Susan Mendus, ed., *Justifying Toleration* [New York: Cambridge University Press, 1988]). Hobbes's skepticism in the nondoctrinaire sense in which Oakeshott uses and I have here used the term is a prominent theme in Richard Tuck's exemplary little *Hobbes* (Oxford: Oxford University Press, 1989), and Tuck has examined Hobbes's stance toward more programmatic forms of skepticism in "Grotius, Carneades, and Hobbes," *Grotiana,* N.S. 4 (1983), pp. 43-62 and in "Optics and Skeptics: The Philosophical Foundations of Hobbes's Political Thought," in Edmund Leites, ed., *Conscience and Casuistry in Early Modern Europe* (Cambridge: Cambridge University Press, 1987).

Along with Oakeshott, the most widely influential students of Hobbes in the last decades were Leo Strauss, Howard Warrander and C. B. Macpherson. As Oakeshott recognized, there are important affinities between his account of Hobbes's ideas and that given by Strauss in *The Political Philosophy of Hobbes: Its Basis and Its Genesis* (Oxford: Clarendon, 1936), and in Strauss's later *Natural Right and History*

(Chicago: University of Chicago Press, 1953). Their respective valorizations of those ideas could hardly be different. Oakeshott sees Hobbes as the theorist of an admirable individuality and civility, Strauss sees him as the theorist of a subjectivist, amoral and dangerously divisive individualism. The more I read Strauss on Hobbes, the better I like Hobbes. Macpherson's *The Political Theory of Possessive Individualism* (Oxford: Clarendon, 1962) shares Strauss's animus against the liberal societies they both think Hobbes did much to inaugurate, but his neo-Marxist reading of Hobbes seems to me to be largely a distraction.

Along with A. E. Taylor's "The Ethical Doctrine of Hobbes" (in K. C. Brown, ed., *Hobbes Studies* [Oxford: Basil Blackwell, 1965]), Warrander's *The Political Philosophy of Hobbes* (Oxford: Oxford University Press, 1957) is the main source of the view that Hobbes combined elements from both traditional Christian and "modern" natural law thinking and anticipations of Kantianism into a strict deontological morality. In the particulars of its interpretation of Hobbes's most specifically moral thinking, this argument generated much illuminating discussion; I discuss issues that are successors to those the argument first raised in Chapters 4 and 5.

Viewed more broadly, Warrander's book can be regarded as an attempt, of which there since have been several more, to eliminate or at least to relieve what appears to be a large difficulty in Hobbes's thinking. Hobbes's manifest aversion to disorder and his insistent political authoritarianism strongly suggest that he wants a system of rule and rules that govern human conduct widely and closely. As Oakeshott in one tone of voice and Strauss in quite another make clear, his skepticism, his egoism, and much else in his thinking call the possibility of such a system very much into question. If, as Warrander argues, Hobbes's moral doctrine is independent of his egoism and is anything but skeptical, this difficulty is partly overcome.

Much of the recent writing concerning Hobbes is done by scholars and theorists who are unpersuaded by Warrander's solution but who nevertheless regard the problem just described as fundamental to Hobbes's thinking. Hence they too attempt to find a solution to it in Hobbes's texts. Partly following Warrander's and more particularly Taylor's lead, some have looked to Hobbes's religious doctrines to provide unifying and controlling forces strong enough to bring and hold Hobbesian human beings in the disciplining order they assume Hobbes wanted. F. C. Hood's *The Divine Politics of Thomas Hobbes* (Oxford: Clarendon, 1964) is a resolute example of this tendency. William E. Connolly's *Political Theory and Modernity,* esp. Ch. 2 (Oxford: Basil Blackwell, 1988) is a more spirited and refined one and is conducted for very different purposes.

Don Herzog, who is as zealous as any recent commentator in insisting that Hobbes wanted an encompassing and tightly controlling social and political governance and order, claims that Hobbes invoked religion, revived conventional wisdom, offered philosophical arguments, deceived, manipulated and did all and anything else that he thought might serve this purpose. See his *Happy Slaves,* esp. Ch. 3 (Chicago: University of Chicago Press, 1989). David Johnston thinks that, partly to the contrary, Hobbes saw religiosity and much of the rest of the inheritance of his time as sources of disorder. Accordingly, Hobbes attempted to effect, by the force of his own reasoning and rhetoric, no less than a "cultural transformation" of his fellow human beings. See Johnston's *The Rhetoric of Leviathan: Thomas Hobbes and the Politics of Cultural Transformation* (Princeton, NJ: Princeton University Press, 1986). To mention but one more approach that is largely governed by this same problematic, members of the game theoretical school of thought are now treating Hobbes as an early practitioner of the mode of analysis they prefer, in particular as having seen the problem of order as a major example of what are now called prisoner dilemma problems. They find him using game theoretic techniques in his attempts to solve the problem and they supplement his efforts with the more refined analytics now available. David Gauthier's *The Logic of Leviathan* (Oxford: Clarendon, 1969) is the first major effort of this kind. Prominent recent examples include Gregory Kavka's book listed under II above and Jean Hampton, *Hobbes and the Social Contract Tradition* (Cambridge: Cambridge University Press, 1986).

As much as I have profited from these works, my own reading of Hobbes leads me to suspect that their authors may be responding more to their own concern for order, one perhaps intensified by their reading of Hobbes, than to Hobbes's own concerns. No doubt in part to persuade his contemporaries of the desirability of a *greater* degree of moral and political uniformity and order than then obtained, Hobbes paints horrific pictures of affairs among "masterless men." It does not follow that he thinks it either possible or desirable to subject those "men" to any very close or encompassing master or mastery. If we question the assumption, which life in the immensely powerful and active states of our own time makes it all too easy for us to make, that Hobbes wanted an extensive and closely controlling governance, the issues and concerns that animate much of this literature take on a quite different character.

The themes of making, unmaking and mismaking I discuss in Chapter 1 receive the best previous treatment known to me in Oakeshott. See also Arthur Henry Child, *Making and Knowing in Hobbes, Vico, and Dewey* (Berkeley: University of California Press, 1953). The many commentators who argue that Hobbes thinks we are or should be made by something other than ourselves, by God, Nature, Reason, Our Community, and so forth, are all in effect challenging the centrality I accord to these notions.

The classic treatment of Hobbes's cosmology and materialist metaphysics is Frithiof Brandt, *Thomas Hobbes' Mechanical Conception of Nature* (Copenhagen: Levin & Munksgaard, 1928), which is of course relevant to my arguments in Chapter 3 as well as 2. Richard Peters, *Hobbes* (Harmondsworth, UK: Penguin, 1956), Tom Sorell, *Hobbes* (London: Routledge & Kegan Paul, 1986), and J. W. Watkins, *Hobbes's System of Ideas* (London: Hutchinson University Library, 1965) provide instructive discussions of his metaphysics and epistemology. Concerning his thinking about God and religious questions generally, in addition to works mentioned above see: "God and Thomas Hobbes," in K. C. Brown, *Hobbes Studies;* Eldon Eisenach, *Two Worlds of Liberalism: Religion and Politics in Hobbes, Locke, and Mill* (Chicago: University of Chicago Press, 1981); J. B. Schneewind, "The Divine Corporation in the History of Ethics," in Richard Rorty, J. B. Schneewind, and Quentin Skinner, eds., *Philosophy and History* (Cambridge: Cambridge University Press, 1984); and especially J.G.A. Pocock, "Time, History and Eschatology in the Thought of Thomas Hobbes," in the author's *Politics, Language and Time* (New York: Atheneum, 1971). I discuss the relationships between Hobbes's religious and political views in greater detail in Chapter 1 of *Willful Liberalism* (Ithaca, NY: Cornell University Press, 1992).

There are valuable discussions of Hobbes's views concerning language, reason and science in J. W. Watkins, *Hobbes's System of Ideas;* in Steven Shapin and Simon Schaffer, *Leviathan and the Air-Pump: Hobbes, Boyle and the Experimental Life* (Princeton, NJ: Princeton University Press, 1985); in M. M. Goldsmith, *Hobbes's Science of Politics* (New York: Columbia University Press, 1966); and in Miriam M. Reik, *The Golden Lands of Thomas Hobbes* (Detroit: Wayne State University Press, 1977). Reik and especially Shapin and Schaffer argue persuasively that Hobbes's philosophy of science (as distinct from the content of his own efforts at science) anticipates views now widely influential in this field. Of course this is in large part because, as I have suggested, his philosophy of language also anticipates views now current. There is, however, need for a closer study of Hobbes's philosophy of language. Reik's concern with Hobbes's conception of language and concern with rhetoric is valuable in opening a window unto Hobbes's relationship to classical and renaissance humanism, particularly the emphasis of the latter on what Stephen Greenblatt has called "self-fashioning" (*Renaissance Self-Fashioning: From More to Shakespeare* [Chicago: University of Chicago Press, 1980] to which I owe my epigraph from Spenser) through the performative use of the made instrument of language. This too is a theme that deserves fuller development.

On prudence, morality and Hobbes's relationship to natural law and natural rights thinking, in addition to Taylor and Warrander see especially the following: Tuck, *Hobbes,* "Grotius, Carneades, and Hobbes," "Optics and Skeptics," and his *Natural Rights Theories* (Cambridge: Cambridge University Press, 1979); J. B. Schneewind, "The Misfortunes of Virtue," *Ethics,* Vol. 101 (October 1990), pp. 42-63), and Schneewind, *Moral Philosophy From Montaigne to Kant,* Two Volumes (Cambridge: Cambridge University Press, 1990); D. D. Raphael, *Hobbes: Morals and Politics* (London: Allen & Unwin, 1977). The ways in which Hobbes's prudence does or could be adjusted to support consent to political authority has been a special concern of those who treat him as an early practitioner of the theory of games and is discussed at length in Gauthier ("Logic of Leviathan,") Kavka (*Hobbesian Moral and Political Theory*), and Hampton (*Hobbes and the Social Contract*). There is an especially interesting treatment of the issue in Andrzej Rapaczynski, *Nature and Politics: Liberalism in the Philosophies of Hobbes, Locke and Rousseau* (Ithaca, NY: Cornell University Press, 1987). The historical-social background of Hobbes's views concerning the noble and vain-glorious is illuminated in Keith Thomas's classic article, "The Social Origins of Hobbes's Political Thought," in K. C. Brown, ed., *Hobbes Studies.*

With the possible exception of works devoted primarily to Hobbes's metaphysics and philosophy of science (e.g., Brandt [*Thomas Hobbes' Mechanical Conception*] and Shapin and Schaffer (*Leviathan and the Air-Pump*), virtually all of the works thus far listed speak to the issues I have discussed in Chapters 6 through 8. For a superb analysis of Hobbes's understanding of authority, see Richard B. Friedman, "On the Concept of Authority in Political Philosophy," in Richard E. Flathman, ed., *Concepts in Social & Political Philosophy* (New York: Macmillan, 1973). Friedman's Oakeshottian distinction between *in* and *an* authority is particularly relevant to the question of the subject's identification with the Sovereign's commands and hence to the bearing of the Sovereign's religious teaching on the subject's faith. The religious, moral, and political criticisms leveled against Hobbes by his contemporaries are discussed in John Bowle, *Hobbes and His Critics: A Study in Seventeenth Century Constitutionalism* (London: Jonathan Cape, 1951), in Samuel I. Mintz, *The Hunting of Leviathan: Seventeenth-Century Reactions to the Materialism and Moral Philosophy of Thomas Hobbes* (Cambridge: Cambridge University Press, 1962), and by Quentin Skinner in the following among numerous articles: "Conquest and Consent: Thomas Hobbes and the Engagement Controversy," in *The Interregnum: The Quest for Settlement, 1646-1660,* G. E. Aylmer, ed. (Hamden, CT: Archon Books, 1972); "The Ideological Context of Hobbes's Political Thought," in Maurice Cranston and Richard Peters, eds., *Hobbes and Rousseau: A Collection of Critical Essays* (Garden City, NY: Anchor-Doubleday, 1972).

Index

About the Author

Richard E. Flathman is George Armstrong Kelly Memorial Professor of Political Science at The Johns Hopkins University where he teaches political philosophy. His previous teaching positions have included Reed College and the University of Chicago. Professor Flathman is the author of seven previous works in political theory, including *The Philosophy and Politics of Freedom* (1987), which received the Elaine and David Spitz Prize of the Conference For The Study of Political Thought. His most recent works, *Toward a Liberalism* (1989) and *Willful Liberalism* (1992), explore and promote a version of liberal theory and practice that foregrounds individuality and plurality. Viewing Thomas Hobbes as a theorist of making and especially self-making or self-enactment, in the present work Flathman treats the great 17th century thinker as a precursor of and important source of ideas for liberalism so conceived. This reflection, which he views as a companion to *Willful Liberalism*, will enrich Hobbes studies as well as enliven our own political and moral thinking.

184

The BEAST and the BETHANY

and the

BETHANY

Battle
of the
Beast

BY JACK MEGGITT–PHILLIPS
ILLUSTRATED BY ISABELLE FOLLATH

ALADDIN
NEW YORK LONDON TORONTO SYDNEY NEW DELHI

ALADDIN
An imprint of Simon & Schuster Children's Publishing Division
1230 Avenue of the Americas, New York, New York 10020
First Aladdin hardcover edition January 2023
Text copyright © 2022 by Jack Meggitt-Phillips
Illustrations copyright © 2022 by Isabelle Follath
Originally published in Great Britain in 2022 by Farshore
All rights reserved, including the right of reproduction in whole or in part in any form.
ALADDIN and related logo are registered trademarks of Simon & Schuster, Inc.
For information about special discounts for bulk purchases, please contact
Simon & Schuster Special Sales at 1-866-506-1949 or business@simonandschuster.com.
The Simon & Schuster Speakers Bureau can bring authors to your live event. For
more information or to book an event contact the Simon & Schuster Speakers Bureau
at 1-866-248-3049 or visit our website at www.simonspeakers.com.
Book designed by Heather Palisi
The text of this book was set in Goudy Old Style.
Manufactured in the United States of America 1222 FFG
2 4 6 8 10 9 7 5 3 1
Library of Congress Cataloging-in-Publication Data
Names: Meggitt-Phillips, Jack, author. | Follath, Isabelle, illustrator.
Title: Battle of the beast / by Jack Meggitt-Phillips ; illustrated by Isabelle Follath.
Description: First Aladdin hardcover edition. | New York : Aladdin,
an imprint of Simon & Schuster Children's Publishing Division, 2023. |
Series: The beast and the Bethany ; book 3 |
Originally published in Great Britain in 2022. |
Summary: The beast, who tried to eat Bethany twice and controlled Ebenezer Tweezer
for years, is declared no longer dangerous and delivered back to Ebenezer and Bethany's
house, but the beast's newfound manners may not be as polished as everyone thought.
Identifiers: LCCN 2022037553 (print) | LCCN 2022037554 (ebook) |
ISBN 9781665903820 (hardcover) | ISBN 9781665903844 (ebook)
Subjects: CYAC: Monsters—Fiction. | Behavior—Fiction. |
Humorous stories. | LCGFT: Humorous fiction. | Novels.
Classification: LCC PZ7.1.M46775 Bat 2023 (print) |
LCC PZ7.1.M46775 (ebook) | DDC [Fic]—dc23
LC record available at https://lccn.loc.gov/2022037553
LC ebook record available at https://lccn.loc.gov/2022037554